Goddess Durgā and Sacred Female Power

Goddess Durgā and Sacred Female Power

Laura Amazzone

Hamilton Books
A member of
The Rowman & Littlefield Publishing Group
Lanham · Boulder · New York · Toronto · Plymouth, UK

Hamilton Books
4501 Forbes Boulevard
Suite 200
Lanham, Maryland 20706
Hamilton Books Acquisitions Department (301) 459-3366

Estover Road
Plymouth PL6 7PY
United Kingdom

Printed in the United States of America
British Library Cataloging in Publication Information Available

Library of Congress Control Number: 2010933398
ISBN: 978-0-7618-5313-8 (paperback : alk. paper)
eISBN: 978-0-7618-5314-5

Dedication

To the Divine Śakti in each of us
And especially to:
Kyle Corsiglia,
my Mammy, Lillyann Stephens Delsig,
And my beloved Gypsy
With Reverence, Gratitude, and Love

Contents

Foreword

Goddess Durgā and Sacred Female Power is an erudite and scholarly exposition, rich in descriptive detailed knowledge of ancient and contemporary Indian texts and formal Tantric practices: it can be read as a sophisticated guidebook to understanding the complexity of Goddess Durgā's multifaceted and paradoxical nature. However, the book in no way stops there. Laura Amazzone shares her personal story as a contemporary American woman who is also a fervent devotee ("bhakta") of Durgā, whose luminous agency she credits with redemptive force both for individuals and for the planet. Having accumulated an enormous scholarly knowledge through two decades of world travel, intellectual studies, and intense devotional practices, Laura blends this knowledge seamlessly in the telling of her own personal narrative.

Her aim is no less than to liberate all women from enslavement and abuse, as well as freeing the men who are able to love them. To accomplish this ambitious task, she brings a piercing but compassionate feminist lens to her careful analysis of the rituals, texts, and practices belonging to Durgā. When she sees a patriarchal overlay, she names it—but without needing to throw out the baby with the bathwater. Her profound immersion in the Ten-Day Durgā Festivals in Nepal and India, along with her longtime devotional identification with the deity, give us an inside glimpse into the South Asian cultural experience of Durgā, even as Amazzone never forgets her position as an outsider to that culture. Her lens is that of a serious and respectful pilgrim on a particularly female journey of discovery and healing.

I love the scholarship in this informative book—the many vivid details and knowledge about different Goddesses honored in the festivals, such as Saraswatī on the first day and Kālī on the seventh. Amazzone's vibrant descriptions throughout the book bring her learning to life for the reader. Especially potent is her storytelling ability, such as when she describes her first breathtaking encounter with the young Kumārī, a virgin Nepalese girl whose office is to personally embody the Goddess Durgā. Finally it is her understanding of ancient women's blood mysteries and the erotic power of the Yoginī that informs the book and makes it relevant for contemporary women searching for more meaning than that normally offered in mainstream western culture. The book itself is a bit of a pilgrimage and one that you will want to read more than once.

Vicki Noble
Candlemas 2010

Preface

"Sexual difference is a given reality. It belongs universally to all humans. Being interested in it cannot, in any case, result from any privilege, but forgetting its importance can."[1]

Luce Irigaray

Goddess Durgā is a divine model of female empowerment. Her animating, sustaining and annihilating essence is more ancient than any of the orthodox world religions. To many, Durgā is the Divine Force behind all existence. Durgā is courageous and invincible, and She has sisters: Goddesses in collective form that have surrounded Her throughout history and who assist Her in battling demonic forces that are destroying the harmonic interrelationship between all earthly and cosmic existence. These sister Goddesses across the globe come in every shape, color and size, and move with the natural cycles of this planet. They have governed the cosmos since time immemorial. Most importantly, the divine female force of Goddess is evident in the strength, resilience, hope and love of women's lives.

Goddess Durgā and Sacred Female Power explores foundational tenets within the Śākta Tantra tradition and the myriad expressions of Goddess Durgā in Her South Asian manifestations. It examines Goddess' evolution from earth-based shamanic origins into the rise and development of the Hindu Tradition and beyond. It explores the ways Goddess' original untamable and formidable nature has and has not been respected and demonstrates how the gradual negative shift in Goddess' status parallels the malignment of women's social, cultural and religious roles under patriarchy. *Goddess Durgā and Sacred Female Power* deconstructs orthodox depictions and descriptions of various manifestations of Goddess and shows how the debilitated submissive presentation of the human as well as Divine Female is limiting to both sexes. In the West we lack an empowered image of the Divine Female. It is not my intention to appropriate the religious icons, appearances and symbols by turning to the millennia-old Kaula and Śākta Tantra tradition of the East. The ancient spiritual foundation from which these Goddesses and their rituals thrive have much to teach all of us about human experience and the nature of existence.

In Part One I introduce Goddess Durgā and the religious traditions in which She is most firmly situated. I present one of Her most popular epithets and emanations, Bhagawatī, as a Divine female role model. I provide an overview of the philosophical and spiritual traditions that serve as the foundation of Her rituals and practices.

I also discuss the relevance of pilgrimage.

In Part Two, the day by day account of the Durgā Pūjā or Navarātri, a nine-night autumn festival, offers philosophical, historical, ritualistic and mythological material pertaining to Goddess and Her annual ritual. Throughout the book I share anecdotal highlights of my pilgrimages over the past ten years that have enhanced my research. Ethnographic research on the festival as presented through archaeology, religious studies and practice, art, iconography, mythology, and feminist studies have informed this work. By examining archaeology, linguistics, myth as history, iconography, and Kaula and Śākta Tantric texts, we can glimpse the prepatriarchal forms of the popular Goddesses in the Hindu pantheon and other lesser known, marginalized Goddesses who have something to say to us about our inherent divinity and place in the world today.

As you journey through the days of the Durgā festival that make up the ten chapters of this book in Part Two, please note this is not a chronological tale of my pilgrimage experiences. It is impossible to describe some of the events and the evolution of my consciousness in a linear way. Although I have lived the ten days of the Durgā Pūjā in Nepal, India and the US, as a day by day experience, each day and the Goddess/es related to it have also continued to influence me through different periods outside of the autumn festival days over the past ten years of my life. Time is elusive and cyclical—a process of constantly becoming. My own consciousness about various forms of Durgā has shifted and evolved over the past ten years—revealing layers of mystical knowledge that I have received from books, teachers, the pilgrimages, and relationships with humans and certain animals (especially cats!), and through infinite synchronicities and affirmations in my everyday life. After the first pilgrimage I made in 1998 I began to see patterns, interconnected designs within my life and in life all around me. There have been times when everything has become Goddess—as one of my favorite expressions and greetings reminds me. *Jai Mā!* Victory to the Mother Goddess, Reverence to the Mother Goddess!

In this book I present windows into female consciousness. I do not claim to speak for every woman, nor am I speaking against men. I share what I have come to understand as female consciousness—a consciousness that, like the Śakti, or female power of the South Asian tradition, is constantly evolving and becoming. My use of the word patriarchy and patriarchal male is not restricted to men alone. I am speaking against patriarchy as a male-dominated, exploitative and hierarchical system of power that pervades and controls all levels of society—and human consciousness.

While *Goddess Durgā and Sacred Female Power* is primarily about Goddess, women, and female consciousness, this book was written for men as well. Both women and men hold the keys of peace, love, and social justice for this planet. We live in a world dominated by masculinist/patriarchal thinking and my exploration of the Durgā myth, Her rituals and manifestation as various Goddesses offers a contemporary vision for a sacred egalitarian space. In a world that demands conformity and still privileges the white male race over the female sex and all people of color, this book challenges the status quo. European philosopher, linguist and cultural theorist Luce Irigaray talks about the need for us to deconstruct *everything* in this patriarchal world in order to experience our female consciousness:

> When women want to escape from exploitation, they do not merely destroy a few "prejudices," they disrupt the entire order of dominant values, economic, social, moral and sexual. They call into question all existing theory, all thought, all language, inasmuch as these are monopolized by men and men alone. They challenge the very foundation of our social and cultural order, whose organization has been prescribed by the patriarchal system.[2]

This book speaks directly to ways we can dismantle the patriarchy through spiritual empowerment. Patriarchy and monotheistic religion assert there is one Truth. On the contrary, the female-centered spiritual, social and cultural paradigms I explore in this book focus on multiple truths and ways of knowing. In feminist spirituality communities we talk about embodied knowing—other ways of knowing via our bodies and intuitions in addition to turning to the rational mind and logic. By observing manifold ways of accessing Truth, we realize there are many Truths. Therefore, this book is not about the Ultimate Truth as Durgā and only Durgā. While I consider Durgā to be a Divine Mother, I also cherish and call on Her multifaceted nature. She has as many expressions as there are beings in this world. I honor that diversity, specifically the tolerance of difference that looks to the unity behind the myriad expressions of humanness and divinity. As the great Indian saint Ammachi says, "God is neither male nor female—God is 'That.' But if you insist on God having a gender, then God is more female than male because the masculine is contained within the feminine."[3]

Durgā: An Alternative to "Femininity"

Not only are we missing an empowered model of the Divine female in the West, but also traditional notions around femininity and what is and is not acceptable for women remains limiting, restrictive and problematic. I purposely do not use the word "feminine" throughout this book because it is loaded with traditional and stereotypical notions that attempt to control woman's natural power and essence. Traditional femininity connotes weakness, a need to be taken care of and protected by a man, obedience, willingness to please others—especially men—submissiveness, and selflessness. In reclaiming and redefining femininity, we need more embodied models of what femininity IS outside of the stereotypical and sexist definitions that continue to perpetuate notions of women as the second sex.

One possibility is to look to Eastern and indigenous spiritual traditions around the globe where the often paradoxical reality of female nature is allowed to exist unbridled—at least in the divine pantheons. Although the socioeconomic status of women is most often not equal to the female power and equality these Goddesses embody, they offer an alternative to the virgin mother/whore dichotomy that is often the only representation of femaleness in Western orthodox religion—where even the sacred female is often completely obscured and denied.

One of the reasons I have come to love Durgā is that She defies oppressive Western concepts of femininity. Her presence in both independent and collective forms expresses a broader spectrum of the female psyche than what we are often presented with in the dualistic West. Instead of being either submissive or "aggressive," obedient or subordinate, Eastern female representations of the Divine such as Durgā and Her entourages are fierce and nurturing, terrifying and benevolent, and sensual and ascetic. In fact, these various forms of Goddess offer more possibilities in our consideration of what it means to be a woman in this world. They even put the woman back into mother![4]

Goddess Durgā and Sacred Female Power presents an ancient tradition that extols female virtues of strength, action, and creative dynamism and male virtues of receptivity, quiescence, and grounding. However, these virtues are not restricted to one sex over the other. Within each of us the potential for both and all exists. The tension between the sexes need not be used as a means to dominate one over the other, but to call forth the strengths and complementary energies of both sexes, which ultimately contributes to a greater and more peaceful whole. Ammachi reminds us:

> Women are the power and the very foundation of our existence in the world. When women lose touch with their real selves, the harmony of the world ceases to exist, and destruction sets in. It is therefore crucial that women everywhere make every effort to rediscover their fundamental nature, for only then can we save this world.[5]

In *Goddess Durgā and Sacred Female Power,* I am interested in the possibility of personal and planetary transformation that comes through a more female-centered, even matriarchal reality. While matriarchy has been interpreted as the opposite of patriarchy, matriarchy actually means "from the mother" and refers to a social system that is structured around environmental sustainability and the peacemaking wisdom of mothers and grandmothers. For the past twenty years I have been studying the rich and diverse female lineages across global history. I am especially interested in the potential for spiritual growth, wisdom, inner peace and strength that comes with exploring our relationship to both human and divine women. Clearly, I do not speak for all women nor do I speak for all feminists, for I believe in feminisms. I can only offer my own experience, knowledge and wisdom and hope that some who read this will feel empowered and transformed by my words. I am especially grateful to the words of feminists, poets, activists, leaders, artists and authors like Ammachi, Vicki Noble, Alice Walker, Elinor Gadon, Gloria Steinem, Eve Ensler, Susan Faludi, Audre Lorde, Adrienne Rich, Luce Irigaray, Charlene Spretnak, Starhawk, Luisah Teish, Z. Budapest, Susan Griffin, Judy Grahn, Tori Amos, Toni Morrison, Frida Kahlo, Anais Nin, Marge Piercy, Hélène Cixous, and so many others who have helped me to see my own place in this world. I respectfully continue their work in the spirit of sisterhood and solidarity, and I am grateful I have the honor to do so.

It has taken ten years for me to complete this book, but a lifetime of experience has gone into every word, thought and theory. *Goddess Durgā and Sacred Female Power* reflects the evolution and expansion of my female consciousness since embarking on this Eastern path. Perhaps more importantly it is an expression of my understanding of our place in the cosmos by nature of my female body and female being.

Jai Mā! Victory and Reverence to the Mother Goddess!
Laura Amazzone with beloved cat, Gypsy, on my desk beside me
Venice, California
Vijaya Dasami, Tenth Day of the Durgā Pūjā, September 27, 2009.

Notes on Style

When referring to the *God* of the Judeo-Christian tradition, one rarely sees God written with a small *g*. God implies the Absolute, the Ultimate, the Force (Father behind all existence). I understand that Force to be more female than male; therefore, I capitalize any nouns and adjectives that refer to this concept of the Divine as Ultimate and Absolute. My use of caps also intends to shake the consciousness of the reader. Language *is* consciousness and the vibratory power of the word both on the page and in oral communication has an effect on the recipient. Therefore, my use of caps is intended to remind (and reiterate to) the reader the idea of female expression of Divinity. Many of us go throughout life without questioning or wondering why certain cultural, social and religious "Truths" exist. My use of capitalization in this text not only expresses but also affirms my belief in the Divine Source as female as well as male.

I also do not use an article before Goddess unless I am referring to a specific Goddess or Goddesses. Do we ever read of the monotheistic Judeo-Christian tradition GOD with a *the*? No, we do not. When referring to the Divine in the West, we always hear and read of God, and never *the* God. I can only refer to the Divine Mother as Goddess.

Notes

1. Luce Irigaray, *Why Different: A Culture of Two Subjects. Interviews with Luce Irigaray* (New York: Semiotext, 2000), 166-167.
2. Luce Irigaray, *This Sex Which Is Not One*, trans. Catherine Porter (New York: Cornell University, 1985), 165.
3. Sri Mata Amritanandamayi Devi, "The Universal Motherhood" (Speech given at A Global Peace Initiative of Women Religious and Spiritual Leaders, Palais des Nations, United Nations, Geneva), October 7, 2002.
4. In Luce Irigaray, *Why Different?* her interviewers quote her as saying "bring out the woman in our mothers," which speaks to the lack of female agency patriarchally defined roles (mother, wife, daughter, virgin, whore) offer. Irigaray sees the mother-daughter relationship as the "darkest point of our social order"—we do not interact subject to subject and need to re-establish a genealogy of women outside the patriarchal order. See Luce Irigaray's writings on mothers and daughters (for example: Mothers and Daughters in *Why Different?* and *And the One Doesn't Stir Without the Other*).
5. Sri Mata Amritanandamayi Devi, "The Universal Motherhood."

Acknowledgements

Deep gratitude to all the beautiful souls I have been blessed to know, learn from and love. I think of the cakras (circles) of Yoginīs, Matṛkās, and Navadurgās in my life as well as the sacred men who have embodied the fierce, feminist, inspiring, ecstatic, creative sparks of Śakti. You have shown me myriad and diverse facets of female consciousness. I appreciate the ways you have been fearless, courageous, and invincible teachers in approaching and confronting the darkness within and around us.

I am grateful to many as this book would never have come into form without the support and love of my blessed community. Not only those who have been in my life over the last ten years, but also many kindred going back into my childhood. All these friendships have helped my words flow onto these pages. However, there are several women, who, for years, have offered direct support of my lifelong passion for writing and research that I must honor first. Without their support I would never have been able to birth this book: Vicki Noble, Nancy Leatzow, and Margaret Saraswatī Kruszewska.

I wish to thank Vicki Noble for affirming truths, and for always reminding me of Yoginī Reality and my place in this world. I am especially grateful for more than a decade of countless conversations and emails packed with gems of insight, affirmation, resonance and inspiration, Śakti-full exchanges, reads, edits, and brilliant suggestions on earlier drafts that deeply influenced this book and opened my heart and mind. I am forever indebted to you, Vicki, for your love, your kindness, your understanding, and for the Vajra wisdom you have shined on my life.

Nancy Leatzow, thank you for your radical feminist sentiments and for countless conversations about the life of the contemporary Yoginī. You were the first to read these words as they were shaped into chapters, and I deeply appreciate how you were always available to reread them and share your thoughts. You boosted my courage to continue with this project in the moments when my fears got the best of me, and you cheered me on until I finally finished. I am grateful for our exchanges that often got my Śakti flowing so I could move through the tamas and write, write, write!

Margaret Saraswatī Kruszewska, I thank you for embodying and expressing the poetic wisdom of Saraswatī Mā. Many hours were spent writing this book while listening to your soothing voice dancing off the internet air waves during your radio program, *Sacred Sounds with Saraswatī*. Thank you for rivers of invaluable advice, loyal support, and most of all, your soulful understanding of the life of a writer and Yoginī in this day and age!

I am forever indebted to the many (m)others who directly supported the writing, editing and production of this book:

Immense gratitude to Pat Anderson, the most phenomenal proofreader and editor! With all my funky capitalization and the diacritics on Sanskrit words, proofreading this book was no simple task. Pat, your meticulous eye and exquisite precision for detail as well as your ability to make the most tedious of tasks feel exciting, motivating and joyful has been a great gift. Thank you for connecting me to Alan Gilbertson and for all your help with the design of the layout. Most importantly, I thank you for helping me birth *Goddess Durgā and Sacred Female Power* into its current incarnation. You are this book's matriarchal midwife and Auntie!

And thank you to Meloney Hudson for your enthusiasm for my work and for referring me to Pat Anderson!

Alan Gilbertson of G&G Creative, I am deeply grateful for your wonderful typesetting knowledge, for your sagacious advice around spacing, fonts, and the text, and especially for going on wild diacritic hunts! In moments where I felt I would pull all my hair out from having to focus on yet another tedious textual detail, a witty and informative email from you would appear in my inbox and not only educate and reassure me, but also make me laugh. Thank you, thank you, thank you for your endless assistance and patience with the index, and above all, for being such an amazing and generous support. It has been a tremendous blessing to have your expertise in the final stages of the production of this book!

Thank you Samantha Kirk at University Press of America for inviting me to submit my book proposal for consideration and for believing in this feminist work enough to present it to the selection committee. Thank you for giving me this opportunity to share *Goddess Durgā and Sacred Female Power* with the world! I especially appreciate your patience and understanding as I have extended the deadline numerous times.

I am indebted to Elinor Gadon for creating the Women's Spirituality Program at the California Institute of Integral Studies. She has given all of us the opportunity to study female spiritual history and the rich lineages of female deities and female-centered cultures around the globe from earliest times. I am blessed to have had the opportunity to journey through Orissa to the Hirapur Yoginī temple and especially the Grama Devī sites with you in 2003. Thank you for your encouragement of my research, and for your meticulous research and discovery (in a footnote!) of the Tantric temple to Durgā in a small village in Orissa that houses the image on the cover of this book.

Alice Walker, thank you for reminding me to take naps, drink tea, eat greens, cuddle with my beloved, sit in my garden, pay attention to my dreams, and to love and nurture myself. From you I have learned an invaluable lesson—that I do not need to be in front of the computer, or even with pen in hand to be writing! And I thank you for affirming my deep need to live and be alone to write in my red cottage by the sea.

Jim Ryan, my spirited teacher and co-devotee who is really Kālī in drag, I thank you for all of the Śākta, Tantric and feminist knowledge you have shared as my professor, mentor, advisor on my thesis committee in 2001, and friend. Thank you for encouraging and supporting my research and for countless passionate conversations about Mā and Tantra over Jai Mārgaritas and beyond. The quotable Jim Ryan has shifted and expanded my consciousness more than most texts on Tantra I have read! Krīm!

Kalli Rose Halvorson, my Śākta sister devotee and pilgrim—who I met in 2000 for my first Durgā Pūjā and who I have spent more pūjās with in India, California and Nepal than any other Śākta—thank you for fierce Śākta sister conversations about MĀ, patriarchy, astrology, and female power that influenced my consciousness and this work. I thank you for living female consciousness and for sharing your brilliance, beauty, passion, love, and grace. And especially, dear Kalli Rose, thank you for teaching me some of the deepest lessons I have ever known about illness and death. I miss you, sister.

Betty Meckstroth, who carries the generosity of Lakṣmī and compassion of Kuan Yin, without the unconditional love, support and abundance you have shared over the past two decades (and many lifetimes), this book would never have been written.

Yana Womack, I am forever grateful to you for inviting me to assist you on the Durgā Pilgrimage in 2000, a journey that changed the direction of my life. Thank you for being a channel through which Durgā spoke to tell me to write my thesis on Her!

Blessings and gratitude to Sandy Boucher for mentoring me in the initial stages by helping me create a book proposal, for compassionate support in the often grueling submission process, and for your thoughts and edits on the final draft.

Sophia Washam, thank you for formatting assistance.

Erin Sundari Johansen Hurwitt, thank you for sending me fonts that include diacritics.

I am grateful to Andre Ohland and Rose Malone for reducing my rent on the enchanted red cottage so I could stay and write in a very peaceful, inspiring, beautiful, and sacred home.

Special Thanks to Richard Manomani Watson (Hanuman incarnate) for your very generous Lakṣmī support; to Jayne DeMente and Women's Heritage Project for a grant for my work; and to A Coracle Foundation for a travel grant to Nepal for Durgā Pūjā in 2006.

I would like to thank the cakra (circle) of sisters, brothers, teachers, colleagues, lovers and friends who in no particular order have helped me birth this book through their love, encouragement, mentorship and friendship. I thank you for the ways you have supported not only this book, but all my Durgā projects.

Amma~Sri Amritanandamayi Devi, Lillyann Delsig (Mammy), Kyle Corsiglia, Jen Untalan, Crystal Ulrich, Cassandra English, Marisa Tomei, Angela Gengler,

Anne Meckstroth, Mike Linn, Erich Dolejsi, Elizabeth Binyon, Jessa Walters, Brian Pollack, Reena "Didi" Gauchan, Nicola Graydon, Lisa Leone, Pagan George, Suzy Wiles, Dharmanidhi Saraswati, Nandu Menon, Amma Pratyangirae and Swamiji, Chris Chapple, Garrett Larson, Alicia Jones, Ann Lanning, Melissa Martin, Ryan Adelman, Amy Gattie, Kelly Cann, Erin Isebrands, Karen Meckstroth, Janine Canan, Linda Johnsen, Charlene Spretnak, Arisika Razak, Lucia Chiavola Birnbaum, Behiye Suren, Austin Willacy, Barbara Voinar, my mother Cheryll Armstrong and stepfather Bob Armstrong, Egle Balsiene, Audra Avizele, Alaura O'Dell, Mari Ziolkowski, Marguerite Rigoglioso, Lisa Espenmiller, Vanesa Rey-Hipolito, Kristin Garvin, Lisa Solberg, Kamala Davis, Madhya Randi Levinson, Claudia Anfuso, Laura Inserra, Vaschelle Andre, Katty Renard, Abby Ward, Julia Aditi Jean, Reese Bhaktisukhini Souza, Ava Carpentier Kasrabod, Farzad Kasrabod, John Cotugno, James Baldwin, Yessy Peralta, Elizabeth Wells, Trenten Clark, Chani Nicholas, Carrie Brooks, Gary Townsend, Michael Schumacher, Bonnie Stylides, Courtney Sheets, D'vorah Grenn, Dianne Jenett, Michael Aragon, Leah Kerr, Robert Lugo, Paul Gunby, Cindy Matas, Kristin Koziarski, Maei Thomas, Susan Carter, Mary Beth Moser, Minerva Gow, Marsha Lange, Laura Kray, Jill Leslie, Elaine Mazzoni, David Mitchell, Vajra Ma, Bob Steiner, Jonathan DeYoe, Nancy Wright Cooper, Cindi Boardman, Leslie Kanberg, Jen Marlow, Sarah E.J. Cohen, Anniitra Ravenmoon, Letecia Layson, Laura Janesdaughter, Karen Tate and all the wonderful people I have known and learned from in Nepal and India, but especially Ranju Sharma, Ram and his family, Ratna Māyā Devī Mātā and her family, the Kumarīs, and Lhamo.

A very special thank you from the deepest and highest reaches of my heart and soul to Tori Amos for her muse-ic and fierce feminist Goddess spirit.

Reverence and gratitude to all Devīs and Devas who have inspired, protected, loved, and showered me with grace as well as presented challenges that seemed insurmountable but have ultimately led me to transform, grow and blossom: Durgā, Saraswatī, Kālī, Lakṣmī, Lalitā, Mātaṅgī, the Matṛkās, Navadurgā, the Mahāvidyās, Vajrayoginī, the Dakinīs, Hanuman, Śiva, Yoginīs, Yogis, Yakṣīs, Yakṣas, Yemaya, Mami Wata and all the mermaids.

Blessings and deep thanks to my ancestors and to all my spirit guides.

And finally, I am eternally grateful to Gypsy, my blessed feline companion and familiar who spent hours lying on my desk or across books I was referencing, and who danced across my computer keys to shift my attention—often leading to some invaluable insight—and who often got me to take a much-needed break and play. Gypsy you are one of my greatest sources of inspiration and joy, and your presence in my life has been one of the greatest blessings I have ever known. It is no wonder the ancient Egyptians revered cats as deities! Creative inspiration flowed more freely and fully for the writing of this book thanks to the pure Love I received from you.

Namaste, and Jai Mā!

introduction
encountering durga

I am a Yoginī. I am a devotee and priestess. I am a daughter of Goddess Durgā. Through my initiations into ancient and contemporary Śākta Tantra, Śrī Vidyā and Kashmiri Śaivite rituals in India, Nepal, and here in California, I have been exposed to distinctly female realms of consciousness that are different and more liberating than anything I was presented with growing up in the West. Durgā is a Goddess whose very nature is paradoxical. She is fierce and indomitable, infinitely nurturing and compassionate. She takes charge and succeeds. She is the power inherent in all of existence.

My reverence for Goddess Durgā has taken me on an inner and outer journey; first to the temples of Nepal, then throughout India, and perhaps, most importantly, deep within the temple of my soul. Leading the way through this previously unexplored terrain of my psyche and physical environment was Goddess Durgā. Throughout my journey, I have met teachers, both female and male, who embody qualities of Durgā: invincible strength, fearlessness, spiritual discrimination, deep body and soul-based wisdom, and spiritual power. I have witnessed how these teachers, like Durgā, often serve the dispossessed and disenfranchised. Many speak to social and religious injustice, but above all they help us find ways of accessing our own sense of spiritual authority and agency. I have studied Durgā's mythological and ritual significance; and I have experienced what She represents firsthand, having had to confront the internal and external demons in my own life in order to live more holistically within patriarchal culture.[1] Goddess Durgā is an empowered and Divine Female guiding presence, who appears in human, animal and infinite mystical forms in my life.

My relationship with Goddess Durgā has illuminated the repressed aspects of myself that I have been afraid to live out due to cultural conditioning and past experience; time and again it has helped me to confront and transform my pain and fear into a deep sense of internal power[2], or as it is described on the Indian subcontinent, Śakti. Durgā reconnects us with our body's innate wisdom and forces us to combat demons of shame, pain, rage, and fear. She demonstrates that it is our inherent nature to be ambivalent, mutable and flexible rather than eternally pinned to one pole of existence (e.g. victimhood, martyrdom, manipulator, manipulated, etc.). She reminds us of the rich legacy of female shamans, priestesses, healers, Yoginīs and midwives across the globe who have known how to access both internal and external natural power for millennia. Rather than understanding our place in the universe through a dualistic model, as we are taught in the West, the Śākta Tantric paradigm, within which Durgā thrives, offers an alternative and unified model of living in harmony with Mother Earth. Worship of Durgā demands that we consider our relationship with the female body—that we choose to be sexually empowered, rather than allowing ourselves to feel objectified and exploited. What does such an autonomous, self-determined woman look like? This book explores the significance of embracing the inherent paradoxes of life in order to become one with Durgā, and ultimately one with our own inherently Divine nature.

In 2000 I was invited to co-lead a pilgrimage to the Kathmandu Valley of Nepal during the Harvest festival called Durgā Pūjā, Navarātrī or Dashain. I once heard someone say that a pilgrimage begins once one commits oneself to the journey. Indeed, a challenging and awe-inspiring road appeared before me as I prepared to take this journey and pay homage to the Great Goddess Durgā. I had been a devotee of Goddess[3] in Her various cross-cultural manifestations for years; however, I had not yet known Her in Her Hindu incarnation as Durgā, "the Invincible and Unassailable One." As I delved into the research and began familiarizing myself with what at first I assumed was unfamiliar terrain, I began to notice qualities, patterns, and attributes within Durgā's mythology that had shaped the structures of my own life since birth.

Mythology serves as a road map of the human psyche, providing insight into and explanations for the trials and tribulations of human experience. Myth speaks to the unseen realms of our existence that mysteriously shape and guide our lives in ways that become obvious once we relax the over-controlling logical mind. Synchronicities and intuitive knowing have long fascinated me. Like indigenous and tribal peoples around the globe, I have always felt sensitive to the invisible, yet palpable forces that play some governing or at the very least influential role in our existence. I believe in free will, and I also believe we have guides who give us signs, road markers of sorts, which help us to follow our heart's most cherished desires. Preparing for the autumn pilgrimage and considering the implicit meaning behind the harvest and ensuing yearly cycle of destruction, death, and decay, I realized that it was Durgā, the great Remover of Fear and Difficulty, who had been with me from the beginning.

Durgā's roots stem from the ancient earth-based shamanic cultures. The collective forms of Goddess that appear as aspects of Her—the seven and eight Mātṛkās, Yoginīs, and Nine Durgās—all display shamanic powers. Shamanism is deeply related to female collectivity, in fact, the word *shaman* means female healer, contrary to erroneous popular belief that the word refers mainly to male healers. Vicki

Noble is the first author to rectify the authoritative position of *female* shamans in her groundbreaking book, *Shakti Woman*. Noble shows how the roots of shamanism date back thousands of years and can be found in cultures around the globe. A shaman, she notes, takes on the role of healer, midwife, artist, and ritualist, and for millennia was most often female. The range of shamanic knowledge branches many disciplines. Shamans often specialize in some form of divination; have knowledge of astrology and astronomy, dream interpretation, medicinal herbs; are keepers of the mysteries of birth, sex, and death; can control the weather; read signs from the natural world; and many communicate with spirits. Many shamans serve as mediums calling on the wisdom of the dead, or working with lost souls who do not know how to pass into the next realm of existence. Most often a shaman is someone who goes against the grain—someone who knows how to navigate many realities, not just this waking reality. She is an expert at traversing liminal states of consciousness, a person who defies societal norms.

Shamans take up their calling in a number of ways: they may be born into a family of shamans, or they may awaken to their path through severe illness and repetitive trauma. Shamanic initiations almost always entail a period of severe testing—of having all of one's emotional, mental, spiritual, and physical limits violated. They involve near-death experiences, and often otherworldly experiences that take one into places sometimes literally, sometimes figuratively, that one never imagined s/he could handle. Again and again, those on the shamanic path are challenged by extreme circumstances, forced to face up to test after test, and eventually come to a deeper, more integrated understanding of consciousness within themselves and the universe.

I had been on a shamanic path for years: one that began during my early childhood when I had to endure years of severe physical, mental and emotional abuse. As a child my body and spirit were so traumatized that as a young woman my body responded first with Guillian-Barré, a paralyzing virus of the sensory nervous system that left me hospitalized and paralyzed for weeks. I came down with Guillian-Barré in 1992 only days after I cut all contact with my biological father, the main perpetrator of the abuse I experienced. Guillian-Barré, the ensuing spinal tap and three-week hospitalization were only the beginning of a decade-long health crisis. What followed was years of severe gynecological disease (endometriosis, chronic urinary tract and vaginal infections). I was in almost constant physical, mental and emotional pain as I traveled around the world visiting both Western doctors and indigenous healers, trying to find solutions and remedies for the pain and infections that were waging war within my body. In my anger, my pain and the further wounding of being sick for so long, I came to realize that it was only Goddess Durgā who heard my cries and offered me spiritual relief.

During that decade of severe suffering, I became familiar with basic principles of shamanism (premonitions, embodied knowing, waking and night dream visions, healing abilities, a worldview that all is animate and interconnected) and realized that I had been having "mystical" or shamanic experiences my entire life. To me, these altered-state experiences (both with, and mainly without, the use of substances), served as a refuge from the painful reality of the disconnected, inanimate worldview in which I grew up.

Almost two years before the pilgrimage in 2000, I had been called to the Kathmandu Valley for the first time. I had been living in Vienna, Austria, and had embarked on a yearlong backpacking adventure through Southeast Asia. I traveled, even though I was ill. I suffered mainly from severe menstrual cramps and chronic pain due to endometriosis and ovarian cysts. I was furious that Western medicine had not been able to help me, and discouraged by the many alternative remedies I had tried that offered only temporary relief. I insisted on traveling despite extreme pain and discomfort, still trying to connect with something outside rather than within myself. Healers in Austria, Malaysia, Indonesia and Lithuania all told me the same thing: it was I who was inviting the pain back. They believed that in some respect I had psychically taken on the pain of womankind—first through the abuse I had endured as a child and then through the physical pain of reproductive illnesses. Why? In part so I could teach myself and, eventually, others about female power and female consciousness. But, I would have to experience firsthand how it felt to be so totally dis-empowered. Often I was not sure if it was I who was crazy, or if these healers were. But one thing was for sure: as I would lie writhing in my bed, screaming out in pain, I would cry for the African and Muslim women who had undergone female genital mutilation; for the women around the world who were being raped, molested and beaten; for women who did not have access to health care and were suffering from painful vaginal infections, STDs, pelvic inflammatory disease and other reproductive illnesses; for women who were pregnant or in labor and at the mercy of uncaring doctors. I cried for women past and present and the excruciating suffering our bodies must endure. The female body, the gateway through which each and every human being enters this world, is too often a battleground for suffering. I felt it acutely, my own pain and that of the oppressed female, in my yoni (Sanskrit for vagina and uterus).

While I continued to work with shamans, healers and doctors in the many different countries I visited and was hospitalized five times during this period, I did not fully make the turn into healing and personal power until I went to Nepal and was introduced to Goddess as the Kumārī, a virginal form of Durgā. Nepal and India had always intrigued me, but a deep part of me always knew that when it was my time to go to those places I would be called by Goddess. Shortly before I had to return to the States, strangers—both local Asians and travelers alike—would spontaneously approach me in Thailand, in Indonesia, in Malaysia, and in Vietnam, and ask if I had been to Nepal. What at first seemed amusing, and perhaps even part of the usual travel talk, gradually came to feel like a mysterious calling, one that I could not shrug off as banal and insignificant. Strangers came up to me quite frequently and randomly posed the question, *Have you been to Nepal?* even before the usual, *Where are you from*? I began to consider going to Nepal, perhaps in the spring. However, my beloved grandmother, my Mammy,[4] was experiencing declining health, and I began to wonder if it was best I return to the States to be with her.

One of my greatest fears since early childhood had been her death. Mammy had been the only adult I could fully trust as a child. She was the only one who showed me unconditional love in its purest, truest sense. She was always my sanctuary from my conflict-ridden home life. Being so far away from her while I lived abroad was a continuous inner conflict for me; however, she always encouraged me to follow my heart. She promised me that she would let me know when she needed me to come home to her. I traveled for both of us, and as often as I could recorded my experiences into a tape recorder and sent the tapes to her so she could live through me.

In those days (mid-nineties) communication to the States was only possible via snail mail, or phone calls from public phones. I rarely had a number at which my family could reach me. Although today it may be hard to believe, the majority of travelers did not have email accounts, nor were there even internet cafes. Cell phones with international plans were far from affordable for those of us on a traveler's budget. Therefore, the lines of communication I often tapped into were shamanic: intuition, premonitions, tarot readings, and dreams.

In December of 1997 I had such a dream: my grandmother was calling to me, asking me to come home. I phoned my mother the next day and she told me it was "time." Mammy was "seeing" her ancestors. She would ask about loved ones who had died years before, pointing them out in various corners of the room. They had come for her, I was certain. And my mother affirmed that Mammy kept saying she wanted to "go home." I returned to the States to be with her, to help her cross over, to release her to the ancestors. I was devastated by the thought of losing her, but honored to be part of such a powerful rite of passage. This was the work of Goddess, of the ancient priestesses or Yoginīs who oversaw all sickness and funerary rites.[5]

The Yoginī is an independent woman, unfettered by her relationships, not bound to social conditioning. She is a woman who defies the all-too-limiting social expectations and carves her own path. She, like Goddess whom she serves, is a great navigator. She can traverse the realms between life and death, sickness and health, sorrow and joy. She revels in the liminal realm, a realm that is potent with possibility, yet can feel unstable and intimidating to the uninitiated. This is a realm where "normal" human rules do not apply. It is a realm governed by unseen forces both benevolent and malevolent, a realm of consciousness sadly unfamiliar to many of us today as our "modern" culture rejects and denies the cosmic reality of this inherent part of the life cycle. We must not always be fixated on the pleasure of existence. Death. Pain. Sorrow. Suffering. Each has something to teach us and each is an equally valid part of life. In a sense conflicted experiences serve as doorways to a life that is perhaps in many ways richer from the experience of our having survived and confronted such formidable forces.

The greatest fear of my life was losing my grandmother. From the age of four I spontaneously began to declare that when she died, I was going with her. Without her loving light and presence, I believed, life would not be worth living. Considering the severe abuse I experienced during my childhood, it is not surprising I made such declarations. Over twenty years later, my time had come to face what I dreaded most, the loss of Mammy. Here was the ultimate test of the modern Yoginī: to confront, embrace, then transform that which she fears will utterly destroy her. Despite the chaos and utter dissolution that is occurring all around her, can she still notice the signposts wavering in the winds of change? Can she courageously begin to walk down the unfamiliar path that will inevitably appear before her?

During this time a friend called and told me she had had a dream of me resting under fir trees on the Himālayan mountain, Annapurna. Annapurna is also the Nepalese Goddess of Grain and Abundance. She is a Goddess of Nurturance, Plenty, and Strength, qualities I needed as I navigated the terrain around Mammy's death. I listened and wept as Kelly related this dream. Once again, someone was telling me "out of the blue" to go to Nepal. Goddess was asking me to pay homage to Her, not only here, but also there.

As if to affirm this realization and the reality of the call, a day later I met for the first time one of my Mammy's caregivers, Audra, a wise Lithuanian healer. She hugged me, looked deep into my eyes, and then told me how happy she was to be reunited with me again. *It has been lifetimes!* she said knowingly, then asked in all seriousness, *So, when are you going to go to Nepal?* We had never spoken before this meeting, and yet once again Nepal, a land of Yoginīs and Yogis, fiercely compassionate and fully empowered Goddesses, was calling me.

One of the many Goddess manifestations to whom I was devoted during those years before Mammy's death was Hecate, the Greek Goddess of Death and Transformation. She is the Goddess who stands at the crossroads. Crossroads have long been associated with other realms. They are a gateway of sorts, a place where we must choose in which direction to head, and once that choice is made, never look back. Crossroads are places of power in Nepal and India. They are the stomping ground of Greek Hecate, and they are also the terrain of a collective form of Durgā, the Mātṛkās. At the time of Mammy's death, I did not know Durgā by name, nor did I know much about the Hindu tradition.

My Mammy died on December 29, 1997 at the age of eighty-seven. I held vigil for days as she lay dying, her breath labored, her body weak and ailing. I brushed her hair, patted her parched tongue with a wet cotton sponge, and massaged her face, hands and feet. I sang to her. I promised her that she could live through me—that I would live despite my lifelong belief that I would die with her. I was holding her hand as she took her last breath.

Despite my reverence for Goddess and what I thought then as well as what I believe now about death, it still rips my heart and soul open to think of her passage from this reality. The pain of the physical loss of someone we hold so dear, the mysterious disappearance of their life-force energy, the listless shell of a body that remains—none of it can be grasped and understood with the logical mind. And yet, the peace I have experienced at that moment when soul leaves the body with both my grandmother and a cherished cat I lost in 2005 was like nothing I have ever experienced before. A portal opens and our loved ones disappear into the ethers putting us in contact, for a moment, with the most profound sense of peace and clarity. An ancient wisdom comes streaming through, perhaps it is Goddess Herself. Yet, to most, that sense of deep embodied knowing soon becomes forgotten, remaining inaccessible and incomprehensible: to all but the shaman, Yoginī and Yogi who must learn to navigate these terrains.

After Mammy's death I returned to Southeast Asia and spent several months traveling off the beaten track in Vietnam and Thailand. I stayed in places without electricity and other modern comforts. I needed to live as close to the land and as much at the mercy of elemental forces as possible. As I was experiencing an inconsolable sense of grief and loss, the only solace was to surrender to the natural rhythms of my environment and live the simplest life possible.

In April I traveled to the Kathmandu Valley of Nepal. I had come home. The medieval red brick buildings and streets bathed in the glow of the South Asian sun were strangely familiar. Immediately I was drawn to the temple of the Kumārī, at that time a seven-year-old living incarnation of Goddess Durgā. I entered Her temple courtyard wearing red (which signifies the life-force energy specifically known as Śakti), without realizing until later that this is part of the ritual custom in approaching and worshiping Goddess here. I stood there in awe of the intricately carved temple struts, the small deity plaques above doors, the yantras (geometric forms of Goddess) carved into the ground. Within moments She appeared wrapped in red and gold glittery robes and laden with necklaces, earrings, bracelets and rings. The Virgin Goddess, who within the Nepalese political structure has even more power and authority than the king, is chosen around the age of two, put through a series of tests that only a truly awakened being can conquer, and searched for thirty-three auspicious marks on Her body. The process of choosing male lamas in the Tibetan Buddhist tradition is similar to the Kumārī's. The power of Durgā remains within the Kumārī until She begins to bleed—either from the loss of a tooth, a cut, or, most importantly, when She menstruates. This sudden loss of divine power with

Her menstruation is suggestive of patriarchal religious customs that have exploited and stripped females of their human rights for millennia—a point I will return to later. When women's creativity and sexuality are exploited or abused, illness can develop. I later learned that women who have menstrual disorders go to the Kumārī and pray for help. Reproductive illnesses are part of Her domain. She embodies a fierce Goddess of female sexual and creative power. Is it any wonder that I had instinctually gone directly to Her temple upon arriving in Nepal?

I was not prepared for the arresting sight of a young girl decked in rich red robes, and bejeweled with gold necklaces and amulets. Her forehead had been painted bright red and traced with yellow to accent the rest of Her face. In the center was a carefully-placed glittering gold and black eye. Around Her human eyes were thick black lines, to ward off evil spirits. She leaned out the intricately carved window frame, held up by two attendants on either side of Her, and watched me, the only person in the courtyard, with all three eyes. Her stare went right through me, and seemed to rearrange and remove some of what was inside. I received Her darśan, an auspicious and very potent blessing from the deity. In many respects, darśan, which means to see and be seen by the deity, is the ultimate goal for a pilgrim. At the time I had no conscious understanding of any of the ritualistic or even spiritual significance of this. I felt Her energy and knew She was different than the other humans I had met. This young embodiment of Durgā has undeniable power. To me the Kumārī was and is a living Goddess, and yet the qualities of her human life trouble me. Until recently, She was not allowed to be educated, for She is believed to be omniscient. Her feet are not allowed to touch the ground for the ground is deemed polluting to orthodox Hindus and Buddhists, so She is carried everywhere. Even more concerning, after Her short "reign," the pubescent girl is returned to her village and often ostracized by the community, mainly out of fear that they somehow may incite the wrath of the Goddess She once was. Little is done to help acculturate her into everyday life. The status of the Kumārī tells much about how the status of women has shifted and remains maligned—a point I shall return to later. However, what interests me deeply is the universal acceptance of this *female* child as Divine if only for a ten to twelve year period. I often wonder, how would my life and every other woman's I know be different if we knew from an early age that we are not separate from the Divine, but like the Kumārī, hold this sacred power within our female bodies?

During the next two months of my stay in Nepal, a path opened before me, one that I had longed for and dreamed about for ages. I worked with a Tibetan shaman, a woman called Lhamo, who embodied Dorje Yudronama, a fierce manifestation of Goddess to the Tibetans. Spirit possession or channeling deities is a shamanic art, one that in ancient Tibet was often a spiritual art passed from mother to daughter. People travel from all over the world to seek Lhamo's divine healing powers. Lhamo, or Mrs. Dolkar, which is her married name, fled from Tibet before the Chinese occupation and took refuge in Ladakh. As her reputation as a healer grew, His Holiness the Dalai Lama invited her to come to Dharmasala to perform a healing. Before she moved to the Kathmandu Valley, the Dalai Lama certified Lhamo as a "reliable exorcist for all mental and physical ills."

I learned about Lhamo during a four-day intensive Reiki course at the Kathmandu Healing Center. In addition to my gynecological problems, I had begun experiencing overwhelming feelings of grief for my Mammy. I felt possessed—as if my Mammy was at times living in my body. I craved foods she liked, colors she wore, and would hear her favorite songs in my head. I felt as if I was only half in this reality, and more often walking in the land of the dead. I began to wonder if I was being called to cross over as I had promised Mammy so long ago. I also feared I was losing my mind. When someone told me about Lhamo I knew I needed to go.

The technique Lhamo uses is paradoxical in nature and can best be described as "fiercely compassionate."[6] The friendly woman, Mrs. Dolkar, who greeted me at the door, became a shockingly different personality once the ritual was in progress, she had gone into a trance and Dorje Yudronamma had entered her body. She cackled, she screamed, she whipped rice and corn at those of us in the room. About twenty people—Nepalese, Tibetans, Newari, a few Europeans, a Tamil Singaporean family, and myself—were in the audience. A Singaporean woman, who had leukemia and had traveled all over the world seeking medical help, was told that her Western medications were going to kill her before the disease would. To heal her, Lhamo lightly hit her with a metal stick and then sucked out a thick black liquid from her head. She fiercely bit each of the woman's breasts without breaking the skin and sucked out large bloody clumps and spit them into a bowl.

Needless to say, after witnessing a few of such seemingly violent sessions, I approached Lhamo with much trepidation. But to my surprise she took my hand and started stroking my cheeks. "Your mama. Dead." she said in English before turning to her translator to help her give a more detailed analysis of my condition. I cried as the translator told me my Mammy was still in my aura, in fact her spirit was feeding off of my body because neither of us was willing to let go of each other. She warned that if I did not do a ritual to release her it would be harmful to us both. I was not frightened, but relieved. Lhamo's words were of great comfort to me. Although Mammy's physical body was no longer here, her spirit had indeed lived on. I understood that Mammy had work to do in the spirit world, and I, on this physical plane. Even though I could not see her or touch her, I could feel her spiritual presence and knew we would always be part of each other. I had never before felt so calm and sure about any of my convictions about life after death before.

Days later I returned for the special fire pūjā bringing nine different kinds of flowers and a photo of Mammy. The fire pūjā was a special exorcism. Elements of the ritual, in particular the significance of offerings in the number nine (flowers, grains, meats), the spirit possession, prophesies, burning of photos of loved ones and other belongings associated with the spirit of the possessed, and the brutal techniques she used to dislodge the spirits and entities from our auras and bodies all are shamanic in nature and are evident in the later research I did on Durgā. In fact, I later came to see that the fiercely nurturing Dorje Yudronamma and Her set of twelve goddesses was a Tibetan equivalent of Durgā and her collective entourages of 7, 8, 9, and more Goddesses pointing to the matriarchal and shamanic roots that underpin the Tibetan, Nepalese and Indian traditions.

Totally convinced of Lhamo's divine healing powers, I returned again and again. During another session Lhamo looked at my belly and shrieked *Tumor! Tumor!* She proceeded to bite the skin over my right ovary and sucked out a large black mass and several stones. I left with an herbal remedy knowing she had just prevented me from having to undergo a third surgery. For almost a year my gynecological problems got better. I was not plagued by such painful menstrual periods, the infections decreased, and overall I felt stronger, more vibrant.

Lhamo is a shaman, a medium for Goddess, communicator with the dead, healer and herbalist, exorcist and ritualist. My visit to her and to the Kumārī during this first visit to Nepal activated my kuṇḍalinī—that serpentine energy that lies coiled at the base of our spines and rises through intense spiritual practices and experiences. I had a low fever the entire time I was in Nepal, but I did not feel sick. In an energetic sense I was blazing with Śakti. I felt like karmas were being burned away and knew I was changing in ways that were irreversible. Every time I looked in the mirror I was shocked by the way my eyes shone. Being in the presence of the Kumārī and Lhamo had opened portals long forgotten: they were helping me to remember who I am. Before I left the country I returned to the Kumārī's temple in tears. Having found Her again, I was reluctant to leave Her. I felt she was in some way responsible for my having been led to Lhamo for it was due to a synchronicity on the way to Her temple on the first day I had arrived that I had heard about the healing class, and there received the information about Lhamo. So, I returned to pay homage. I stood in Her courtyard, silently weeping, filled with gratitude and love. I promised I would finally return to the States and devote the graduate work I had been considering doing for the past six years to Her if she would help me find a way back to Her. And soon.

One year later, as promised, I returned to the States, and moved to San Francisco to begin a Master's program in Women's Spirituality at the California Institute of Integral Studies. The program offered courses on women's spiritual history and ancient and contemporary cultures that venerated the Divine as female, as Goddess. On my first day of the *Mary: Goddess of the West* class, a woman I had met at a gathering the night before approached me and admired some jewelry I was wearing from Nepal. "Yesterday you told me you have been to Nepal and feel a strong connection to the people and the land." I nodded enthusiastically, then Yana continued. "I am leading a pilgrimage to Nepal for the Durgā Pūjā next fall. I need an assistant. Do you want to come?" I remembered my prayers to the Kumārī, my almost desperate request to return to Her soon. And here was an opportunity. Yana told me that she would do research on Tārā, the Vajrayana Buddhist manifestation of Goddess, while I could focus on Durgā. I then knew the Kumārī, the virgin manifestation of Durgā Herself, had been listening. My prayers had been answered. I was going to return to my beloved Nepal.

Notes

1. My use of the word and concept *patriarchy* throughout this book refers to social, political, cultural and religious systems of dominance, hierarchy, and competition that have only existed for the past 5000-7000 years. At the core of this male-centered worldview are values of *power over* rather than a *power that comes from within* or is shared. Patriarchy is a system that "elevates male domination to universal status by the androcentric focus of Western social science." Peggy Reeves Sanday, "Antigone in Sumatra: Matriarchal Values in a Patriarchal Context," in *The Rule of Mars: Readings on the Origins, History and Impact of Patriarchy,* ed. Cristina Biaggi (Manchester, Connecticut: Knowledge, Ideas & Trends, 2005), 95. This is a tradition that perpetuates unnatural death and violence, oppression and exploitation to achieve its agenda for an elite, predominantly male, few.

   "In terms of social life, patriarchy constantly creates chaos like wars, conquests, oppression, revolutions, and civil conflicts, all which have been laboriously choreographed by the rulers of their day. In its relatively short history, patriarchy has proven to be extremely turbulent and unstable, as shown by the quickly changing 'world empires' with their high consumption of human life. And today the destructive tendency to devalue all life—a tendency inherent in patriarchy from the very beginning—has reached gigantic dimensions in such areas as nuclear overkill, overpopulation of the earth with increasing poverty, and climatic catastrophes." Heide Goettner-Abendroth, "Notes on the Rise and Development of Patriarchy," in *The Rule of Mars,* 38-39.

   I do not consider all men to be patriarchal and so I will use the term "patriarchal man" to refer to men who carry these limiting and life suppressing values. I also believe there are women who exhibit patriarchal qualities in order to fit into the dominant system and get what they want without regard for others. However, patriarchy privileges the white male race over all others.

   In a later chapter I will discuss an alternative to patriarchy or the rule of the father—matriarchy—and how it differs. In brief, matriarchy is not the opposite of patriarchy nor does it mean "the rule of the mother." Matriarchy is a social order where women are at the center (Cristina Biaggi, *The Rule of Mars,* 13). Drawing from the Greek *arche*, which means "origin, beginning and sovereignty," (Sanday, "Antigone in Sumatra," 96) we can consider female-centered traditions such as the Śākta, Tantra, and Kaula traditions that value the importance of the female lineage and clan (kula) as having matriarchal values.

2. Power has come to take on negative connotations within today's world for it most often refers to dominance, hierarchy, usurped authority and competition. Heide Goettner-Abendroth offers an alternative definition to the patriarchal concept of power as a power that means "possession of authority/fortitude/ dignity as a property of nature in one's personality." (Heide Goettner-Abendroth, "Notes on the Rise and Development of Patriarchy," in *The Rule of Mars: Readings on the Origins, History and Impact of Patriarchy*, ed. Cristina Biaggi (Manchester, Connecticut: Knowledge, Ideas & Trends, 2005), 27. One important distinction is that the sense of empowerment I refer to throughout this book "is not based on an enforcement staff or structure." (Ibid.) I define power as an energy that comes from within and when expressed holistically is an energy that is shared. In the Hindu Śākta Tantra tradition, the term Śakti means "power." This kind of power is viewed as the animating *female* and creative force behind all existence.

3. I am choosing to use Goddess without the article "the" to refer to what I consider to be the *Divine Force* of all existence. As my dear Śākta sister Kalli Rose Halvorson pointed out to me years ago, in the Judeo-Christian tradition the white male father god is never referred to as *the God*, but God. In the Śākta Tantra tradition, Durgā and other goddesses like Her are referred to as Devī in Sanskrit or Goddess.

4. Although she was of Danish descent, my grandmother chose to be called Mammy when I was born. Some of her closest friends were African Americans, and one of them was an early role model for me. I do not wish to appear disrespectful to African Americans in my use of this term, *Mammy*. Alice Walker discusses the racist implications of this name and how the African mother became demonized in her essay, "Coming in from the Cold" in *Living By the Word* (New York: Harcourt Press, 1981). I am deeply disturbed that *Mammy* was "expropriated and popularized by whites and used to designate a kind of contented, white-folks-comforting black woman of enormous girth, of whom black people felt ashamed"(Walker 1981, 59). However, I do not believe my grandmother was being racist in taking this name. Knowing her, it seems she was aligning herself with her African American friends by trying to reclaim the essence of this name by honoring it and becoming a Mammy, a mother to me. It is interesting to consider the possible origin of this term. The ancient Ghanians refered to the moon, who was experienced as maternal, as *Mame*. Dr. Lucia Chiavola Birnbaum postulates that the oldest Divinity on the planet is African and female and memory of our "dark mother" is encoded in our DNA (*dark mother: african origins and godmothers,* (Lincoln, Nebraska: iUniverse, 2001)). Perhaps on a subconscious level my Mammy remembered the name's ancient lunar and maternal origin: the all-nurturing and loving mother, who could also be fiercely protective of her kin.

5. Vicki Noble, *Double Goddess. Women Sharing Power* (Rochester, Vermont: Bear & Company, 2003).

6. China Galland was the first to coin this expression of the fierce yet compassionate nature of Goddess. She calls Durgā, "Goddess of Fierce Compassion."

part one

the teachings of goddess durga

Chapter One
Durga: Goddess of Paradox

The Great Mother Goddess Durgā astride her tiger, brandishing eight to eighteen arms, each carrying a distinct weapon or tool, is one of the most ubiquitous images on the Indian subcontinent today. She is stunningly beautiful: her long dark hair cascades down her back and over her shoulders; each arm is adorned with bangles and decorated with hennaed tattoos, golden earrings dangle from her ears and on one side are connected to a delicate chain that leads to a ring in her nose. A garland of orange and yellow marigolds flows over her breasts; the folds of her sari enhance her sensual feminine features, and intricate symbols emulating the wondrous patterns of Mother Nature are portrayed on her feet.

To the Indian and Nepalese people of past and present, Durgā is the Divine Mother Goddess who presides over the seasons of life, death and birth. To many She is simply Devī, which means Goddess and comes from the Sanskrit root *deva* (to shine). In Her more peaceful forms She is known as Saraswatī, Goddess of Creativity; Lakṣmī, Goddess of Abundance; Lalitā, Goddess of Delight. In Her fierce and wrathful manifestations She appears as Kālī, Goddess of Death and Transformation; Vajrayoginī, Goddess of Power; or Caṇḍīkā, The Angry One. Although She comes to us with as many names and forms as there are beings on this planet, Durgā, which means the invincible, unconquerable, and unassailable one, is the name She takes when She comes to help us calmly face our fears and difficulties. A liberator of the oppressed and the marginalized, Durgā is not a warring Goddess by nature. She comes because we need Her help. When called upon She leads us through situations that feel insurmountable. It is no wonder one of the meanings of Her name, Durgā, is fortress. Durgā indeed reminds us of the fortress we each carry within ourselves and can call on when we need to fortify our emotional, physical, mental and spiritual boundaries.

To many in the West, Durgā remains an esoteric deity; however, the richly compelling Eastern symbolism that is associated with Her is too often greatly misunderstood. Goddess Durgā radiates great confidence and authority. She is formidable and fearsome: four of Her hands hold a scythe, a spear, a trident and a club. She is beneficent, generous and reassuring: three other hands hold a conch shell, a lotus, a discus, and another gives the mudra or hand gesture of *Fear not, I will protect you.*

The sacred objects Durgā carries in each of Her eight to eighteen hands, like the Great Goddess Herself, carry the power to create and destroy. Symbolically they serve as guides and tools we can use to help us get through the inevitable cycles of death, destruction and suffering as well as life, blossoming and joy. For example, Durgā's knives are not to be used for violence, but are a symbol of liberation. The knife is a tool that cuts away; it severs or excises that which no longer serves us whether it is a destructive belief, an unhealthy relationship, or a toxic situation in which we find ourselves embroiled. Her sword also points to the focus and discriminating wisdom that is necessary in life—particularly to those committed to a spiritual path. All the sharp weapons Durgā carries cut through obstacles that impede our progress and clear the path for spiritual growth.

Often She carries a shield for protection, a bow for determination and focus, and an arrow for penetrating insight. When She holds a bell it is to be used to invoke mental clarity and to clear the air of negativity, when Her fingers play with a string of beads (mala), Her worshipers are reminded of lessons on concentration and spiritual growth. The club She wields can be used to beat a new path, and the three pronged trident pierces through the veils of the past, present and future and teaches us about birth, life and death. The conch shell represents the vibratory powers of manifestation, while the lotus refers to both spiritual and material abundance. The discus refers to the cycles of existence, especially in the physical world. The skull or severed head, a common motif also associated with Durgā in Her fiercest of forms, represents the ego and all the ways we become slaves to our egos. The ego mind conceives of situations as bad or good, positive or negative, while Durgā is here to show us the paradoxical nature of our reality and the divine unity behind all existence.

Goddess Durgā Herself embodies the paradoxes of our very existence: She is both Warrior Goddess and Divine Mother, both Death Bringer and Creator. Durgā can help us open to the complete picture of our human existence: that fierceness coexists with tenderness, death walks hand in hand with life, that pain and suffering are the polar and complementary reality of joy and ecstasy. No matter who we are, how old we are, how much money we have or what we believe or desire; no living being on this planet is free from the inevitability of death and decay. In the West we are taught to look away, to deny, repress and ignore our emotions; we avoid consciously facing the inevitable reality of human pain, suffering and death. Although we cannot stop all suffering, we can find more embodied and life enriching ways of approaching such realities—rather than denying them through various mind numbing means. Now more than ever we need the guidance of a role model like Durgā to lead us through the horrors, the fear, and the pain that riddle this world. Durgā takes us right to the center of the chaos that is upsetting our lives and shows us that no matter how harsh reality may seem, we can survive and come through feeling more empowered and more alive. For centuries Durgā's myth known as the *Devī Māhātmya* has been used to guide Her devotees through tumultuous life experiences. Let us turn to it now and see what wisdom and insight it may have to offer us in the twenty-first century.

The Great Goddess Durgā's Mythic Battle of Balance and Liberation

Durgā's myth, the *Devī Māhātmya,* dates back to the fifth century C.E. Today, different episodes from the myth are recited on each day of Her autumn and spring festivals that take place around the equinoxes each year. However the fall festival, since it marks the end of the harvest and the beginning of the season of death and decay, is in most places the more significant of the two yearly festivals. Just as the equinoxes mark a time on the planet where day and night are in perfect balance, each autumn Durgā's myth is recited over a nine-day period to invoke balance within people's individual lives as well as within the entire community. On the tenth day of the festivities Her followers celebrate the Goddess' victory and mimic the mythological celebration that takes place in the story. Here then is the tale of how the Great Goddess stopped the demons from destroying the equilibrium of the Earth, and how She came to be called Durgā:

It has been said that when life becomes full of suffering, when no relief seems to be within reach, when forces beyond our control threaten to destroy our very existence, it is then that the Universal Mother Goddess will appear to Her devotees and free them from the forces that bind them to their anguish. Although the Great Mother Goddess is always with us, Her devotees know that She does not always reveal Herself. Her ways are mysterious and often hidden. In this patriarchal era it seems She has offered some of Her responsibilities to the male gods Brahmā, Viṣṇu and Śiva. However, as Her tale shows us, the male gods are by no means as powerful as She. Although the male gods have their place within the universal scheme of things, there are times when it is only the Divine Female Force who can respond to the desperate call of those that need Her. As an embodiment of unconditional love, the Goddess in Her forms as Ambikā, Caṇḍīkā and Pārvatī will come with Her entourage of wildly fierce, amazonlike Goddesses and fight the asuras or demons that threaten our very existence. To those who know Her, the Goddess is Time and the Goddess is Place. She is the Earth and the Cosmos, the Reality and Unreality of every realm. She is Existence Itself. In the timelessness of Her Ultimate Reality there is a demon known as Mahiṣāsuramardinī or Durgāma, the shape-shifting buffalo demon, who visits the land of the gods in search of the God of creation, Brahmā. The buffalo-headed demon is exceptionally large, strong, and very greedy, but unlike the immortal deities who are watching over different aspects of earthly life, Mahiṣa is a mortal. Having a mortal soul is the one weakness the demon cannot tolerate for he has grand plans for himself. After years of prayer and penance, Mahiṣa goes to Brahmā and asks him for a boon. He finds Brahmā dreaming away and wakes him to ask that he be given the gift of immortality. Although he has been asleep and neglecting his duties since the beginning of his reign, Brahmā still has enough sense to refuse. He is wise enough to know a demon should not be given the gift of immortality, but he does agree to grant Mahiṣa's second request: that he die only at the hands of a woman.

Off the demon goes, determined to conquer the universe. For over a thousand years, the demon and his ruthless armies wage war in every realm of the cosmos. They derive great pleasure from their terrorizing games. First they take over the earth, then they march off into the heavenly land of the gods. Unfortunately, the male gods do not pay much attention to the demon nor do they even attempt to intervene and come to the aid of the other beings in the various worlds whose existence is being annihilated. Only after the demon has conquered their realm do they take notice and try to stop him. However, they are unsuccessful. It seems that nothing can be done to stop the demons' ruthless bloodshed and now they threaten to rule over the land of the gods. The head of the demons has even taken on the name Indra, King of the Gods. Finally, the holy male trinity is summoned by the lesser gods. Śiva, God of Destruction, Viṣṇu, Lord of Preservation, and Brahmā, God of Creation all meet and try to devise a plan to stop the demons. Not only are they too late, but also they do not possess the natural power necessary to stop the violence and restore balance on the earth. It is only through the grace and will of the Divine Mother Goddess who pervades the entire universe, and who ultimately is the force behind these gods' own existence, who can stop the demons. But will She come? They remember Her promise to always come when called and call a meeting of all the gods.

The gods convene and out of the fiery rays of their anger the Goddess appears. Śiva offers Her his trident, Brahmā, his rosary, Viṣṇu, his discus, Varuṇa, God of the Waters, gives Her a conch, while the wind god Vayu gives Her his bow and arrow. Each of the gods approaches the formidable Goddess and offers Her one of his weapons as well as a jewel. She is adorned with glittering anklets, shimmering bracelets and rings sporting faceted jewels the size of mountains. The brilliant rays of the sun radiate from Her skin, the glow of the moon shines from Her face, and the stars lend their sparkle to Her teeth and Her three eyes. Never before has a more beautiful and powerful being existed. She is Ambikā, Mother of the Universe, and the gods owe their very existence to Her divine grace. They each bow before Her and offer Her praise while Devī summons Her mighty tiger and climbs onto his gold and black striped back.

Undaunted by the thought of battling this vicious demon and his minions, Devī roars in delight at the task before Her. Her laughter sends a tremendous echo across the skies and causes tremors in all the worlds. Mountains tremble and shake, and rivers, lakes and oceans swell and whirl into tsunamilike waves. Suddenly the worlds the demons so arrogantly thought they had conquered have been shaken into a different kind of turmoil than that which they themselves had created. Mahiṣa and his demon armies are shocked that there is still another power that they must reckon with. When Mahiṣa learns it is a Goddess, he is delighted for he mistakenly thinks he is more powerful than She. The demon king Mahiṣa sends two of his favorite and most repulsive little demon spies, Caṇḍa and Muṇḍa, to find the Goddess. They are ordered to do whatever it takes to bring Her to him. The demon king has decided that a woman of such beauty is meant to be his possession. He will take Her for his wife.

"If She does not come willingly, then drag Her by Her hair!!!" he foolishly commands them. He then sends them off to find the beautiful Goddess who is waiting for them in the Himālayas. Devī has taken the form of Pārvatī, the stunning mountain Goddess with skin as dark and rich as the earth. When the demons find Her, they are dumbstruck by Her radiant beauty. However, they remember their mission and attempt to regain control of themselves. They tell Her they have come to take Her to their king for he wants Her as his wife. "If you even dare refuse," they tell Her as they snicker, burp, and rub their balls, "we have been told to drag you by the hair."

"Oh really?" the Goddess replies. "But I will only marry the man or god who can defeat me in battle."

The demons, Caṇḍa and Muṇḍa laugh and joke with each other about how easy it will be to fight Her—after all She is only a woman. The Goddess listens to them carry on, but soon becomes bored by their childish antics and ridiculous egos. She lets out a long sigh that stirs the trees across all the lands, and then points Her finger at them. The rays of the sun reflect off of Her faceted carnelian stone ring and for a brief second blind the demons' sight. They do not even have a chance to be alarmed, for as She shakes Her finger flames stream out its tip and annihilate the demons.

When Mahiṣa learns that two of his most beloved generals have been tricked by the Goddess he is outraged. He sends his army of hundreds of thousands of demons to defeat Her. They descend upon the mountains where She is waiting for them and has transformed Herself into one of Her fiercest forms. Caṇḍīkā, the angry Goddess with Her three eyes that can see past, present and future all at once stands ready. She raises the various weapons in each of Her eighteen arms while She and Her tiger calmly wait for the demons to approach them. As soon as She sees them She rings Her bell. Its sweet chime confuses them and sends them scattering in every direction. Her sword slices through thousands of demons in one fell swoop, Her club pounds them into the earth, and Her arrows pierce the empty chests of demon after demon. However, Mahiṣa has another trick that cleverly keeps him in power: with every drop of blood that falls from the demons—another demon springs up from the blood. Enthralled by his own cleverness, Mahiṣa watches the battle from his palace while demons and demonesses oil his horned feet and massage his hairy limbs. His pride grows more immense by the second, and he feels increasingly certain that even the Supreme Mother of the Universe cannot defeat him, the king of the demons. The battle wages on and on and more and more demons appear with every drop of blood that is shed. The Goddess knows She must change Her tactic. She decides to call on Her own powerful army of female warrior deities and in Her rage summons eight Goddesses or Matṛkās who spring from Her third eye and with various animal companions leap onto the battlefield. The Matṛkās send out ululating war cries that stop every demon in his tracks. Arrows fly through the air and before the demons' blood can even fall to the earth, one of the Matṛkās, Kālī or Cāmuṇḍā unrolls Her long snaky tongue and laps up every single drop. Furious that he is no longer winning, Mahiṣa throws a temper tantrum. He calls out to Caṇḍīkā and accuses Her of cheating. He demands that She take back Her army and promises he will do the same. It is time for a duel between the two of them. Knowing that the Matṛkās are only aspects of Herself, the Mother of the Universe, the Goddess inhales and Her sweet breath draws them back inside Her luminous body.

For a moment the land and all beings are silent as Ambikā waits for Mahiṣa to appear. Behind Her a river of blood from the felled demons streams across the land. Above Her the gods cautiously peek through the clouds eagerly waiting for the next epic drama to unfold. Finally, Mahiṣa comes storming onto the battlefield in his form of a buffalo. He is further enraged by the sight of the terrible massacre of his demon army. He snorts and growls and charges Ambikā's tiger. The tiger roars and rips open the demon's chest with his sharp claws. The buffalo demon cries out in pain and kicks mountains up with his back hooves. The mountains come hurling at Ambikā who punches them away with Her ringed fists. The demon shakes with fury and transforms into an elephant. In his elephant form he comes barreling at Her with every intention of trampling both the tiger and the Goddess. But She is too quick for him and throws a noose about his neck just as he attempts to slay Her tiger with his tusk. Again the demon changes form. He becomes a lion and lunges at Her. Ambikā raises Her sword and chops off his head, but the demon turned lion now assumes the form of a man. The Great Goddess and Her tiger roar together as they leap onto the man's chest and force him to the ground. Mahiṣa shapeshifts back into his original form of half-buffalo/half-man just as She pierces his chest with a trident in one hand and lops off his head with a scythe in another. The terrible demon cries out in pain and fury, then falls lifeless to the ground. As She stands with one foot on his torso proudly holding his severed demon head in one of Her hands, Ambikā decides that from then on when ever Her devotees call Her to help them with any difficulty She shall be called Durgā after the buffalo-headed demon.

The gods are elated and sail down from the clouds. The Matṛkās emerge from the Great Goddess' body and dance ecstatically across the mountainous slopes. Gandharvas (demigods) Apsaras (celestial Goddesses) and all the sages from throughout the cosmos come and join in the celebration. Not only has the Goddess defeated the horrible demon and stopped the bloodshed and terror that was destroying the precious equilibrium of all the worlds, but also She has freed them from their vicious ego-bound forms. In the realm where this battle takes place, there is no such thing as physical death, only transformation and liberation. The Goddess' victory is one of justice and fierce compassion. Durgā has annihilated the egos of each and every demon She destroyed, thus allowing it to rediscover its own true and divine essence.

Goddess Durgā and the Matṛkās dance and sing in ecstatic bliss with all the other beings for hours. But soon, it is time for Her to retreat back into the formless void, into the Yoni of the Great Mother, who is ultimately Herself. Durgā blesses each and every being and promises to return whenever they need Her aid. She reminds them that it is only the fiercely compassionate Goddess, the Supreme Mother of the Universe, who can take on the demons in all their insidious forms and win. "Remember that just as each of you and every other being is part of me," She tells them, "so too is every demon part of my great body. This is my sacred and most mysterious play." She turns to leave on Her majestic tiger, then suddenly asks him to stop. There is one more promise She wishes to make. She assures them that if they call on Her and create ritual festivities, She will come every year in the fall and in the spring and give Her blessing of balance between the forces of light and dark, day and night. She will come calmly, with composure, and battle any asuras (demons) with Her fierce gaze of measured intent. She will take action with unyielding ferocity, tenderness and grace. She will always come to liberate the oppressed and ensure that none of Her creation's egos get too grossly out of hand. They all know that it is only Goddess who can ultimately restore balance to this world and all the others. She will come to remind us that it is we, Her devotees, who must awaken the fierce creative force of Goddess within ourselves.

That is Durgā in Her first classic appearance—a stunning and powerful figure whose significance may be richly evocative. But who is She to Western women in our contemporary culture? What does She have to teach us?

The paradoxical nature of Durgā and the collective forms of Goddesses who represent Her offer a model of the complexity of the female psyche that holds both benevolent and terrifying qualities. She embodies the untamed, wild woman who lives her life according to her own standards. She is autonomous and independent, courageous and strong. She is creator of her life instead of passive participant. She resides at the center of her life rather than having it defined for her by the patriarchal culture and its limiting institutions. She carries many tools in her eight to eighteen arms that symbolize qualities such as self-reliance, confidence, fierce determination, and unyielding passion. These qualities help a woman to carve out a more female-centered existence for herself and her loved ones.

Durgā models an essence of femaleness that has been denied and repressed for most of us. As the Remover of Fear and Difficulty, She finds no obstacle too great to overcome. She will not tolerate any form of injustice. She embodies the profound strength, courage and complexity of women's emotional and sexual power. She is distinctly different from traditionally defined experiences of womanhood for She embraces the full spectrum of human experience, moving gracefully between death and life, darkness and light, the periphery and the center. She is fierce and compassionate, wrathful and sensual, nurturing and furious, embodied and Divine.

Durgā is often the embodiment of a righteous female rage that when provoked swells up against the injustices perpetuated against humanity. However, Her battles are nonviolent for they represent the slaying of the ego. They are revolutions, fought only to overcome oppression and corruption. She fights to liberate Her devotees from the dominating forces that keep them from experiencing and expressing their true natures. Her name, Durgā, means fortress and stronghold. These qualities of strength, fortitude, courage, and grace are the gifts She offers. Nevertheless, they are not so easy to come by. Mrinal Pande, journalist and author of *Devi: Tales of the Goddess in Our Time*, talks about what happens to a woman who "closely observes these wild Goddesses and their actions" and how challenging it can be to follow in Durgā's footprints. Pande describes "an untethering of secret wants, emotions, and desire for creativity" that can arise for women who begin to work with Durgā energy. She notes, "One cannot come by such power easily. Like Durgā, all those that wish to ride a lion must be proud, and watchful of compromises, even if it means losing security and friends of a certain kind."[1]

To have our power, to fully express it is not an easy task. There are many layers of conditioning to break through. Women on this path often stand alone in the face of the infinite ways patriarchal values have seduced and captured so many women and men. We keep our mouths shut to avoid a fight with a lover, friend, colleague, or family member. We smile and pretend that everything is okay, when it is not. We feel self-conscious, unconfident, and insecure about ourselves and our gifts. We refrain from saying the truth in order not to disappoint the other. We compromise our desires so that we are liked, loved, and accepted. Despite these attempts to stay in control and not become too "emotional," these denied and often lost aspects of our self will ultimately demand to be expressed. If there is no creative outlet for our inherently wild natures to come through, intense emotions can erupt through illness, self-destructive rage, isolation, loneliness and depression.

In many respects, Durgā and Her bevy of Goddesses carry the hidden aspects of the female psyche. They are Dark Goddesses, whose darkness holds their primal power, the power of those fierce, angry, passionate, sexual and powerful parts of women's selves that we have been taught to repress and deny. Durgā in Her myriad forms provides a model of expressing anger toward injustice in a constructive rather than destructive manner. Her anger does not oppress: it cuts and liberates. She holds the paradoxical nature of a woman who can feel anger and pain, yet still feel love and compassion for herself and others. She helps personal and societal transformation take place by getting in touch and releasing her pain and anger in constructive ways: art, writing, yoga, dance, song, political activism, social justice, etc. She teaches us how to free the pent up energy that has kept us bound and victimized and transform it into creative power. Looking at the ways in which women have been denied full participation in a liberated human experience under patriarchy inevitably brings up feelings of rage and betrayal. It is important that we allow ourselves to feel furious at the ways women and people of color, indigenous peoples, animals and the environment have been abused, exploited, and oppressed. And then it is crucial we work with our anger and let it go.

Courageously challenging restrictive conditioning that is harmful to our mental, physical, emotional and spiritual well-being and willfully embodying our rage and sexual passion is a direct act of working with, even embodying, Durgā. We can call on Durgā in any of Her fiercely loving forms to help us dis-identify with the intense emotions that the patriarchal reality evokes in us yet feel them fully, understand, and navigate through them. A Yoginī (practitioner) does not simply react to life and its various situations, but learns to respond consciously and without causing further harm to herself and others. Perhaps the greatest lesson that Durgā teaches is for us not to turn away from our suffering, but to learn to confront it and walk through it, no matter how terrifying reality may seem.

Ultimately, Durgā in all Her forms brings us back to our selves, to our true nature, and reminds each of us of our purpose here. She is powerful, and therefore, so are we. She has come to teach us to reclaim our power. As Cynthia Ann Humes writes in her essay, "Is the Devī Māhātmyā a Feminist Scripture?"

> Rather than adopting masculine ideas of power over things or events, one can argue that a superior stance would be to adopt an attitude of exalting strength from within, and power with. . . Power from within is not a power of control, but one which comes from valuing self, community, and experience. It is the power which can heal and renew, a power which—like the Goddess of our text—exemplifies compassion even when violent, and strives to contribute to an ultimately positive outcome for the greater good.[2]

Durgā is a Goddess invincible to patriarchal constructs and control. She is the amazon, the 'no husband one' as defined by Vicki Noble, who may choose to have lovers or consorts but is not possessed by them. Nor does She lose herself and her desires to them. She is the virgin in the original sense: whole unto herself regardless of whether or not She chooses a lover. Durgā and her entourages carry a vast legacy of empowered leaders, healers, and artists. They offer multiple models of female existence. She and Her collectives of fiercely compassionate Goddesses remind us of the ancient and contemporary women on this planet who gather together and pray for healing, for peace, for each other's families, for their communities, for animals, and for the world. Goddess Durgā is a female-centered realm of consciousness that views and experiences the female as subject rather than object thereby allowing a woman to be the agent of her destiny instead of forcing her to hand all authority over to the dictates of patriarchal man.

Notes

1. Mrinal Pande, *Devi: Tales of the Goddess in Our Time* (New Delhi: Penguin, 1996), xvi.

2. Cynthia Ann Humes, "Is the Devī Māhātmyā a Feminist Scripture" in *Is the Goddess a Feminist? The Politics of South Asian Goddesses*, eds. Alf Hiltebeitel and Kathleen M. Erndl (New York: New York University Press, 2000), 148.

chapter two
tantra, kaula, and sakta tradition

Tantra

In order to understand the essence of Durgā and all that She offers, we must understand the principles, practices and ideologies of the Tantric tradition.[1] Let's look at some essential principles of Hindu Tantra[2] in order to understand the nature of Durgā, Her bevy of goddesses, and the Goddesses that are central to the Durgā Festival and Tantric rituals.

Tantra is the weaving of science, philosophy, ritual and yogic methodology. Yoga itself is an important aspect of Tantric philosophy: yoga means union and refers to any unifying practice including but not restricted to the popular āsana (posture) practice that is blossoming in the West. Tantra is a yogic path of integration. It is a path that embraces opposition and paradox. It involves practices that attempt reconciliation between disparate parts or thoughts. Tantra works to heal all dichotomies; particularly the dichotomy of spirit and matter, which has been so prevalent in the West. In Tantrism, all reality is seen as One. This Oneness must be realized through the integration of all dualities; male and female, active and passive, higher and lower, good and evil, joy and sorrow, birth and death, pure and polluted, divine and human. By merging all oppositions through ritualistically internalizing them in the form of a deity and oneself, the Tantric practitioner experiences the sense of Oneness that is inherent in the universe. Union with the Divinity is the yoga of Tantra.

Central to Tantric ideology is the concept of microcosm/macrocosm. The human body is believed to contain all the wisdom of the macrocosm or universe. By understanding the human body as a microcosmic reflection of the greater universe, we become active agents in the divine drama of existence. The body and senses are highly valued in Tantra and are understood as the locus for the interplay between cosmic and earthly energies. Tantric Scholar Madhu Khannu explains: "Whatever forces govern the outer cosmos also govern the inner planes of the body cosmos. It is held in the Tantras that we do not experience our consciousness as external to our bodies. The subtle aspects of consciousness of the unity of creation manifests in, and through, the subtle channels of the body cosmos."[3] The concept of any reality being a microcosmic mirror of the cosmos extends to all creatures in the natural world and to the organization of a village, town, city or house. Tantric temples are conceived as the body of Goddess and are therefore a microcosmic representation of the Divine. Spirit and matter is not separate in this tradition. Every aspect of reality is imbued with Divinity. Seen and unseen realms as well as the presence of disembodied beings are equally valid. Realization of the divine nature of existence, particularly for those who are embodied is crucial in realizing spiritual liberation in this lifetime. Spiritual liberation is a state of non-dual consciousness in which we are no longer bound and limited by our egos, and we experience a deep sense of acceptance, contentment, integration and bliss.

Tantra cannot be neatly defined and classified. Its meaning cannot be contained in a limited form. A single definition would defy the true meaning of Tantra, which is an all-encompassing, all-embracing philosophical and spiritual system, and ultimately includes and transcends all boundaries. Professor Jim Ryan, Director of Asian Comparative Studies at the California Institute of Integral Studies, defines Tantra as "the expansion of consciousness and the offering of protection."[4] It is a path that expands our awareness so that we move beyond dualistic thought and action, which limit our consciousness from experiencing the entirety of Existence.

The word, *Tantra*, comes from the Sanskrit, *tanoti* and *trayate*. By breaking down the word into its two roots, *tan*, meaning to stretch, and *tra*, to protect, Tantra has unifying and merging implications.[5] Ultimately it is this sense of Oneness with the immanent and transcendent universe that a Tantric practitioner seeks. The protection which Tantra offers provides an opportunity to more consciously experience ourselves as divine beings. We learn to find comfort and solace in natural cycles of existence. The Tantric path teaches us to embody the omnipotence, omnificence, and omnipresence of our own Divinity. Tantra also means "warp on a loom"[6] and conjures up the image of weaving the strands of indigenous practices and beliefs, and creating a new tapestry. There are at least sixty-four different schools of Tantra within both the Buddhist and Hindu religions, which all have roots in the early Kaula tradition. The Kaula tradition evolved into the similar female-centered Śākta Tantra tradition.

Unfortunately Tantra in the West has become something of a new age term implying free love and wild sex with multiple partners. Tantra is grossly misunderstood as a practice for improving one's sex life and capacity for intimacy. However, the "California" notion of Tantra has nothing to do with its original essence. Tantra is a complex heterodox tradition; however, as Khanna points out:

> Few attempts have been made to identify areas within Śākta Tantra that have a positive value for women. Unfortunately, much of the debate in the context of women and Tantra has centered on women's roles in sex-yogic ritual, whereas the role of women

has to be viewed in the context of the larger issues of Śāktācāra (rules of conduct followed by the Śākta), which in some areas may alter our perception of the tenuous relationship of dharma and gender in Hindu thought.[7]

The Kaula, Śākta and tribal shamanic traditions from which Tantra later emerged all honor the tension between opposing energies. Śakti, the female, dynamic, all pervading creative force is constantly in a cosmic dance of birth and destruction with Śiva, the male, receptive and quiescent ground of being. The female is not repressed, excluded, oppressed, or denied. Instead, a deep reverence for the female principle as a pervading and animating force of existence is central in Śākta Tantrism and the earlier Kaula tradition. Madhu Khanna writes of the "goddess-woman" equation that can be found throughout Śākta texts and shows how women are by no means subordinate to men as we find in other religious doctrine. In fact, Śākta texts "claim that at birth all women, of all cultures, naturally assume the power and divinity of cosmic energy and that they are to be looked on as the Goddess' physical counterpart on earth."[8] Other female-honoring statements that emphasize women's divinity include: "Every woman in this world, is indeed, my [human] form" and "All women are Thee, and all men are Myself, O beloved. Merely by knowing this, the devotee attains spiritual powers."[9] It is noteworthy to add that Śākta texts do not denigrate or chastise men as most orthodox, especially Judeo-Christian texts and dogmas, do to women. Instead there is an acknowledgement of the complementary energies between women and men as well as "a code of ethics and rules of conduct that are entirely in favor of women."[10]

The Tantric dictum, "Śiva without Śakti is but a corpse" is important in Śākta Tantra. It demonstrates that both the male and the female aspects are essential to the whole. Several scholars in the comprehensive work, *Hindu Tantrism* assert, "It is often emphasized that Śakti is the active partner in the cosmic act of procreation, while Śiva remains purely passive and would be unable even to move without her impulse."[11] Rather than viewing opposing forces as mutually exclusive, Tantra emphasizes their complementary qualities and allows for a *both/and* rather than an *either/or* paradigm. The Tantric path encourages us to fully accept all our desires, feelings and situations as human beings. Through our full participation in life without judging and polarizing our experiences, we are able to recall our original identity with the Source of the Universe. This does not mean we act on all our desires, but that we learn to approach life through a path of moderation. We learn to not give our power to another person or a substance, or let ourselves become stuck on negative and painful memories. Nor do we attempt to dominate or control people or situations. We can understand that extreme and complex experiences and emotions can stretch our consciousness and allow us to embrace a more comprehensive and empowering understanding of life.

In *The Tantric Way*, Indian scholars Ajit Mookerjee and Madhu Khanna discuss Tantra's prehistoric roots. They write: "Tantric ritual symbols are found in the Harappan Culture (Indus or Saraswati Valley Civilization, c. 3000 B.C.E.) in the form of yogic postures, and in the Mother and the fertility cult."[12] Ancient ritual elements that center on the female principle have had enduring relevance and later became integral to Tantric beliefs. While many aspects of Tantra possibly date back to the Saraswati Valley, Tantra flourished between 700 and 1600 C.E. It was during this period of Tantric revival that worship of Goddess, particularly in Her temperamental and fiercer aspects, became more deeply entrenched in Indian and Nepalese counterculture. Tantra developed as a response to the orthodox and highly conventionalized practices within both the Hindu and Buddhist traditions. Beginning around the second century C.E. societal and religious codes known as the Laws of Manu or Manusmṛti became more limiting and restrictive for the female sex in South Asia. The Manusmṛti:

> expound the brahminic attitudes on caste, theology, and law. The Laws of Manu laid the foundation of their social, legal, and moral code and introduced several innovations that concerned women. It eulogized the eternal nature of dhārmic marriage and introduced a husband-deifying ideology, according to which the spouse must be worshiped as a god by a faithful wife. Manusmṛti was also instrumental in abolishing female property rights and prohibiting widow remarriage. . . . Marital restrictions placed on women decreased their authority considerably and introduced an era of sexual double standards that perpetuated the theology of subordination and weakened the autonomy of women.[13]

Despite the codification of these misogynistic laws, Tantric practices and ideologies have always offered the possibility of earthly empowerment and enlightenment to all members of society regardless of gender, sex, or caste. Tantrism offers very useful and applicable philosophies that could remedy many of the societal, religious, personal and even environmental problems we encounter today. Tantrism expresses a level of tolerance, integration and acceptance that is perhaps theorized, but not practiced in orthodox tradition. Ideologically, Tantra is inclusive of subaltern people, a fact which contributed to its medieval popularity—for this was a period in South Asian history when royal courts dominated the culture. It is an ideology that is anti-brahminical in that it is neither hierarchical nor exclusive. Tantric practices are a direct response to the Indian caste system. In a sense, we could say that classical Tantra is antipatriarchy for it is not about dominance, competition, or any form of subordination as we find within organized religion. It even "takes a strict stand against wife beating and sexual abuse of women.[14] Śāktā Tantra also supports lowcaste, outcaste and marginalized women emphasizing their equality and divinity. Moreover, "Tantra stands apart from other orthodox traditions in India, for here we find more than a mere triumph of the divine feminine, as energy of the cosmos. We get a glimpse of pro-woman codes for ordinary and secular women who are at par with their male partners."[15]

Inevitably, Tantrism had a strong effect on Hinduism, Buddhism, Jainism, and other religious groups and has remained in practice to this day. While other forms of Hindu practice and dogma desacralize the body, thus placing importance on transcending the body, Tantra seeks to sacralize the body and through somatic experiences achieve liberation.[16] Tantric rituals such as nyāsa: worshipping the body as a deity, the recitation of mantras, worshipping yantras: geometrical drawings of the Divine, and sacred sexual practices aid Tantric practitioners in their quest.

In his classic work, *The Tantric Tradition*, Agehananda Bharati considers Tantra as a "psycho-spiritual speculation." He writes: "What distinguishes tantric from other Hindu and Buddhist teaching is its systematic emphasis on the identity of the absolute and phenomenal world when filtered through the experience of sādhanā." Sādhanā refers to any spiritual endeavor the devotee undertakes.[17] Angela Dietrich gives a detailed definition of sādhanā in her book *Tantric Healing in the Kathmandu Valley:* "Sādhanās focus on the usage of mantras (chants), then on yantra (sacred diagrams of the divinity), mudrā (gestures evocative of the deity) and nyāsa (sacralization of one's own body). . . . Its emphasis is on gaining spiritual power (bhukti) through tapping active spiritual energy (Śakti) with the achievement of final empowerment through its integration with male energy."[18] Dietrich goes on to point out:

> In Tantrism, there is an elaborate, subtle geography of the body that must be learned, controlled, and ultimately resolved in unity. By means of the body, both the physical and subtle bodies, the sādhaka may manipulate levels of reality and harness the dynamics of those levels to the attainment of the goal. The sādhaka, with the help of the guru, undertakes to gain his goal by conquest—by using his own body and knowledge of that body to bring the fractured world of name and form, the polarized world of male and female, sacred and profane, to wholeness and unity.[19]

On a personal level, Tantric practice includes the relationship between guru or teacher and student or disciple. The Tantric guru initiates her/his student into the practice of sādhanā, in order to reach liberation (mukti or mokṣa). While the guru is crucial in Tantric traditions, the original earth and female-based tradition did not require the guidance of a guru for both sexes. Instead, the female *is* the embodied guru who transmits the teachings. In *Kuṇḍalinī: the Energy of the Depths*, Lilian Silburn states "to her alone should the guru impart the whole of the secret doctrine; and through her, by practice of union, it is imparted to men."[20] The Supreme Guru is Goddess in Her immanent yet transcendent form and any sincere practitioner can have a direct experience of Her. Khanna cites Śākta texts that "claim that women are the purest source of transmission of sacred revelation." In fact, "Knowledge of the Tantras must be transmitted through the 'yoginīmukha,' the lips of the self-realized female yoginīs and spiritually accomplished women."[21] She goes on to state how the origin of both Kaula and Krama (Kashmiri Śaivite) schools of Tantra can be traced to a Yoginī and that male gurus within the latter tradition were first initiated either through a living Yoginī or through receiving transmissions from a Yoginī in a dream. Although women lack agency in the orthodox sphere of religious practice, Tantra, specifically the Śākta Tantra tradition offers not only contemporary opportunities of female spiritual agency, but also provides over two thousand years of textual history, much of which still needs to be translated, as well as even more evidence of a many millennia old female-centered oral tradition. Not only do women have the power to impart dikṣā (initiation), but according to one of the Tantras Khanna cites, "initiation given by a woman is considered more efficacious than initiation given by a man."[22] Today more and more non-South Asian practitioners are finding their way to female gurus for spiritual and worldly guidance. Ammachi, the Hugging Saint from Kerala, Shree Mā of Kāmākhyā, Karunamāyī and Gurumāyī[23] are some of the more known examples of South Asian women who are both guru and living Goddess. Female gurus and Yoginīs are stepping forward in communities all over the world. Indeed the myriad and varied displays of female consciousness are becoming more and more visible and accepted in every day life.

Regardless of sex, gurus in a human body, (who do not abuse their power), are undeniably helpful, even crucial as teachers or guides—especially when such a challenging path disorients us by presenting us with experiences and encounters that disrupt our egos and rational minds. When we first open ourselves up through the various spiritual practices, we are vulnerable and impressionable. It is a dangerous state for we are changing at a core level. The guru teaches us how to transmute potentially harmful energies and how to harness our own Śakti power.

Let's turn now to some key components of any Tantric and yogic practice.

Meditation

The foundation of Eastern spirituality and religion is a meditation practice. Different meditative techniques are taught depending on various schools even within the Tantra tradition. Certain schools of Tantra offer very systematic and elaborate philosophies and practices on the nature and function of the mind. The goal of meditation is to uncover the judgments and emotions that keep us unconscious and cloud our most authentic expression. Regardless of theoretical and practical differences between various Tantric schools, a key component of meditation is to observe the rising of thoughts and memories in our minds. Meditation is a practice that helps us align with our essence or the "background" of being against which our everyday dramas, thoughts and actions play out. Meditative practices aid us in seeing every moment and every aspect of our self with discernment. From a non-dual Tantric perspective, energies are constantly expanding and contracting: the nature of the universe is constantly in flux. We can observe this in the outer and inner manifestations of our reality. For a Tantric practitioner, meditation helps us to navigate various levels of consciousness.

Nyāsa

It is important to look more closely at the philosophical concept, nyāsa, which means to ritualistically transform oneself into the Goddess. Through nyāsa one links the transcendent and immanent nature of the Divine by becoming the deity. This recalls the ancients' understanding of our interconnectedness with the cosmos. There is no separation between sacred and profane; rather they are united through Tantric practice. "Nyāsa is the rite by which the aspirant consciously enters the sacred space. It is the cleansing and purifying process in which the body, its key points and zones of renewal are sensitized by the placing of fingertips."[24] In stricter Tantric terms, nyāsa involves the practitioner visualizing herself as Divine by doing finger mudrās on different parts of the body and reciting mantras. In Tantric ritual, we do not merely worship Devī, we embody Her, become Her, see Devī in our own reflection, and feel Devī in every cell of our being. By calling the Divine into our being, we invite Her into the physical world, and thereby participate in a Tantric act. Nyāsa involves the human being becoming a mediator between earth and cosmos; however, this experience is not restricted to priests or other religious heads. Instead, it is open to everyone on the Tantric path including those who have been marginalized. The body becomes the vessel for Her grace and wisdom, and we only need surrender and allow Her to work through us.

Mudrā

Mudrā is a term deriving from the root *mud*, 'to please' and signifies a bodily posture designed to please the gods which can include ritual hand gestures or even yoga āsanas.[25] Mudrā is the ritualized body-language both of offering and surrender. Mudrās (finger positions) are connected with nyāsa in Tantric ritual. Mudrās accompany mantras (chants) and āsanas (poses) and aid in the various stages of the pūjā. They present a beautiful visual dance as the pujari's hands flow gracefully over and through the altar space.

Mantra and Japa

While a prayer is an emotional act, often spoken entreatingly to the Divine, a mantra is a combination of sounds that affects and transforms the subtle levels of our reality. A mantra serves as an instrument of thought, speech, sacred text, song of praise, or prayer. Mantras can also be used as spells and incantations. Through the recitation of certain syllables with a focused intention the powers of these words actually do manifest certain realities.

The recitation of mantras or sacred sounds is an ancient method of meditation that considers the whole manifested Universe a result of an all inclusive vibration called nāda. All existing things in the Universe are forms or fields of this vibration. Everything that exists has a different wave length and density. Certain tonal vibrations can alter energetic and even physical qualities of manifest and unmanifest realms. Vibrations not only create forms, but also influence difference states of consciousness. Through japa, the repetition of mantras, we change our consciousness, increase our intuitive powers, and expand our perspective. It helps us to see the underlying unity behind all diversity and opposing thoughts, qualities, and realities. It works on a subconscious level and also alters our brainwaves. Scientific studies have shown how mantra entrains our brain so that left and right hemispheres are in sync. Every sound is believed to possess its own vibration, producing a desired mental and spiritual effect when properly intoned. Such changes the mantra provokes ultimately manifest in the physical realm.

Etymologically the root, *man* is associated with the mind, thought and intentionality. *Tra* has protective implications.[26] Through the recitation of mantra (japa) we strengthen our mind, thus protecting it from unwanted thoughts or persuasions that influence our essence. Mantra is a necessary preparation for more advanced practices (sādhanā) in Tantra. Mantras activate particular powers within us. The mantra of the deity connects to that divine aspect inherent in our self and activates its energies. Mantra is a state of being indicative of the presence of the deity.[27] Mantras for female deities are called vidyā, which means knowledge. Mantras are usually intoned to a certain rhythm. Certain meters influence the efficacy of the mantra. In the Śākta tradition the Tantric deities have a seed syllable that embodies their essence. Reciting one or a combination of the following syllables, Hrīm (Durgā), Aīm (Saraswatī), Śrīm (Lakṣmī), Krīm (Kālī), and Klīm (graceful Kālī or Lakṣmī) opens portals of consciousness and aligns our own consciousness with Source. Bīja mantras also purify our nāḍīs. However, to experience the full potency of these bījas, they must be transmuted through a teacher, especially a Yoginī. Mookerjee notes,

> The bīja mantra repeated according to the rules of the doctrine serves to centre and support the aspirant's auditory perception by its very continuum. In this way it contracts and intensifies the field of awareness to a single point, under pressure of which, Kuṇḍalinī stirs toward awakening.[28]

Yantra and Prāṇayama

Yantras are not merely geometric symbols but actual dwelling places for the deities. They are consecrated space. They are portals that stimulate our consciousness to open into profound dimensions of reality. While mantra and its particular vibration is the deity Itself, yantra is the body of the deity. Yantra is a powerful centering device, but needs to be activated by a ritual practice called prāṇapratishṭhā. The practitioner invokes the prāṇa (life force) of the deity and uses mantras to energize the space. "Every yantra creates a power-field, a cosmicized circuit (kshetra) in which the powers of the sacred are invoked. The lines and planes localized within the yantras, though distinct from all the spaces that surround its outer circuit, are an expression of a transcendental reality."[29]

Another important Tantric practice is prāṇayama. "Yoga has developed systematic techniques of breathing, regulating its speed, depth and rhythm."[30] Prāṇayama combined with āsanas directs our breath to flow in certain energy centers which stimulate our awareness.

Nyāsa, mantra, mudrā, prāṇayama, and yantras are practices that integrate subtle and gross energies and are foundational to Tantric and yogic practices. They originate from early earth-based cultures that revered the female body as divine.

The Śākta Kaula Tradition

In the Śākta tradition, *Śākti* (power or energy) is the all-pervading dynamic energy of the universe. Perceived and personified as ultimately female, Śākti is the divine consciousness behind the never-ending cycle of birth, life, and death. Goddess weaves the fabric of all existence. The Śākta tradition "views the divine as a female body of which women, earth, and the Goddess are but different manifestations."[31]

The sacred female sexual power that is at the heart of all rituals and beliefs around divinity is referred to by many names: *Śakti*, *Kuṇḍalinī*, and its earlier form, *kula*. Therefore, what we refer to as Śākta and in some cases Tantra, is essentially synonymous with the Kaula tradition. The understanding of Śakti evolved from an earlier clan-based system known as *Kaula* or *kula*. Within this culture the kula—or female sexual fluids and menstrual blood—are understood as potent power. Activating and harnessing these substances' energetic properties in ritual can bring about creative or destructive means. Kula is the power of Goddess.

In the Kaula, Śākta and Tantric worldview the Divine resides in all things, therefore how could sexual practices, or even mind-altering substances, be impure or bad? Sex is a powerful and beautiful expression of the Divine. Sexual rites within this tradition lead one to ecstatic union with Goddess. In Kaula sexual practices Goddess is sometimes referred to with such poetic epithets such as "Our Lady of Love, She who is Garlanded by the Vulva (Bhagamālinī), and She Who Is Always

Wet (Nityaklinnā)."[32] The yoni and her fluids are deemed sacred, even necessary for achieving enlightenment.

> While this fluid essence of the goddess flowed naturally through female beings, it was absent in males. Therefore the sole means by which a male could access the flow of the supreme godhead at the elevated center of the maṇḍala, the clan "flow" chart, was through the yoginis who formed or inhabited its outer circles. Only through initiation by and continued interaction with the yoginis could these male practitioners access this fluid essence and boundless energy of the godhead. It was therefore necessary that male practitioners be inseminated or insanguinated with the sexual or menstrual discharge of the yoginis—rendering the mouth of the yogini their sole conduit to the membership of the clan.[33]

According to David Gordon White's interpretation, drinking female sexual fluids such as blood or female ejaculation in a ritualized context is one of the most important ways for a man to achieve access to a divine and non-dual realm consciousness. Female sexual fluids are recognized as being ultimately divine. During such rites, sex is an act of reverence and a direct opportunity for union with the Divine. Due to the esoteric nature of this tradition, it is not clear what exactly went on and still goes on in Tantric circles, however we learn from various texts that the most potent Tantric practices require menstrual blood and female sexual fluids because of the vibrational potency of these fluids to alter consciousness. We learn through the iconography, myth, and textual descriptions that the yoni is sacred and held in high regard. In the anthology, *The Roots of Tantra,* André Padoux notes ritualized sexual practices allow for the body to be seen as "a structured receptacle of power and is animated by that power and the somato-cosmic vision upon which these practices are based."[34]

Originally, these practices equated the female body as a channel for female deities, and practitioners respected the inherent power within female sexual fluids and venerated the female body. Such practices utilized women's bodies to achieve certain supernatural powers (siddhis) and as a means to gain liberation (mokṣa). Such activity is peripheral to traditional religious practices because it involves elements considered threatening and polluting to the civil order, namely, functions related to the female body and intricately tied to the reality of human existence—i.e. menstruation, pregnancy, and sexuality. In this conception, the "untamable" female body is equated with the "untamable" Earth as Mother, Herself. Reverence for the female body and an integrated understanding that divine power naturally flows through women is central to the Śākta, Kaula and Tantric worldview but missing from Western ideology. Kaula Śākta Tantra ideologies are a celebration of the female body, blood, and sexual fluids. The fear, disgust, and overall malice toward these very aspects of femaleness in Western culture are nonexistent within this Eastern tradition. Kaula/Śākta Tantric tenets ask that we confront our fears and embrace all that is considered taboo by the dominant culture. Anything we resist, whether a thought, experience, relationship or desire, must be consciously examined and transmuted.

Kaula practices include conducting rituals in charnel grounds, using alcohol and blood to feed and propitiate deities, inducing spirit possession in ceremony, and employing transgressive sexual behavior as a means of achieving union with the Divine. Padoux sees ritual elements such as transgression and "erotic rites and sexo-yogic practices as antedating Tantra," yet they still persist because they are a "universal category of human behavior."[35] Although these practices may be "universal" and have continued through the ages, they have never become part of mainstream society. Vicki Noble contends "Ancient purely matriarchal societies were almost certainly practicing those rites, even though Tantra hadn't yet been invented. Tantra is probably a more codified version of what was once the natural way societies practiced their religious rituals."[36]

Tantra developed as a response to the restrictive, judicious, orthodox views on sex, alcohol, certain foods, and women. As Michael Allen notes: "Tantric doctrine and practice constitute quite explicit inversions of the ascetic, and often even misogynist, values that underpin both Brahmanism and monastic Buddhism."[37] Contrary to these orthodox traditions, Hindu Tantra is "directly predicated on a positive evaluation of human sexuality as a source of ritual, meditative and cognitive power. . . the devotee celebrates coitus as a cosmic force of great generative power."[38] This power is not fully inherent in men, but can come through engaging in practices with "a woman who represents the power that is so vital for the success of his (the priest's or male practitioner's) ritual objective."[39]

On the Kaula path, Yoginī practices emphasize the female body as the medium through which liberation is achieved. As we shall see in the Yoginī chapter of this book, the Yoginī is a Tantric practitioner who is devoted to Durgā in any of Her fiercer and sensual forms. Through the various prescribed yogic practices of mantra (chanting), yantra (visualization), mudrā (gesture), āsana (physical postures), meditation, and prāṇāyāma, (breath practices), the practitioner is able to consciously engage in the maithuna sexual ritual. The sexual energies that are invoked take the participants into divinely inspired states. They experience each other as Śakti/Śiva as Goddess/God, or more importantly, the union of the Divine. It is difficult to say if Śākta texts speak to strictly heterosexual unions because the majority of Śākta texts have still not been translated. We do know that while conceiving of the Divine in a gendered form is useful in some practices, Śiva and Śakti are ultimately not to be interpreted as restricted to male and female sexes, but as qualities of Divinity. Tantric sexual practice is ultimately focused on harnessing the differences between opposing energies;

allowing them to dance, merge and shift our consciousness into more expanded states of awareness. A divinely inspired sexual union brings tremendous boons to the participants regardless of sexual orientation. Raising kuṇḍalinī energy through the various cakra (energy) centers evokes joy, transformation, and a sense of union between the tensions within life. While we may not stay in these states for long, the after effects can be long lasting. After a ritual, energies can be channeled into creative forms and expressed in infinite ways. From the wellspring of female sexuality flows creative inspiration for the arts. It is a consciousness focused on the sensual, the beautiful, the transformative, the ever-becoming and the spiritual. Through ritual worship we are led to the mysterious realms of the Goddess, who will weave Her magic and take the sādhaka (practitioner) to the next stage of his or her spiritual development. Such practices also help the devotees to achieve worldly success.

Although it may *seem* that Tantric sexual practices could have a liberating effect on the orthodox world, I wish to point out that Tantra is by no means restricted to sexual practices, as the trendy California "Tantra" workshops imply. Sex is an integral part of the practices, but there are many levels one must accomplish before s/he starts having sex as a spiritual practice. Due to the powerful and ultimately elemental nature of the energies which the practices generate and harness, the practitioner must be trained on many levels to handle the intensity of energies. Above all Tantra is a path of expanding consciousness, of stretching the limitations of our perceived awareness and opening to other forms of power within our very being and the cosmos. Ultimately, the practitioner views the Divine as both immanent and transcendent. The Tantric worldview is not the dualistic, either/or model we find in the Western world, but embraces a *both/and* paradigm. Tantra is a path of confronting and embracing the paradoxical nature of our existence, seeking to bridge all oppositions as complementary energies, and striving to find the unity behind all diversity. Contrary to racist, sexist, homophobic and prejudicial attitudes in the orthodox religions, diversity is highly esteemed in the Tantric worldview. In particular, reverence for the female sex enhances society as a whole.

Based on years of field research in the Kathmandu Valley, Michael Allen suggests, "Such a high cultural evaluation of specifically female powers and potencies, especially as regards female sexuality and reproductivity has, I would suggest, effectively *precluded the possibility of such restrictive institutions as child marriage, no divorce and widow immolations.*"[40] However, Allen also sees the reality of the "politically dominant and caste-structured Hindu world" and the "contrary negative views of women so distinctive of such a world" as "encapsulating" even the most unorthodox populations.[41] It is obvious that the more deeply entrenched women are in organized religion, the fewer rights we have. Under such traditions women often have little or no ownership over our own bodies—especially in regard to our reproductive and sexual choices. We cannot fully escape the ideological and structural problems of the modernized world, but I ask, how might such an understanding of the beauty and potency of the female body, not only for its power to conceive and give birth, but also for its ability to expand consciousness through sexual rites, make a difference in the way women are treated and treat ourselves today?

Notes

1. Although Buddhism is a dominant religion in the Kathmandu Valley of Nepal, my research has focused on the Śākta and Kaula roots of the rituals, Goddesses and practices. My own experiences have been rooted in the more shamanic, elemental and female-centered practices and worldview. Therefore, I will not discuss the origin of Buddhism nor the way Tantric Buddhism differs from the Hindu Tantric tradition. While my references to and discussion of Tantra primarily focus on the Śākta and Kaula origins of the tradition and practices, some of the history can be applied to the Buddhist Tantric tradition. However, it is beyond the scope of this book to provide a comparative analysis or even to go into much discussion about the Buddhist tradition here.
2. While I speak of Tantra in more general terms to present an overview of key aspects of this philosophy, I am mostly referring to the Śākta Tantra tradition, which is a tradition that "embodie[s] a critical and controversial attitude toward women, sexuality, their relationship with their bodies and senses, social classes and traditional notions of purity and impurity." Madhu Khanna, "The Goddess-Woman Equation in Śākta Tantras," in *Faces of the Feminine in Ancient, Medieval, and Modern India*, ed. Mandakranta Bose (New York, Oxford: Oxford University Press, 2000), 111.
3. Khanna, "The Goddess-Woman Equation," 116.
4. Dr. Jim Ryan, "Hindu Tantra"(lecture for graduate level course on Hindu Tantra at the California Institute of Integral Studies in San Francisco, Sept. 4, 2001).
5. Ibid.
6. Sanjukta Gupta, Dirk Jan Hoens, and Teun Goudriaan, *Hindu Tantrism* (Leiden/Koeln: E.J. Brill, 1979), 5.
7. Khanna, "The Goddess-Woman Equation," 110.
8. Ibid., 114.
9. Ibid.
10. Ibid., 115
11. Gupta, Hoens, and Goudriaan, *Hindu Tantrism*, 55.
12. Ajit Mookerjee and Madhu Khanna, *The Tantric Way: Art. Science. Ritual* (England: Thames and Hudson Ltd., 1977), 10.
13. Khanna, "The Goddess-Woman Equation," 110.
14. Ibid., 113.
15. Ibid., 116.
16. Ibid.

17. Agehananda Bharati, *The Tantric Tradition* (London 1965, 15, 18), in Angela Dietrich, *Tantric Healing in the Kathmandu Valley* (Delhi: Book Faith India, 1998), 18.

18. Dietrich, *Tantric Healing*, 18.

19. Ibid., 30.

20. Lilian Silburn, *Kuṇḍalinī: The Energy of the Depths: A Comprehensive Study Based on the Scriptures of Nondualistic Kashmir Saivism* (Albany: State University of New York Press, 1988), 190.

21. Khanna, "The Goddess-Woman Equation," 120.

22. Ibid.

23. See Linda Johnsen, *Daughters of the Goddess: The Women Saints of India* (St. Paul, Minnesota: Yes International Publishers, 1994).

24. Mookerjee and Khanna, *The Tantric Way*, 31.

25. Dietrich, *Tantric Healing in the Kathmandu Valley*, 22.

26. Ibid., 25.

27. Ajit Mookerjee, *Kuṇḍalinī: The Arousal of the Inner Energy* (London: Thames and Hudson, 1982), 30.

28. Ibid., 29.

29. Madhu Khanna, *Yantra: The Tantric Symbol of Cosmic Unity* (London: Thames and Hudson, 1979), 30.

30. Mookerjee, *Kuṇḍalinī*, 19.

31. Kartikeya C. Patel, "Women, Earth, and the Goddess: A Shakta-Hindu Interpretation of Embodied Religion," in *Hypatia* 9 (4, 1994), 69.

32. David Gordon White, *Kiss of the Yoginī: "Tantric Sex" in Its South Asian Context* (University of Chicago Press, Chicago, 2003), 99.

33. Ibid., 11.

34. André Padoux,"What Do We Mean By Tantrism?" in *The Roots of Tantra*, eds. Katherine Anne Harper and Robert L. Brown (Albany: State University of New York Press, 2002), 21.

35. Ibid.

36. Vicki Noble, personal conversation with the author, June 2009.

37. Michael Allen, *The Cult of the Kumari: Virgin Worship in Nepal* (Kathmandu: Mandala Book Point, 1996), 128.

38. Ibid.

39. Ibid.

40. Ibid. (Italics mine).

41. Ibid.

chapter three
durga as bhagawati: the power of the yoni

Durgā has thousands of names—one of Her most beloved is Bhagawatī: Goddess of the Resplendent Yoni or Vagina. In Sanskrit *bhaga* means power, yoni, and dazzling light. Bhaga also means "go with the divine light." Accordingly, Bhagawatī recalls the power of woman's yoni and the divine light of passion and love that ignites our will and governs our creative and sexual desires. Durgā in Her epithet as Bhagawatī, as She is known in Kerala, Nepal and Assam, is worshipped as the womb or yoni of existence. Throughout South Asia one finds shrines of natural rock formations or vulvic openings in trees that resemble the yoni. Cleft rocks are smeared with red vermilion powder reminding the devotee of the powerful essence of a woman's menstrual blood and her yoni. Such sacred places hosting a natural form of the yoni have been worshipped for millennia. There are thousands of them. Devotees pay homage to the yoni as the source of all life, the "womb and tomb" of our existence.[1] It is from Her, through the cosmic gates of Her sacred yoni that we all enter this reality, and it is through Her vulvic gates that we will eventually return.

Worshipping the Divine as Bhagawatī, as a Goddess of Female Sexual Power offers a vastly different worldview than life under God the Father. To explore Her mysteries, we must know Her history. We must understand the traditions and philosophy from which She emerges. Bhagawatī represents female consciousness, which cannot be separated from its intrinsic sexual and creative energies. Bhagawatī's elemental instinctual nature is one of Her distinguishing characteristics. She does not abide by rules of social convention and orthodox religion. Bhagawatī is a singular form of the Goddess' Śakti power. She is the embodiment of creative and sexual expression. She *is* Durgā, they are one and the same Goddess. Groups of Goddesses such as the Sapta or Aṣṭa Mātṛkās, Navadurgā and Yoginīs are also emanations of Bhagawatī or Durgā. All these Goddesses, whether in singular or collective form, speak to the myriad expressions of the natural sexual power of women.

Durgā's epithet, Bhagawatī, She of the Resplendent Yoni, recalls this Goddess' ancient female-centered roots in highly creative cultures that held women and sexuality in high esteem. The ideologies and practices surrounding Bhagawatī offer an alternative, yet equally real and valid way of experiencing life from the female perspective.

The Power of Bhaga, the Yoni

The yoni is the oldest iconic representation of divinity on this planet.[2] Downward pointing triangles found in cave art dating back to the Paleolithic are a prevalent symbol that honor and express the creative force. The power and sacrality of the yoni whether expressed through cowry shells, triangles, flower imagery, or other shapes is a prevalent symbol of creation from earliest times all over the planet. This is not surprising given the undeniable interrelationship between the female reproductive cycle, the lunar and seasonal cycles—and the life bearing and preserving role women have held since earliest times. The interconnection between women's bodies, and in particular women's menstrual cycles, with the lunar-based agricultural cycles still honored in certain parts of the world has been expressed in both aniconic and anthropomorphic forms since at least 3500 B.C.E. in South Asia. Vegetative Goddesses such as Śakambharī and Lajjā Gaurī (1st to 4th CE) were perhaps an earlier stylized form of Goddess Bhagawatī as we know Her today. Common motifs representative of these Goddesses include naked female bodies with vulvas fully exposed. Known as the uttānapad pose, the woman's legs are drawn up into an M shape near her torso. While such images are erotic, they are not primarily or only focused on sexual eroticism. The pose of a woman with legs open to give birth is similar to a woman who is sexually receptive. In her study of Lajjā Gaurī Carol Radclifffe Bolon notes, "The human form and the intercourse/birth pose are used as a metaphor for creation."[3] Instead of heads these Goddesses often have pots that are either empty or filled with vegetation. Sometimes a lotus will take the place of a human head. The presence of such Goddesses is an expression of abundance, fertility, sexuality and desire. The essence of this Goddess goes beyond being a Mother Goddess, Universal Mother and/or Divine Woman. "She is the elemental source of all life, animal and plant." She is creative power personified.[4] Today the pot with and without vegetation continues to be recognized as a sacred aniconic embodiment of the Goddess' great womb, especially the terracotta or earthen pot. This vessel is a central icon of worship during the Durgā Pūjā.

The connection between women's bodies, earth and Goddess are not metaphors, but living realities of female power. The centrality of the female yoni in these ancient artifacts expresses a deep reverence for the mysterious interconnectedness of the female to the earth, moon and cosmos that has persisted to this day in the Kathmandu Valley and parts of India. In his article, "Women, Earth, and the Goddess: A Śakta-Hindu Interpretation of Embodied Religion," Kartik Patel notes:

> For a Shakta-Hindu, however, menstruation is not simply a biological fact, and for that reason it cannot be separated from the concepts of women, female, and the feminine, or for that matter, from what is cultural, psychological, and biological. . . . For a Shakta-Hindu menstruation is a holistic concept. It is a religion (dharma). The term

ritu, which signifies menstruation, also signifies the cyclical changes of the season as well as the orderliness of the cosmos. Thus, it is believed that the menstrual cycle in the female body corresponds to, and represents, the cyclical change of seasons and the orderliness in the universe.[5]

We find shrines and sacred sites to parts of the Goddess' body all over the Indian subcontinent. Many cities, temples, even houses are constructed based on ancient spiritual systems linking the physical and spiritual realms in a way that reveres and honors yoni as source. In fact, Nandu Menon, a Tantric priest and teacher from Kerala, teaches that the collective forms of Bhagawatī or Durgā, the Mātṛkās and Navadurgās, actually evolved from nine cosmic yonis. We find esoteric geometric triangle designs known as yantras (representations of deities) in Tantric ritual art. For example, one of the most popular, the Śrī Yantra, consists of nine interlocking triangles, which on one level represent the union of the yoni and lingam (phallus). The nature of this union is not merely a reference to the sexual act of intercourse between a woman and man, but is indicative of union with the Divine. The various triangular formations also point to a profound cosmological and philosophical depiction of the universe and our bodies. The yoni goes beyond the status of symbol: it is a portal of becoming, of possibility and power.

In the West, on the contrary, the yoni is not spoken of openly in orthodox culture and is still regarded as something taboo. In Western cultures there is no notion of woman constantly *becoming*, rather her identity is static, fixed, pinned to one aspect of existence. For example, in the Western Judeo-Christian tradition, we have the "virgin mother or the whore complex" where female sexual expression is restricted to one of these representations. Despite the fact that Mary gave birth to God, she not only has no Divine status of her own, but she is said to have conceived Christ immaculately—thus stripping her of her sexuality. Recent scholarship by Dr. Marguerite Rigoglioso suggests that the parthenogenetic nature of Mary's pregnancy is suggestive of the powers of ancient priestesses whose sexual rituals centered on embodying the Divine, and perhaps, even conceiving a child without a man.[6] Although women within the Judeo-Christian and Islamic orthodox traditions must look behind and beyond the patriarchal layers that conceal the original nature of the Divine Female, we can find Divine models of females who are and remain sexually empowered and autonomous in Eastern religious traditions.

Bhagawatī and Durgā are models of female potential. The Goddess' myriad forms offer alternative female models of creative expression. While Bhagawatī and Durgā are not mothers in a procreative sense, there are other Goddesses in their circles that offer that possibility. And there are others that express the creativity of the artist, professional and lover. The female universal energy, Śakti, is dynamic and creative. Śakti is the divine essence of constantly becoming; the endless flux of creation, fruition, and destruction that pervades existence. In the Śākta Tantric tradition Goddess is constantly in a state of flux—She is the ever changing force behind all reality. Worshipping and honoring the yoni as the Source of all existence remains one of the most powerful and central aspects of the Śākta spiritual tradition today.

The most important Kaula and Śākta site of the Goddess' yoni is in the tribal state of Assam in Northeastern India. Goddess Kāmākhyā, Goddess of Desire, is worshiped as a split rock through which water bubbles up from the earth. These waters turn red for one month (in June) every year and are believed to be the Goddess' menses. The direct correlation with women's menstrual cycles and the female body's mysterious relationship with the Earth as Mother is not only noticed by local participants and pilgrims from afar, but also plays a central role in contemporary rituals.

India, Navarātri 2005

In 2005 I am in Guwahati, India at the temple of Kāmākhyā when Durgā Pūjā begins. Conch shells ring out signifying the arrival of the new moon. I hear shouting, chanting, bells and horns beneath the earth I am standing on. Their resonance vibrates up through the earth into my feet and body. The shrine to Goddess' yoni is about 30 feet below me, deep in Earth Mother's body. The priests are invoking Her presence for the pūjā. On the first day of Durgā Pūjā, they are praying. They are asking Mā to come so She can be worshipped as the Great Cosmic Mother, Destroyer of Demons, Remover of Fear, and Goddess of Desire. Kāmākhyā is one of the most ancient sites of continual Goddess worship on the Indian subcontinent. And it is perhaps the most potent of all Śākta sites. Here She is worshiped as a moist rock over which a natural spring has trickled for millennia. Kāmākhyā is a Śakti pīṭha, or one of 50 sacred Goddess sites that are associated with a myth about the Goddess Satī and Śiva. Each pīṭha or seat is one of the Goddess' body parts.

According to the myth, Satī's father, Dakṣa refused to invite his daughter to a great ceremony for the gods because he did not like the appearance or behavior of Her wayward husband, God Śiva. While the ganja smoking Yogi could care less about Dakṣa's conventional concerns, Satī was outraged. One version tells how Śiva tries to stop Satī from crashing Her father's party. In Her rage She transforms into the ten Mahāvidyās, Great Tantric Goddesses of Liberation, showing Her husband that She has multiple forms and none of them are the demure, submissive, and obedient wife. In a more popular version, Satī storms into Dakṣa's party, uninvited. The immensity of Her grief at Her father's insults and rejection is too much to bear: She immolates Herself on the ritual fire. Śiva, totally bereft at his loss, takes his beloved's body and wanders the worlds, stomping and trampling anything in his way. Viṣṇu, the God of Preservation is concerned that Śiva's despair over losing his beloved will destroy all existence. So he follows Śiva and hacks away at Satī's body until the weight of Śiva's burden has been lessened. The Goddess is reborn in another form so She can reunite with Śiva. Each place where Her body fell became a very powerful shrine or temple to Goddess. Satī's yoni fell at Kāmākhyā.

The ten Mahāvidyās, Tantric Goddesses of fierce, impenetrable natures reside on the mountain of the Kāmākhyā temple. To pay homage to these fierce emanations of Goddess, the pilgrim must carefully traverse slippery often crumbling stone stairs into cavernous pits or duck into small dark shrines where the pungent scents of incense and fresh blood intermingle. The dark almost overpowering air seduces us into feeling as if we are entering the yoni of the Mother again and again. Throughout the temple grounds and mountain itself, Yoginīs and Yogis wander about asking for alms and offering blessings—and sometimes, if unsatisfied, curses. Many sit in meditation, for what to the commoner would seem like eons.

On one side of the mountain, there is a shrine to Bana Durgā, or Durgā of the Forest. It has been there for thousands of years linking Durgā to the fertile power of the vegetative world. At Kāmākhyā Bana Durgā is worshiped as a huge wall of rock that like so many of Her other ancient sites, has been smeared with red vermilion powder and blood and draped with garlands of marigolds, carnations, and roses. In this open mountain shrine, Bana Durgā is a giant yoni. She is the Great Cosmic Mother of Sexuality, Birth, and Death from Whom we all come, and to Whom we will return. Water, red sindoor paste, and blood from animal sacrifice commingle at the base of Her stone lips and flow down a long trough. It is not June, the month Kāmākhyā always menstruates, but it is the first day of Durgā Pujā and I am at the temple to Kāmākhyā and my own yoni is bleeding. Every time I attend a ritual to Durgā—no matter where I am in my menstrual cycle—I begin to bleed. She asks for the woundless blood sacrifice, and over the past several years, my body has synchronized with the pūjā and teaching cycles. My blood is a reminder that She and I are one. On this first day of Durgā Pūjā at the holiest of temples to Goddess, I dip my fingers in the red blood of Bana Durgā, and dot my forehead and throat with the viscous fluid.

The Assamese beehive style temple in which the Goddess' sacred yoni is housed is located on the top of a mountain. I am reminded of the Ancient Bee Goddess, found in cultures around the globe, but especially in the Mediterranean. She is the essence of female leadership and authority. For many this form of Goddess radiates sexual power. Perhaps it is the connection coming from the sweet buzz of bees that emulates the hum of internal sounds during orgasm—or the aphrodisiac qualities of honey and the mention of this sweet ambrosia so often in song and poetry. Brahmārī, the name of the bee Goddess in South Asia, is also the name of a yogic breathing practice that calms the nervous system. It helps with our memory and concentration. And Brahmārī is one of the names of the Navadurgās in some regions. I have been enveloped by that electrifying hum as I have knelt at Her mūrti (image) at so many of Her temples and shrines.

No detail, no relationship to the natural world goes unhonored in the Śākta Tantric tradition. Even the temple architecture, also known to be the embodiment of Goddess, carries layers of symbolic meaning. And the mountain on which this temple resides? Śiva Himself. While the temple is Her yoni, the mountain is the lingam of Śiva, God of Transformation and Destruction and the foundation of Reality. In Śākta Tantrism there is a sacred precept: Śiva without Śakti is but a corpse. Without Her animating essence, Śiva cannot exist. And yet Śakti needs Śiva too, for it is the tension of opposites that creates existence. He is the foundation of Reality, the cosmological ground upon which She dances. Without his calm and cooling presence, She could burn Herself out. As I stand before the beehive temple, I feel an invitation to remember the sacred hum of existence and experience this as Śiva and Śakti in their sacred lovemaking.

My co-pilgrim, Kalli has been here before and has established relationships with local priests. This is a very useful connection to have, as the lines outside the temple wind down the mountain and are hours long. We are led inside through a side gate, then down the steep narrow stairs into pitch blackness. The air pulses with Śakti. All around me people are shouting, pushing, chanting, crying. I hear them chanting: Aum Kāmākhyā Varade Devī Nīlaparvatavāsini /Tvam Devī Jagatām Mātaryonimudre Namo'stu te'. *The crowds are thick and impenetrable. My co-pilgrims are so fervent with devotion and an all-consuming anxiety to bow before Her rock hewn labia, they push forward to get closer to Her and the pressure of their bodies lifts my feet off the ground for a brief moment. My heart is pounding. I know if I fall, I will be trampled. But I remember why I am there. I remember that She is the Remover of Fear. I feel awe to be waiting here in the temple to Her yoni. A fierce love overcomes me. She will not let me get trampled today, I think. But if I did, if that is Her will, then it would be a tremendous blessing to die at the labial gateway of one of Her most ancient of shrines.*

When it is my turn to bow before Her, I lose sense of who I am and what I am doing. I feel my body being pushed down before Her great yoni by the priests and attendants. My hands float down into the moist darkness and touch the cool fluid. This is Her blood, Her sexual fluid. I try to chant along with the priest whispering in my ear, but I can't move my lips. The mantra is merging into one long vibratory tone that mesmerizes and unifies my consciousness. A hum builds in my heart and flows out into my limbs, it stimulates my throat and MAAAAAAA spills from my lips. I feel emptied, completely—in such a profound way that there is no longer a sense of separation between myself and Goddess.

I am led out of the inner sanctum and stumble behind my friend Kalli to several other shrines. She too wanders around with a beatific look on her face, a lightness to her step. We leave offerings of fruit, flowers, rupee notes and coins, I hear other devotees calling out Jai Mā! Jai Mā! *Victory to the Mother Goddess. Kalli and I join them chanting* Jai Kāmākhyā Mā! Jai Durgā Mā!

I am in a daze. I feel shaky, hot, and delirious. I am coming down with a fever—again. The Śakti at these sites energetically cracks me open. Karmic impurities must be burned away. My kuṇḍalinī begins to stir and my body temperature rises. I cannot follow my rational mind. Instead I let my body lead me.My feet pull me forward and I get the sense that I will begin my circumambulations—three times around the main temple to complete the morning ritual. But before I even go ten feet my feet root into the ground and I notice a very special shrine on the side of the temple. There in the niche is a squatting Goddess, Her yoni perfectly exposed, Her entire body bright red. Jai Bhagawatī Mā! I cry out! And then bow before Her. After all these years, I finally have come to pay homage to the Great Yoni. After years of painful illnesses in my yoni, mantras and rituals to Her have helped me to heal. I thank Her for how the experiences I have been given, however devastating and painful, are helping me break from my past conditioning. Over the last few years, She has stripped me bare— taking everything I identified as me. Illness after illness have made me more aware of the power of my yoni and my creativity. Her teachings have required I look heartbreak after heartbreak in the face and offer up shame, rage, jealousy, and fear. She has tested me until I thought I would break. And then until I did. My mind! My ego! She has forced me to surrender and dissolve into Her. And here I finally stand at the temple of Her yoni and remember the power of my yoni.

The Vagina: Sheath for a Sword

Etymologically, the word *vagina* means sheath for a sword. It serves as the resting place of the male "weapon." The phallic sword that fights and kills ironically seeks and takes refuge in the house of creative energy. While women naturally embody the creative and destructive dance of the universe and manifest it through our cyclical natures, patriarchal man has taken on life's mysteries by being a perpetrator of war and death. Within patriarchal language, even the very word vagina pathologizes the female body. The name in and of itself sounds like a disease, when in fact it reflects the dis-ease patriarchal man has with women's bodies.

If we are to reclaim words like vagina, then it would behoove us to reclaim the sword as well. Durgā and Her bevies of Goddesses are depicted and described as carrying swords. Their swords are not to kill in a physical sense, but to cut through deceit and betrayal. The Goddesses' swords aid them in discriminating between what is just and unjust. They help them to cut away that which no longer serves humanity, the planet, or themselves. These Goddesses use knives and swords to slay the ego, forcing their "victims" to return to a more embodied way of knowing and being in this world.

We live in a culture that exploits female sexuality. Women's bodies are objectified, sold, exploited, mutilated, and severely abused. Despite decades of feminist activism, we are still fighting for the right and freedom to make choices about our own bodies, sexuality and reproductive cycles. Within the patriarchal paradigm, women are not allowed to fully define and manifest our wants, our needs, or our desires. Our erotic nature is often repressed by societal rules and conditioning. Those of us who do are marginalized, deemed threatening, and often demonized as vixens, vamps and whores.

The sacrality of sex has been almost completely erased, repressed, and denied. The erotic is exploited and controlled, and fear and misogyny have taken its place. But Kāmākhyā is the Goddess of *Desire*, and She takes the form of the *Resplendent Yoni* as Bhagawatī and as the Goddess of *Power* as Durgā. These Goddesses inhabit worlds where female sexuality is portrayed and honored as completely sacred, where female sexuality is central to spiritual rites and practices. Instead of objectifying women, exploiting our natural power, and reducing us to our breasts and genitalia, women are worshipped as powerful and hugely sexy, holy and mysterious, creative and empowering. Female bodies are honored as expressions of Divine Consciousness.

Goddesses, priestesses, countless females can be found on temple struts throughout the Kathmandu Valley, central and Northeastern India. Voluptuous bodies twisted in erotic postures—classic yoni encompassing lingam, legs wrapped around each other's necks, women and men tenderly fondling each other while others stand by and observe with expressions of reverence. Such visual imagery is not meant to repulse or shock, nor is it meant only to arouse and stimulate. Instead such depictions are explained as "coded." To an experienced Tantrika, they offer a roadmap of energetic portals on the body, of gateways to other realms of consciousness. For the non-initiate, they express the erotic as sacred and mysterious. Beautiful and egalitarian. Empowering and potentially healing. These erotic expressions depict the state of bliss that comes with union with the Divine.

Female Orgasm, Female Consciousness

While consciousness is ultimately One and genderless, most philosophical and orthodox religious traditions have excluded the perspective and consciousness of the female. Male consciousness, which can be considered patriarchal and evident in the dominant culture, is not restricted to men, nor is female consciousness the private terrain of women. In her essay, "The Goddess as Metaphoric Image," Nelle

Morton addresses the deep-rooted necessity of a divine female image that reflects who women are and celebrates their full femaleness. She writes, "The Goddess ushered in a reality that respects the sacredness of my existence, that gives me self-esteem so I can perceive the universe and its people through my woman self and not depend on the perception conditioned by patriarchal culture and patriarchal religion."[7] Experiencing and considering God in the form of a woman's body is important to many of us. Without a reflective image of ourselves, how can we see ourselves as Divine? Here we must consider the Tantric both/and perspective and how our experiences in a female or male body on a biological level may influence our consciousness. How do we even know if there are differences in the way women and men perceive and experience the world, when everything: language, science, history, etc. is dominated by patriarchal male thought? When looking to the past, or to indigenous ontological views, we are offered alternatives to the dominated reality that we have consented to accept as "real" and the only way to live.

Śākta Kaula texts hold female sexual mysteries at the core of their teachings, while the orthodox world in both East and West does everything in its power to control the female sexual experience. A male-dominated world is always fixated on sex whether it be through repressing natural desires, exploiting female body parts through pornography and the market economy, or restricting women from acting outside the lines that the male mind has placed around the female sex. Poet Audre Lorde notes that the female sexual and creative force, which she calls, *the erotic*, "has often been misnamed by men and used against women. It has been made into the confused, the trivial, the psychotic, the plasticized sensation. . . pornography is a direct denial of the power of the erotic, for it represents the suppression of true feeling."[8] We all know the kind of world Lorde is referring to: one where art, culture, sensuality, beauty, life are expendable, where the female body is exploited, raped, abused. Any expression of the instinctual and wild erotic becomes threatening. A patriarchal world is dominated and permeated by male consciousness, which often translates into linear ejaculatory reactions and the need to control anything that is other, that is chaotic and different. What if there were more female leaders in the world? Would our lives and choices be any different? We need not look only to the East to search for answers. Women are becoming leaders in many places around the world at this time, which is a very hopeful sign.

Two European feminist philosophers Luce Irigaray and Hélène Cixous have written numerous books on the power of the female body, and what Irigaray calls *sexuate* difference. Irigaray has coined the term *sexuate* to refer to the biological differences between women and men that are not of a strictly sexual (pertaining to the sexual act) nature.[9] What is an ethics of sexuate difference? In part, it is the recognition of the biological differences between women and men without reducing us to restrictive, oppressive and traditional notions of femininity and masculinity.

It is our very sexuate differences, namely the female capacity to menstruate, to create life through birth (and if we choose, end it with abortion), and the power of the female orgasm and our sexuality, whose colonization lies at the heart of female oppression and male dominance and control. However, by even pointing out our obvious biological differences, some would criticize me as being *essentialist*. Within this viewpoint, *essentialism* suggests that women are restricted to and defined by their biological functions of birthing and mothering, when it is quite the contrary. Irigaray's ethics of sexuate difference presents an honoring and a deep recognition of the profound relationship between women's menstrual cycles and the lunar cycle, tidal ebb and flow and agricultural cycles. From this perspective, essentialism is an expression of the deep interconnection between women and the cosmos.

Irigaray and Cixous philosophies have helped me understand my place in the world, how my body, and my sense of otherness and difference is influenced by male-dominated consciousness. Both authors present philosophical explanations of the differences between the sexes, especially on a physical level, and the effect this has on consciousness. Cixous insists that one cannot talk about "a female sexuality, uniform, homogenous, classifiable into any codes—any more than you can talk about one consciousness resembling the other."[10] Goddesses are personified and anthropomorphized expressions of consciousness. Durgā, or Bhagawatī and Her myriad collective forms, carry a sense of multiplicity, or varied ways of being. These Goddesses are guides for all aspects of reality; especially our varied and complex expression of sexuality. We find Durgā/Bhagawatī surrounded by 7, 8, and 9 Goddesses and then 49, 64, and 81 Yoginīs in Her surviving temples. Perhaps this expresses multiple forms of female experience and infinite modes of female consciousness.

When we consider female sexuality, our sexual natures cannot be reduced to one pointed experience. Not virginal, not whorish, and just about everything in between. So what qualifies as an expression of female sexuality? "Almost everything is yet to be written by women about femininity: about their sexuality, that is, its infinite and mobile complexity."[11] Looking to Goddess ritual, mythology, symbolism, and iconography and how these are uniquely expressed in our own lives is a fascinating place to start.

The parallels between Tantra and Irigaray's philosophies are intriguing—especially the idea of woman and man as Divine. In her essay, "Divine Women" Irigaray presents the following ideas,

> Divinity is what we need to become free, autonomous, sovereign. . . .[12] God forces us to do nothing except become. The only task, the only obligation laid upon us is: to become divine men and women, to become perfectly, to refuse to allow parts of ourselves to shrivel and die that have the potential for growth and fulfillment. . . .[13]

And yet, without the possibility that God might be made flesh as a woman, through the mother and daughter, and in their relationships, no real constructive help can be offered to a woman (or a man). If the divine is absent in woman, and among women, there can be no possibility of changing.[14]

From a Śākta Tantric perspective, we can understand the Divine as Śakti in any of Her forms. She is the energy of becoming and the divine female entourage of Goddesses that embody Her. Śākta Tantric practices open our energetic channels and allow us to connect with the Divine on a very intimate level. Becoming one with the Divine in Tantric rituals offers the potential of liberation and spiritual autonomy, exactly what Irigaray describes is necessary in this day and age.

Sexuate Difference

Let's now consider how Irigaray's theories on male and female sexuate differences, (that are considered so potent and essential to Tantric rituals), might give key insight into how sexuality and biology impact our consciousness and self-expression within this world. Female sexual fluids have long been considered ambrosia in Tantric culture. Their sacred flow holds the power to alter consciousness into more blissful, pleasurable states of being. Texts on Tantric rituals speak of the ways the smell and taste of sexual juices shift our awareness. Sexual experiences clearly alter our consciousness, and orgasm especially gives us access to an experience that is very different from waking reality. Few would disagree that at the moment of orgasm we lose sense of the boundaries of our physical being. The ego seems to dissolve leaving us with a deep sense of unity with our partner and the world around us. We merge with a non-ordinary state of be-ing which is all-enveloping, highly pleasurable, and for some, charged with electrifying energies. We achieve a non-dual state of awareness, which is the goal of sexual Tantric practices. Could a women's experience of orgasm give us insight into the essence of female consciousness and in fact, distinguish our consciousness from male ego-based consciousness that we have been conditioned to accept as the norm?

In her essay, "The Laugh of the Medusa," Hélène Cixous asks: Is the female orgasm an expression of female consciousness? Cixous contends it is. If we understand language and our use of language as an expression of consciousness, then the idea of our bodies influencing our consciousness does not seem so radical. In fact, Tantric and yogic texts teach how the body and the earth have consciousness. If our consciousness is so intrinsically tied to the body and yet also *is* the Divinity, wouldn't our thoughts and actions in the world give insight into our own sense of Divinity? The great sages say that language is consciousness. Words have an effect on our psyches. Sanskrit is a scientifically and philosophically advanced language. So powerful is the *word* that in ancient India, Panini, the country's great grammarian, was considered a sage.[15] Correct pronunciation in addition to intention is essential to bring the mantras or spells into manifestation. And language itself is considered to be the Goddess. Feminism has taught us that the political incorrectness of words like policeman, mailman, etc. impact our sense of power as women. Racist language also perpetuates debilitating stereotypes and strips us of our humanity. Gender and racially neutral words are slowly replacing degrading language. The connection between language and consciousness is undeniable. Freudian Slips are said to reveal our unconscious predilections; song, poetry, rap, hip hop, spoken word, chanting are all creative expressions of the divine stream of consciousness.

Besides the power of the words themselves, *how* we communicate is yet another important indicator of our relationship to consciousness. Cixous finds the way women communicate to be an expression of creativity and consciousness. Women circle around a subject, often flowing off in different directions, only to later return and pick up where we left off. Women do not always complete sentences in a linear way. We sometimes tell stories beginning with one, wandering off into another, only to circle off on a tangent of relevant but not directly related thought, then finally coming back to the initial spark and proceeding with the story we originally began to tell. We do not naturally think along rigid lines. This does not mean women are incapable of this thinking in a linear way, but rather we have been forced to communicate in ways that are masculine at their core. Cixious metaphorically describes how evident male consciousness is in the use of language. Like the hard penetrating penis, men write and speak along a linear trajectory. With the history of reason comes a phallocentric tradition that is "self-admiring, self-stimulating, and self-congratulatory."[16] Masculine logic is different, not necessarily worse, or even better, but different. It is linear, probing, piercing, and trenchant. The dividing lines are made clear, what is right and what is wrong is strictly categorized. There is one mission that has a search and destroy quality to it—as there is no room for other or both/and. "As a dick is finite structure, with a visible beginning and end, so too is the potential for male orgasm. As a cunt is infinite—how many bloody mysteries and future generations are hiding up there, somewhere?—so too is the potential for female orgasm." writes Inga Muscio in her radical, humorous and thought-provoking book, *Cunt: A Declaration of Independence.*[17] On the other hand, women's experience is not usually linear, nor can women be confined to the straight and narrow and still be able to thrive.

Luce Irigaray also posits a connection between sexuality and consciousness. She notes that the male operates sexually and consciously by tension and discharge while the female experience (when allowed to be expressed freely) seems to center around becoming attuned to the cyclical time of the universe.[18] Relating femaleness to cycles and maleness to singularity and linearility is the essence of Tantric philosophy. Śakti is the cyclical dynamic aspect of existence, Śiva, the pillar, the quiescent and receptive foundation, the ground of being. To represent this concept, stone yonis with lingams are some of the most ubiquitous icons in Śākta Tantrism. Like the coded Tantric temple struts lined with couples in erotic embrace, the physicality and biological nature of our genitalia perhaps can inform us of culture and power, Divinity and humanness. However, we have not yet fully embraced the power of the yoni.

To Irigaray, our labia speak of a culture of two—a culture that is not dualistic but always in a process of communication and becoming.[19] It is a culture that holds the possibility of *both/and* rather than *either/or*. Both pain and pleasure. Both sorrow and joy. A culture constantly transforming, eternally becoming. It is the fluidity between two: between two labia and what comes or does not come between them; between two people; two ideas opposing or unifying. This fluidity is inherent to the female nature which naturally expresses Śakti. The flow between two encapsulates the constant movement between death and life, growth and decline. Those who revere the Divine Mother have long believed that life and death, ecstasy and even pain all flow through Her labial gates. This understanding is naturally transferred onto women as embodying these universal forces. Irigaray and Cixous would probably agree that "While men tend to be logical, women are cosmological."[20]

Participating in the linear structures of patriarchal reality (as has been constructed by the male ego) leaves little room for women to expand and flourish let alone for us to have the opportunity to express our authentic selves. Creativity in any form is the best way for us to access our deepest nature. Regardless of medium, it is essential we create from our bodies, from our experience. Cixous suggests that "women must write through their bodies, they must invent the impregnable language that will wreck partitions, classes, and rhetoric, regulations and codes, they must submerge, cut through, get beyond the ultimate reserve—discourse"[21] Through expressing ourselves more freely, women can create environments that are more conducive to our mode of being in the world. In knowing our body's potential and how the yoni has been the seat of worship for millennia, we have the opportunity to find ways to awaken our truly erotic natures and find expression for our deepest desires. Lorde writes,

> For once we begin to feel deeply all the aspects of our lives, we begin to demand from ourselves and from our life-pursuits that they feel in accordance with that joy which we know ourselves to be capable of. Our erotic knowledge empowers us, becomes a lens through which we scrutinize all aspects of our existence, forcing us to evaluate those aspects honestly in terms of their relative meaning within our lives. And this is a grave responsibility, projected from within each of us, not to settle for the convenient, the shoddy, the conventionally expected, nor merely the safe.[22]

To many of us it feels scary and uncomfortable to manifest our creative desires. We risk losing the often meaningless comforts that we have surrounded ourselves with, but which take up space and keep us numb to these inner promptings. Without the erotic we are left with our dissatisfaction and "disaffection from so much of what we do."[23] To open to this force is empowering to women. Men too can open by honoring and respecting the women in their lives and by honoring the intuitive, dynamic power that motivates them from within. But it is not always so easy. Societal conditioning, negative emotions, greed, shame, fear all can get in our way. And yet, we must remember that Bhagawatī carries a sword.

Fortunately, more and more women are addressing these issues and doing the much needed work of raising consciousness around women's sexuality. There are many books available focusing on these very issues. There is a new wave of sexual consciousness flowing through many of our communities, but it needs to include reverence and women need to be placed at the center. Woman's Divinity, the sacred reality of her body needs to be recognized, honored, and cherished. Our elemental instinctual natures need to be expressed. Celebrating the indistinguishable, inseparable nature of the sacred and the sexual is a necessary step in women's liberation and self-fulfillment. We have a right to sexual autonomy. All women, from the earliest of ages, need to be made aware of the rich, juicy, stimulating history of Matṛkās, Yoginīs, Tantrikas, shamans, healers, midwives, artists, courtesans, temptresses, seductresses, and sacred whores that present us with alternative ways of living in this world. When not bound to a linear either/or model, the roles and modes of female expression within society are as infinite and varied as the waves of women's orgasms. Our power, the erotic, or Śakti is a creative force which can be expressed in multiple ways: the creation of a child, a work of art, the initiation or completion of a project, a relationship—the possibilities are infinite. When women's sexual energies are fully allowed to flow unbridled, without fear of punishment, violation or pain, a different consciousness and reality can and will emerge on this planet.

Notes

1. Marija Gimbutas, *The Civilization of the Goddess: The World of Old Europe* (San Francisco: HarperSanFrancisco, 1991).

2. Lucia Chiavola Birnbaum, *dark mother: african origins and godmothers* (Lincoln, Nebraska: iUniverse, 2001).

3. Carol Radcliffe Bolon, *Forms of the Goddess Lajjā Gaurī in Indian Art* (Delhi: Motilal Banarsidass Publishers, 1997), 5.

4. Ibid., 6.

5. Kartikeya C. Patel, "Women, Earth, and the Goddess: A Shakta-Hindu Interpretation of Embodied Religion," in *Hypatia* 9 (4, 1994), 72-73.

6. Marguerite Rigoglioso, *The Cult of Divine Birth in Ancient Greece* (New York: Palgrave Macmillan, 2009).

7. Nelle Morton, "The Goddess as Metamorphic Image," in *Weaving the Visions. New Patterns in Feminist Spirituality*, eds. Judith Plaskow and Carol Christ (San Francisco: HarperSanFrancisco, 1989), 115.

8. Audre Lorde, "Uses of the Erotic," in *Sister Outsider: Essays and Speeches by Audre Lorde* (Trumansburg, New York: Crossing Press, 1984), 54.

9. Luce Irigaray and Elizabeth Grosz, "Sexuate Identities as Global Beings Questioning Western Logic." in *Conversations* (London: Continuum, 2008), 123-137.

10. Hélène Cixous, "The Laugh of the Medusa," in *Signs* 1, no. 4: summer, (1976): 309.

11. Ibid., 315.

12. Luce Irigaray, "Divine Women." in Sexes and Genealogies, trans. Gillian C. Gill, New York: Columbia University Press, 1993, 62.

13. Ibid., 68–69

14. Ibid., 71

15. Linda Johnsen, *The Living Goddess: Reclaiming the Tradition of the Mother of the Universe* (St. Paul, Minnesota: Yes Publishers, 1999), 27.

16. Cixous, "The Laugh of the Medusa," 311.

17. Inga Muscio, *Cunt: A Declaration of Independence* (Emeryville, California: Seal Press, 2002), 109.

18. Luce Irigaray,"How Old Are You?" in *je, tu nous: Toward a Culture of Difference*, trans. Alison Martin, (New York: Routledge, 1993), 115 and 113-117.

19. Luce Irigaray, "Sexual Difference," in *An Ethics of Sexual Difference*, trans. Carolyn Burke and Gillian C. Gill (London: Athlone Press, 1993), 18.

20. Vicki Noble, personal communication with the author, December 30, 2005.

21. Cixous, "The Laugh of the Medusa," 315.

22. Lorde, "Uses of the Erotic," 57.

23. Ibid., 55.

chapter four
the art of pilgrimage and the durga puja

Pilgrimage has been an enduring expression of reverence and devotion within spiritual and religious traditions since earliest times. Within the Hindu tradition, it is called tīrtha-yātrā, which literally means "undertaking a journey to river fords."[1] Rivers and fords are considered natural places imbued with much power. Groves, caves, hilltops and mountain peaks are other equally important places of worship, especially in Goddess cultures around the world. Many of the most potent Goddess sites in the Hindu and Buddhist tradition can be found at places within the natural landscape. We can consider all of South Asia in the following statement: "The number of Hindu sanctuaries in (India) is so large and the practice of pilgrimage so ubiquitous that the whole of (India) can be regarded as a vast sacred space organized into a system of pilgrimage centers and fields."[2] While some places may be the focal point for Hindus or Buddhists all over South Asia, others may be more local and attract the visitation of that area's inhabitants. Regardless of whether pilgrims travel thousands of miles or a few footsteps, these sacred places are repositories of spiritual and religious knowledge and ritual tradition.

Pilgrimage means to "partake of a shrine"; however, the "shrine" can also be a quality of truth in addition to and sometimes instead of a physical place. Pilgrimage can be understood metaphorically, and the journey can equally be an inner one that takes place during meditative practices. The *tīrtha* or "ford/crossing" can refer to qualities we mentally invoke such as kindness, devotion, compassion, and presence to deal with our struggles and conflicts. In this sense we must cross over the obstacles in the mind that prevent us from achieving our goals and focus on cultivating purer states of awareness.

From a religious perspective, pilgrimages are performed to purify the soul and to help us obtain specific goals within the mundane world. According to Surinder Mohan Bhardwaj, author of *Hindu Places of Pilgrimage in India*, there are two main categories of intention in a pilgrimage. The first involves a specific and more mundane motive. It usually includes prayers for a blessing, help, success or protection. It can also involve a specific rite of passage such as a child's first haircut, menstruation, pregnancy or birthing rites. Other societal passages from childhood into adulthood or any experience where one undergoes deep transformation and wishes to mark their crossing over into the next stage of being or life are valid reasons for physically or metaphorically undertaking a pilgrimage. Often vows (sukhnā or vrata) are made to help focus the pilgrim's intention and to strengthen their commitment toward achieving the desired result. Sacrifices, both monetary and animal, are another way they expresses their vows.

The second category of intention does not involve mundane requests or rewards, but focuses on achieving religious or spiritual merit and alleviating the effects of our karma. Karma is a complex system that goes beyond its popularized and generalized meaning of cause and effect. Sometimes the pilgrim participates to lessen the effects of karma s/he is experiencing. Others may go purely to express and deepen their reverence and devotion to a deity or their religious path. While some pilgrims may perform or participate in certain rites or ceremonies, these rituals are not always necessary for a successful journey. Often darśan (the act of seeing and being seen by the deity) is the most salient goal for the pilgrim. Darśan is a central ritual concept, especially within Tantra. Darśan focuses on the relationship between devotee and the Divine. It refers to the exchange of energy between them that is sometimes the most desired and ultimately transformative experience. Diana Eck illuminates the deep significance of darśan in her book, *Darśan: Seeing the Divine Image in India*. Eck explains,

> The pilgrims who take to the road on foot, or who crowd into buses and trains, are not merely sightseers, but "sacred sightseers" whose interest is not in the picturesque place, but in the powerful place where darśan may be had. These powerful places are called tīrthas (sacred "fords" or "crossings"), dhāms (divine "abodes"), or pītha (the "benches" or "seats" of the divine).[3]

In addition to darśan there are many other ritualistic means to pay homage on a pilgrimage: bathing in a tīrtha, sacred river, lake, or pond; giving alms; singing bhajans, devotional songs to the deity; or kirtan, group devotional expression through song and dance, as well as other rites that relate more specifically to the deity or place the pilgrim is visiting. "For the pilgrims a whole cosmic event is being reenacted, one in which they actually feel they are participating. The myth is re-actualized, at the specific time and at the specific place."[4]

Pilgrimage leads us toward self-realization and spiritual liberation. For orthodox Hindus spiritual liberation means transcending this earthly reality and breaking free from the cycles of karma that bind us to this world. For the Tantrika (Tantric practitioner), freeing ourselves from karma is essential; however leaving this body and world is not the ultimate goal. From the Tantric perspective, the Divinity is immanent as well as transcendent. Instead of trying to escape this existence, engaging with the world around us in all its beauty and all its horror is crucial to the

Tantric path. For a Tantrika, the body is a vehicle and the senses are utilized rather than denied. Therefore, pilgrimage is an effective way for the practitioner to earn religious merit. Achieving such merit will ultimately bring improvement to this life and future ones, should the soul not achieve full spiritual emancipation in this lifetime. Regardless of sectarian affiliation within the Hindu or Buddhist traditions, there are various paths one can follow: jñāna yoga (the path of knowledge), karma yoga (the path of action), rajas yoga (the path of passion), and bhakti yoga (the path of devotion). My own personal quests tend to involve bhakti, the devotional aspect, most strongly; however, jñāna, knowledge, has been a salient path for me as well.

Traveling to sacred places with a devotional intention or specific request allows the pilgrim to step away from the responsibilities, stresses, concerns and problems of everyday life. S/he has an opportunity to fully immerse themselves in spiritual contemplation and prayer. Such periods can prove rejuvenating for the practitioner, enabling her to return to her daily life with renewed clarity and strength, even with insights into solutions to problems or difficulties that may have been limiting her.

In order to fulfill one's spiritual destiny there are various paths the practitioner can follow. The practice of pilgrimage follows four dominant ideas within Hindu philosophy that are attributed to attitudes towards life: dharma (work, duty, virtue), artha (material gain, worldly advantage, success), kāma (love, pleasure, desire) and mokṣa (liberation). For orthodox practitioners dharma, artha and kāma all lead one to the final stage of liberation—mokṣa, which will hopefully lead one into spiritual bliss and enlightenment. For unorthodox practitioners, for example Yoginīs and Yogis, an unconventional path may be chosen, one that will lead them directly to the final stage so that they can spend their life cultivating and expressing qualities that lead them to mokṣa. All rites and rituals help one liberate oneself from the bondage of thoughts and actions that keep one caught up in the endless cycle of death and rebirth.

Navarātri—Nine Nights, Durgā Pūjā

Each year millions participate in the annual Durgā Pūjā, the largest contemporary Goddess festival on the planet, and pay homage to Durgā . In the Kathmandu Valley there are nine tīrthas (fords/crossings) that form a pilgrimage route for the festival in the Valley. Each of these sacred places is associated with a body of water in which the pilgrim could take a ritual bath before the sacred rites. However, today, the water near the majority of these places has unfortunately become too polluted for bathing. Instead of bathing near each respective site, many pilgrims perform such rituals at home, or at the tīrtha near the Shob Bhagawatī temple—an important temple site during the festival. Rather than rules being rigid about how and where one should worship, devotees do adapt with the times and shifting landscape. Certain ritualistic aspects are important, but there is some flexibility especially in the Valley, which houses people from various ethnic backgrounds and animist, Buddhist and Hindu beliefs. Let's consider why the Durgā Pūjā serves as one of the largest pilgrimage experiences within the South Asian world. What purposes does it serve and what does it have to offer not only those in the East, but others, like myself, who are not Hindu by birth?

Celebration of Durgā's victory over the buffalo-headed demon takes place all over the South Asian subcontinent as well as other parts of the Hindu world each fall. Despite the universality of worship of the Divine as Goddess, the length and some aspects of this three-to-ten-day ritual vary depending on region. The recitation of the *Devī Māhātmya* or *Śrī Śrī Caṇḍī* text that narrates Durgā's victory over the demons in three stories or caritas is a common element of worship and practice throughout the Hindu World. The *Caṇḍī* serves as a mythological guide demonstrating the immeasurable powers Durgā embodies, which, from a Tantric perspective, are inherent in each of us. Durgā's name "may denote worldly adversity (e.g. dangerous passages) or an unassailable fortification. Devī thus aids one in overcoming difficulties and traversing hardships, or is herself an impenetrable mystery and difficult to overcome."[5]

Durgā is called because earthly existence has reached a critical juncture. She is invoked to restore balance to the earth and to help us enter into the natural decaying and dying aspect of the yearly, even cosmic cycle. Images of death appear all around us—in the media, in film. We hear stories of torture and war; patriarchal man-inflicted causes of violence and death. Images of death from unnatural and violent causes have become so prevalent most of us have become desensitized and cannot see how it is rupturing the natural web of existence. To speak of death is taboo, and, in fact, it is feared by all of us. And yet to a Tantrika or Yoginī, our entire lives are a great preparation for death. Undertaking a pilgrimage is a very effective way for us to confront this natural aspect of the life cycle. There is always something passing away in our lives—at every moment we experience loss.

In Hinduism we find reverence for the full cycle of existence and practices that guide us to focus on our breath—each breath out, a mini-death, each breath in, an affirmation of life. Buddhism also speaks of the impermanence of existence. In the earth-based roots of every religion we find an understanding of the complementary reality of death. Traveling to sacred sites can serve to amplify the ever-present reality of death through various expressions that are personal to each of us. Pilgrimage provides us with an opportunity to learn to see and to honor the patterns of death in our daily lives as much as we love and honor the birth and fruition stages. Death in the literal sense is also a motive for pilgrims, especially in regards to religious and ceremonial duties associated with a deceased family member. When a Hindu dies, their physical body is cremated in a ritual ceremony. The consecrated ashes must be returned to a river, a tīrtha. This practice is called *muṇḍana* and is an especially important practice at Goddess sites.[6]

The Durgā festival offers us an opportunity to fully participate in the mythological and philosophical aspects of the Hindu tradition. We are active participants in the entire life cycle. We live and express the myth through ritual. When we participate in rituals, we become Her. There is a Tantric precept that says: *In order to know Goddess, one must become Goddess.* When we open to Goddess, new layers of consciousness are revealed. Mystical signs abound. We are swept up by profound feelings of devotion. Another reason to undertake a pilgrimage is so that this numinous state can be spontaneously triggered at Her sacred sites. The devotee does not merely call for the Goddess, or ask Her to return, s/he speaks of a nearness that is intimate, familiar and mesmerizing.

Although knowing Hindu philosophy and mythology is not necessary for reaping the benefits of the pilgrimage, such knowledge will also help us understand our experiences and the age-old layers of meaning they contain. One striking variation between the Kathmandu Valley and Bengal, Assam, (as well as other parts of India: Orissa and Gujarat) is the reversal of the first three days of the Pūjā. In the *Devī Māhātmya* text the first three pūjā days are devoted to Mahākālī and the final three to Mahāsaraswatī. In the Kathmandu Valley the first three days are devoted to Mahāsaraswatī. I found that Saraswatī was indeed very present for me when the Durgā Pūjā began in the Kathmandu Valley. I continued to follow the rituals and philosophies as they were expressed in Nepal without any reservation. Both systems' approach to the cyclical nature of death and birth were evident in the rituals. We could begin the Pūjā approaching a Goddess of death, or of birth, for in this tradition death leads to rebirth. Ultimately you cannot separate them.

In keeping with the philosophical basis of the rituals, it is necessary to outline the powers of these three aspects of the Goddess Herself and explain how they relate to our worldly existence and spiritual paths. While these qualities are inherent in everyday life regardless of where we are, they seem to become heightened and more visible and tangible during spiritual festivals and rituals. Inevitably any pilgrim will experience their influences on a personal as well as cosmic level. Within the Hindu tradition the cosmos is made up of three universal energies known as *gunas*: tamas (inertia), rajas (dynamism), and sattva (purity). Esoterically, the three forms of Durgā worshiped during the Pūjā—Mahākālī, Mahālakṣmī, and Mahāsaraswatī—each are the embodiment of one of these gunas. Mahākālī is associated with the denser, heavier energies; Mahālakṣmī with the passionate and juicy; and Mahāsaraswatī with the pure and luminous. Mahā means great and signifies their authority with the universal governing forces of our existence. As a backdrop to the Pūjā itself, these Goddesses provide a spiritual path for the devotees to follow. At the early stages of a pilgrim's spiritual journey, these gunas are not fully manifested and are accessible through the various mūrti (statues, images) and ritualistic icons that symbolize, and in fact embody, their qualities. Therefore, every aspect of the ritual offers the initiate an opportunity to come in touch with the formless powers of Durgā's cosmic nature. Devadatta Kālī notes:

> A physical image such as a sculpture or painting or a mental image visualized in meditation allows us to approach the Infinite through finite symbols and to interact with divinity. Such symbols correspond to psychological or spiritual truths, and every gesture, posture, color, or object associated with a deity stands for a particular attribute or power. A few symbols have universal significance, but others are esoteric, with meanings not readily obvious or easily understood.[7]

Worshiping the holy female trinity around the Pūjā time precedes the fifth century textual description and points to Goddess' inseparable association with the natural landscape. In the Devī Māhātmya we learn that Durgā comes from the Vindhyachal Mountains just outside of Banaras or Varanasi. Still today, pilgrims "will perform a triangular (yoni-shaped) pilgrimage circuit to the temples of Mahālakṣmī, Mahākālī, and Mahāsaraswatī in the hills surrounding the Vindhyavāsinī temple."[8] It is common to find important temples to Goddess naturally forming a yantra or sacred geometric pattern in the landscape. Sometimes the temples have consciously been constructed in such a pattern; however, natural places of millennia-old worship do form patterns that express a greater consciousness behind it all. Due to thousands of years of attendance and the persistence of devotion at certain sites, the Śakti at Goddess sites is much more intense than in places that have not been such constant sites of worship. Making a pilgrimage to these places involves immersing oneself in layers of meaning and centuries of consciousness. Even if we do not understand the philosophical or religious tenets associated with these places, we will feel the Śakti. And we will be changed.

The Bhakti or Devotion of a Pilgrimage

Pilgrims and spiritual teachers of past and present know that a pilgrimage begins once one is called to the journey. Usually the call is unmistakable; synchronicities abound. People and situations spontaneously appear and guide one toward manifesting a vision or dream. The numinous shimmers Her radiant, revealing light through each encounter and experience along the way. Slowly, all aspects of a pilgrim's life seem to be redirected toward the journey at hand. A theme often reflecting one's inner yearning becomes more apparent. What the pilgrim will undergo before even embarking on the journey is a unique and often mystical process, sometimes as indescribable as the numinous signs and symbols that seem to be summoning one. A pilgrimage is not your everyday vacation to "get away from it all," but a profound commitment and act of devotion to a great and all-powerful force. And yet ultimately, in addition to traveling to a sacred place, it is a journey to the divine power that is within our selves. In 2000, as I have said, I was called to Nepal for a second time. When I had left Kathmandu in 1998 I asked the Kumārī, the young living Goddess who is an incarnation of Durgā, to help me find a way to come back to Her, because I sensed there was much more for me to explore in this ethnically and spiritually diverse Himālayan Valley. However, I never imagined the call to return would come less than a year later, and that within two years I would return. Then, in the first weeks of my Master's program in 1999 I was invited to undertake a pilgrimage to the Kathmandu Valley of Nepal during the annual Durgā Pūjā.

At first I was unsure if I should take time off from graduate school. Only months before I had completed a 15-month backpacking journey through Southeast Asia and felt I needed to stay in California for a while. But the signs around me showed me it was time to return. My friend Yana who had created the trip seemed to be a channel for Goddess. For years she had been a Tibetan Buddhist scholar and practitioner. The Kathmandu Valley is the only place in the world where Buddhism and Hinduism coexist and deities from both traditions are worshipped interchangeably regardless of one's affinity for a particular tradition. Yana shared my love for Nepalese culture and Nepalese people. She spoke to my passions and innermost dreams. She told me about thousand-year-old Goddess sites we would visit and living Goddesses we would meet. Conversing with her about this possible pilgrimage brought back vivid memories of my time there: dusty brick red streets, pomegranate vendors, Goddess shrines with erotic imagery decorating the temple struts, disgruntled rikshaw drivers with grapefruit-sized calves, and the majestic Himālayas encircling the Valley. She was interested in the Buddhist sites and Goddesses like Tārā and Vajrayoginī, and had a lot of research to share with a group of Western pilgrims. She told me we would lead the group to various Hindu, Buddhist and shamanistic or animist sites in the Valley, and also we would participate in the Durgā Pūjā.

Since I was writing my Master's thesis on Durgā, Yana told me, I should focus on teaching the group about Durgā and Her mysteries.

Although Yana cannot remember how or why she came up with this, I will never forget the moment she said that about me and Durgā. I was lying on my bed looking at the purple and lavender sari draped over the Indonesian canopy in my room. Time stopped and everything became totally still as soon as she said it. I sat up and heard her words "since you are writing your thesis on Durgā" repeat like a mantra in my head. The room began to spin. It was almost as if I was sitting in the eye of a storm.

I focused my sight on a circular pattern on my white bedroom wall. I felt calm, clear, and expansive. "Yes," I heard myself saying. Up to that point I had not consciously decided to do research on Durgā. I was interested in the Kumārī but had not realized She is a living emanation of Durgā. I loved Goddess, but was only beginning to understand the vast family of Goddesses and Gods in the Hindu tradition. Still those words came through Yana. It had been decided. Me and Durgā. Who was this Goddess to whom we were making a pilgrimage? I was to come to realize that through divine grace She had been with me and *in* me all along.

As I prepared for the pilgrimage in 2000, I learned that Navarātri has many divisions and layers of ritual and beliefs. Although it is a festival to Durgā, the Great Goddess who slays the ferocious and tenacious buffalo-headed demon, and who is the force behind all life and death, many other Goddesses are worshipped as different manifestations of Her immense all-pervading power. On each of the nine days a different form of Durgā is worshipped. Each Durgā is one of the Navadurgā who have individual names. They represent a manifestation of Durgā, who is responsible for different functions involved in the creation, sustenance, and destruction of the universe. They govern the realm of time and relate not only to the nine nights of the festival, but to nine months out of the yearly cycle. On each of these nine nights during the festival, Tantric rites are performed that honor and celebrate the Mother Goddess in Her multiple and singular forms. Mary Anderson, author of *The Festivals of Nepal* explains that during Durgā Pūjā or Navarātri:

> the infinitely ancient mother-cult of Mother Earth and Mother Nature takes form in the worship of Śakti, where the Life Force is embodied in the Divine Energy or Power of the female, depicted as Goddess Durgā in all her many forms. All Mother Goddesses who emanated from Durgā are known as Devīs, each with different aspects and powers, nine of whom, collectively called Navadurgā, are listed in the scriptures, but many more are worshipped in Nepal.[9]

Every autumn Goddess shows us how everything that comes to fruit must ultimately return to Her great body, the earth. Her ancient roots associate Her with the harvest and the agricultural cycle upon which Her devotees see themselves as interdependent. Even today, despite the spread of urbanization and the consequent disconnection of humans from the natural world, Hindus, Buddhists, animists, shamans, Moslems and Christians alike all come together in India and Nepal each autumn and ritually re-enact Her myth in ways that express a deep reverence for Earth as Mother and ultimately, Durgā.

At the autumn equinox, worship of Durgā begins on the dark moon and ends on the full moon with nine nights of Tantric worship culminating in the tenth-day victory. Episodes from Durgā's myth are recited on each day and rituals are performed to specific aspects of the Goddess. Many rituals are centered on stages and expressions of womanhood. During this festival young women who have been married off to a man in another village are allowed to come home and be reunited with their mothers, sisters, aunts, and grandmothers. The reunion between female relatives and the centrality of the female role in specific rites around food, healing, birth, the Kumārīs/maidens of the community, and the harvest, point to the matrifocal heart of these practices. In his study on the Durgā Pūjā in Banaras, Hillary Peter Rodrigues comes to the conclusion that "the feminine presence of the reunited women creates an atmosphere in the home that is crucial to the mood of the domestic Durgā Pūjā."[10] He continues, "Devī presides as the arch matriarch, the symbol and embodiment of womanhood, under whose nurturing and protective wing the family's female lineage may gather. The Devī brings them together, and at the end of the Pūjā, like the Devī, they too will depart, leaving only the lingering perfume of their presence until the next year."[11] The reunion of the female lineage is central to this ritual and speaks to a rich "herstory" of the past.

Men participate in this festival, and today Brahmin[12] priests dominate the rituals. Nevertheless the focal points of worship are inherently female: Goddess in various forms, kalaśa (pot symbolizing the womb), the color red, the yoni, menstrual blood, plants, trees, stones, and so forth. And each icon or symbol triggers memories, a sense of interconnection and respect. They seem to offer a portal into layers of meaning about my own experience of being female.

Although each day of the ten-day festival is associated with different Goddesses, it is ultimately a festival of Durgā as the Supreme Deity of Existence. All other deities are an emanation and expression of Her Great Consciousness. The nine days of Navarātri (nine nights) with the tenth being Durgā's victory day, are divided into three sets of three. Saraswatī is the birth, creativity and generating force; Lakṣmī is the life, growth and preserving force; and Kālī is the death, transformation and empowering force. One of the eight Matṛkās and/or the nine Durgās each has a particular festival day and their rituals are connected to the cosmic and earthly order as are the qualities each of these Goddesses express. Other names for Durgā include Vajrayoginī, Kāmākhyā, Bhagawatī, or Taleju and forms of these Goddesses are honored on each day. In Assam the predominant name of the Supreme Goddess is Kāmākhyā. In Calcutta She is Kālī. In Nepal, She is known and worshiped as Durgā, Bhagawatī and Vajrayoginī.

So, what are the origins of such an empowered and honoring female expression? *Jai Mā* is used to greet and bid farewell—in a sense symbolically embracing birth and death. Originally this was probably a festival where women had high social and spiritual status and were revered for their inherent female connection to Durgā. *Jai Mā*. These women would have presided over rite-of-passage rituals: menstruation, death, and birth. Today some still do; however, given the brahmanic[13] or orthodox Buddhist structures around them, some Hindu and Buddhist women may not celebrate Divine Femaleness as they have in the past, or as they still do in Tantric circles today.

Today in Nepal and some parts of India women are recognized as being Śakti, however, they are not treated as the Divine beings that they are. Certain practices honoring the fierce and female aspect of the Divine remain despite the sanskritization[14] and patriarchalization of the rituals. Although daughters are separated from their natal families, they are taught that marriage is an honor and becoming a mother brings prestige. Independent, unmarried and powerful Goddesses such as Durgā and Kālī are held in awe and fear and the harvest rituals serve to pacify their wrathful natures. They are a force that cannot be ignored. Nevertheless they have been replaced by Goddesses that have been "spousified" and domesticated: for example—Sītā and Lakṣmī are Goddesses women are expected to emulate. Despite the fear of Her undeniable powers, it is Goddess in Her unbridled, untameable Śakti force that comes forth and saves the world year after year.

Whether they are conscious of it or not, the Durgā Pūjā provides women with an opportunity to reconnect with that very primal, instinctual and totally powerful part of their inherent natures. Although the significance of the female bond between humans and the Divine is perhaps restrained in this day and age, it is not entirely lost. Durgā appears again and again to wake us up from the internal and external demonic forces that threaten to overcome us and blind us to our true natures. She reminds Her devotees that She is the force behind all existence. The crops that come to harvest grow due to Her will and grace. To deny Her completely would mean complete destruction of the planet, a direction we are headed if more do not heed Her call and honor the sacrality of Mother Earth and the female sex.

September 2000

Several nights before I embark on the pilgrimage, I dream of a large banyan tree, a tree that has been worshiped as Goddess for millennia. In the dream I feel an overwhelming sense of urgency and desperation to walk over to the tree and place my hands on the snaky trunk. I know that She, the tree, is a Goddess. Twisting vines and roots extend about ten feet around the tree and cover the ground. I cautiously step into the labyrinthine entanglement despite the cries of villagers shouting for me to stay back. The roots and vines have turned into live electrical wires and are electrocuting me. My body is thrown about from the force of this energy and eventually I collapse. All of my power is zapped, or so it seems at first. After a moment of crystalline silence and tranquility, my spirit rises out of my body and looks down at the physical shell lying there tangled in those tentacles, only a few feet away from the trunk I had so wanted to touch. I realize I have died without having reached my destination and know I must return. My spirit reenters my body and I rise, a bit drained and tired, but totally focused on getting to that tree. She is calling me. I slowly make my way and wrap my arms around Her.

When I wake I realize that indeed, this pilgrimage has already begun to test me around issues of power. I am learning how to tap into my own wellspring of power rather than turning to outside sources. The research I am doing on Durgā is my lived reality. I read that "the worship of Durgā offers votaries an opportunity to ally themselves personally with a power more formidable than any adversity they are likely to encounter," and I realize that this Goddess has been very present in my life.[15] *The demons Durgā slays are the demons of my past. I confront abuse, rage, shame, and fear. I study rituals that speak of yoni worship while my own yoni continues to frequently burn with searing pains connecting my consciousness to the countless women suffering similar disease or injury. My body is calling for me to process the abuse I suffered as a child and to express my power through my creativity.*

I learn about boundaries—who to let in, who not to, and painful lessons about giving my power away because I am too afraid to be myself and be judged. Many of the crises I encounter in my personal battles feel like death experiences. Some losses so unimaginable and inconsolable, I feel pieces of me dying from an unbearable grief. I get married and divorced. I say good bye to friends I had thought would be in my life forever. I work on letting go of thoughts that sabotage me. I midwife the death of a sick cat that I love very much. Disillusioned and disappointed I give up on dreams I have thought I wanted for years. I surrender to all these deaths to create space for a new life to emerge. There are other deaths that feel more victorious. Confronting a memory of abuse in neutrality or having conversations with family members about their complicity in the violence I experienced throughout childhood are challenging, but liberating. I fall to the underworld with sword raised and fight the naysayers and critics in my mind until each battle is won.

The dream of the Goddess tree has always remained a lighthouse. In part I understand it as warnings from my subconscious about the electrifying energies that would "kill" those parts of myself that needed to die. However, it also assures me that no matter how difficult any challenge can be, I will rise and make it to Goddess. And when I open to and sync with this female consciousness behind existence, there is tremendous power to be gained.

Notes

1. Surinder Mohan Bhardwaj, *Hindu Places of Pilgrimage in India: A Study in Cultural Geography* (Berkeley, Los Angeles: University of California Press, 1973), 2.
2. Bhardwaj, *Hindu Places of Pilgrimage*, 7.
3. Diana L. Eck, *Darśan: Seeing the Divine Image in India* (Chambersburg, Pennsylvania: Anima Books, 1981), 5.
4. Bhardwaj, *Hindu Places of Pilgrimage*, 149.
5. Hillary Peter Rodrigues, *Ritual Worship of the Great Goddess: The Liturgy of the Durgā Pūjā With Interpretations* (Albany: State University of New York Press, 2003), 17.

6. Bhardwaj, *Hindu Places of Pilgrimage,* 150.
7. Devadatta Kālī, trans., *In Praise of the Goddess. The Devī Māhātmya and Its Meaning. A New Translation* (Berwick, Maine: Nicolas Hayes, Inc., 2003), 49.
8. Rodrigues, *Ritual Worship of the Great Goddess,* 67.
9. Mary M. Anderson, *The Festivals of Nepal* (New Delhi: Rupa & Co., 1988), 144.
10. Rodrigues, *Ritual Worship of the Great Goddess,* 66.
11. Ibid.
12. Brahmin: A member of the highest of the four major castes of traditional Indian society, responsible for officiating at religious rites and studying and teaching the Vedas. Brahmins are the more privileged and dominant group of society. One has to be born into this caste. Typically, Brahmins are an elite caste of scholars, priests and pundits. In a sense they are an Indian aristocracy. Along with the merchant class, Brahmins have been "the historical bearers of much of Indian [orthodox] religious civilization." (White, *Kiss of the Yogini,* 3). However, theirs is a history that is exclusive of subaltern peoples, and carries unfavorable rights for women and darker-skinned South Asians. Brahmins are responsible for the Manusmṛti, sexist and classist laws that were codified around the second century. Generally speaking Brahmins are lighter-skinned (and darker-skinned peoples are demonized and othered as lower castes and/or untouchables). Brahmin is not to be confused with Brahman. Brahman refers to the Great Consciousness of all Existence. Brahmins are described as knowing Brahman, which again reiterates their dominant and exclusive status. From this perspective in order to reach the Divine one must go through a Brahmin priest, i.e., unless you were born into this caste, you do not have the same rights to access the Divine.
13. Brahmanic/brahminic: Pertaining to the dominant, elite and exclusive caste of Brahmins.
14. Sanskritization: Indian Sociologist M.N. Srinivas coined and defined *sanskritization* as a process by which "a 'low' or middle Hindu caste, or tribal or other group, changes its customs, ritual ideology, and way of life in the direction of a high and frequently 'twice-born' caste. Generally such changes are followed by a claim to a higher position in the caste hierarchy than that traditionally conceded to the claimant class by the local community." The concept of sanskritization addresses the actual complexity and fluidity of caste relations. It brings into academic focus the dynamics of the renegotiation of status by individuals from various castes and communities in India. According to M.N. Srinivas, Sanskritization is not just the adoption of new customs and habits, but also includes exposure to new ideas and values appearing in Sanskrit literature. He says the words karma, dharma, papa, mayā, samsāra and mokṣa are the most common Sanskritic theological ideas which become common in the talk of people who are sanskritized. This phenomenon has also been observed in Nepal among the Khas, Newar and Magar people over the centuries. (From http://en.wikipedia.org/wiki/Sanskritisation, August 2, 2009). See, Mysore Narasimhachar Srinivas, *Caste in Modern India: And Other Essays* (Bombay: Asia Publishing House, 1962), 48.
15. Rodrigues, *Ritual Worship of the Great Goddess,* 49.

part two

durga puja: the ten-day harvest festival

day one
Saraswatī: goddess of creativity

Saraswatī and the First Day of the Durgā Festival

The first day of the Pūjā, Ghata-sthāpana is known as the installation of the sacred vessel. Preparations begin weeks before the opening of the Pūjā begins. Durgā in Her various manifestations as Goddess of Creativity, Abundance and Death is constructed out of clay and straw, then hand-painted by local artisans. She is dressed in fine silk saris and adorned with jewels and placed in a pandal or temporary shrine that will house Her only for the duration of the Pūjā. At the most astrologically auspicious time, Durgā is ritually invited into Her worshipers' homes. Nowadays a Brahmin priest or the patriarch of the family performs the rituals to infuse Her energy into the sacred pots and the clay and straw statues that have been painted, dressed, and specially made to embody Durgā during the Pūjā. For the next nine days, daily rituals will be performed; Her epic myth will be read from the *Śri Śri Caṇḍī;* all sorts of offerings will be made: fruits, incense, candles; chants will be sung and recited; special foods, drink, and music will all be part of the festivities.

Inside people's homes an earthen altar, which is conceived as Durgā Herself, is created in the shrine room. Mūrtis or images of Durgā in Her various manifestations are carefully placed on the shrine. On this first day of the Pūjā, Durgā in Her creative aspect as Goddess Saraswatī is honored. One icon that plays a very significant role in the family shrine room during the Pūjā time is the sacred vessel or kalaśa. The clay pot symbolizes the womb of the Goddess and also women's wombs. Since Saraswatī is understood to be the force behind all creation, the womblike kalaśa is an appropriate symbol for honoring Saraswatī's creative and fertile energies. Saraswatī brings all ideas into the manifest world, much like a woman's womb or the dark fertile soil of Mother Earth carries and nurtures new life until it is ready to emerge into the physical realm.

To honor and invoke the fecundity and generosity of the Earth Mother Goddess, the altar is sown with barley seeds that will sprout over the course of the Pūjā. Durgā's yantra or sacred geometrical pattern that in Tantric rites is a portal into a different level of consciousness is drawn into the soil and a clay pot is placed on top of it. At the most astrologically potent moment Durgā in all Her manifestations is invoked into the pot. In the Kathmandu Valley the earthen pot is filled with water and thus represents Bhu Devī (Earth Mother) and Mā Gaṇgā (River Mother), who is the most sacred of Indian rivers. These rituals are all invoked under the auspices of Saraswatī's guidance and Divine presence. As the creative force behind all existence, She imbues the rituals with Her sattvic wisdom—preparing all for purification and new growth. She blesses the ground and offers new life forms through the waters of life, water being one of Her earliest forms. Beginning the Pūjā celebrations in honor of Saraswatī seems fitting since as the kalaśa She is the primordial womb: from Saraswatī the entire world flows into being.

Saraswatī is worshiped as Goddess of Wisdom, Knowledge, Creativity, Music, Poetry, and the Arts. She is also the balancing quality of universal calm amidst all the external and internal activity of existence. Throughout the festival we will find Her inspiring Her devotees and gracing the ceremonies with sacred dance and song. In the Śākta tradition Goddess is everything and everywhere. Every expression of the manifest and unmanifest world is Her great being. She cannot be separated from our existence and so She is especially honored at this fall festival time.

Before dawn on the first day the Goddess' devotees go down to the river to purify their bodies. On an esoteric level they are bathing in Saraswatī Herself for the water *is* Goddess. The Pūjā rituals begin at twilight, a time when the light meets dark, and time and space open to the liminal—a realm that is associated with birth, death and all the betwixt and between states. It is a realm that is governed by Goddess. After their ritual baths the pilgrims wander back through the twilight to the riverside temple gates where they present offerings of bananas, coconuts, rice and sweets to Ganeśa, the Remover of Obstacles. Honoring the elephant-headed God Ganeśa before the start of any ritual or spiritual endeavor is considered essential. As God of Wisdom, He serves as guide and protector and ensures that the path of our devotion and practice remain clear. He is also known to bring obstacles, thus rerouting devotees on a path that is more in alignment with their dharma and karma.

After paying respect to Ganeśa devotees continue on to pay homage to other shrines before heading for the inner sanctum. Family deities, as well as other popular deities of the local pantheon are given offerings and asked to aid families in various areas of their lives. At the Shob Bhagawatī Durgā temple near Swayambhū in Kathmandu, shrines hosting carved images of the Navadurgā line the temple walls. Offerings of red vermilion powder are rubbed on their feet, throats and heads. Often their mouths are covered with a round piece of dough made from cooked lentils, flour and chickpeas. While Gods like Ganeśa and Hanuman, the monkey God who is ever in service to Goddess, receive sweets, the Goddesses receive these lentil and chickpea offerings. It is said that the Goddess's nature is so fiery and active, only savory foods will keep Her grounded, while sugar would make Her even more dynamic and wild!

Proper worship includes appealing to all the senses. Each of these ritual gestures symbolically links us back to the elemental nature of the earth and ultimately, of our existence, demonstrating the complex interrelationship between humans and the natural world. Incense is lit for the sense of smell and the element of air. Devotees bow and touch the earth before entering the temple compound then touch the feet of every deity they pass. Ghee candles are burned for fire. Bananas, coconuts, pomegranates, eggs, lentils, rice, and other ceremonial foods are offered to the deities, then devotees later consume some of these consecrated foods known as prasād and receive a blessing. Bells are rung and devotional chants are sung for the sense of sound. This aspect of the Pūjā in particular is Saraswatī's realm, for She is Vāc, the primordial Goddess of Sound. It is through Vāc's sacred vibrations that the physical world comes into being.

The origins of Saraswatī trace back to the Saraswatī River of the Indus or Saraswatī Valley civilization around roughly 3500 through 1700 B.C.E. *Saras* means both *salt* and *flow,* and the Saraswatī River is said to have been slightly saline.[1] Archaeological remains of this ancient civilization contain an abundance of female figurines, presumably priestesses and Goddesses. On the many seals and other relics that have been discovered in this region, we find an ancient script. Deciphering these symbols has become a controversial area of contemporary scholarship due to disagreement about the translations. Nevertheless, it is fitting to find this ancient writing in a place that is the namesake of the Goddess of Writing. In fact, one of Her earliest epithets from the Vedas, Vāc also means *word*. Saraswatī is flow of water, of speech, of creative inspiration. From the first day onward music, dancing, art, and ritual worship are interwoven and are known throughout the ten-day festival as blessings from Saraswatī.

Durgā Pūjā Reflections 2000

Twelve hours after we arrive I am awakened by drumming and chanting at four a.m. and feel as if I am being called to the river. I am overcome with excitement about being here. I know intuitively that what happens over the next two weeks is going to transform me forever. She is calling me to the river, and my soul is begging me to leap up and join the Nepalese. But fear and confusion, my own demons, inhibit me. I have mixed feelings about intruding on such a sacred ceremony. Although I am a devotee of Durgā, I am not a Hindu. Is it appropriate for me to go down the road to the Bhagawatī temple and observe the twilight rites? I decide to go to the rooftop of our hotel and see if I can see anything from there. I can't, and feel disappointed. I have come all this way, and I feel uncomfortable about even going and looking. This ritual is so sacred to the Nepalese; I do not want to overstep my boundaries. I need a day to talk to local people and gauge what is appropriate for Westerners and what is not.

Now content with my decision to wait, I sit on the rooftop, waiting for the sunrise, and soaking in the sounds. I can feel the drumming reverberating throughout my entire body. I feel the entrainment of my heart to the drumbeat coming from the river. I let it carry me and return to my center. If I can't join them directly, I will join them in spirit. Today is Ghata-sthāpana, the installation of the sacred vessel. I have a revelation that will become a theme throughout my journey. I am a vessel. I am here as a vessel for Devī. I will open myself to Her and allow myself to be transformed. I pray for Her guidance and compassion. I ask Her to show me the way to liberate myself from my fears. I imagine my own kalaśa and ask myself: What do I want to plant in my holy kalaśa and nurture over the next nine days? How can I fulfill the task that Durgā has set before me? And what exactly does that task involve? How can I serve Her? I ask for guidance. I ask for the muse. "Saraswatī bless me with your grace and creative inspiration." I want to write, I want to learn, I want to express the power and wisdom of you and your Goddesses in my art. "Show me how to tap into my inner wisdom and trust myself and my path." In my vessel I nurture seeds of self-love, self-confidence, trust, and the courage to speak my truth.

Jaya Mata, Victory and Surrender to the Goddess
Reflections: September 29-30, 2000

The second morning I wake at 3:45 a.m. in great anticipation of the ritual at the Bhagawatī temple on the river. Ranju, our guide, has told us it is okay to participate. I dress in red and go down to the river with several others. We buy an offering plate of woven leaves filled with rice, red and yellow powder, oiled wicks in ceramic cups, coconuts, flowers, especially marigolds, (a favorite of Durgā), rice, and ropes of incense. I soon become lost within this world. Beyond the bounds of time and space, immersed in the sacredness of every act, I find myself going from shrine to shrine as if I have done it hundreds of times before. All the senses are utilized: the act of darśan, seeing and being seen by the deity, touching our feet or foreheads, listening to chanting and bells ringing, the smell of incense and flowers floating through the air, and the taste of consecrated food.

Our small group follows the procession that winds throughout and around the temple complex. Inside the central gates there is an elaborate temple that houses an image of Durgā as Bhagawatī. To the right, in a separate building, fifteen people are playing instruments and chanting to Durgā. It is necessary to wait in a long line to gain entrance to the main temple. The sounds of devotional music can be heard throughout the compound. We go down to the end of the line, which reaches the riverbank. Women and men must wait in separate lines, and as is common in most religious rituals I have attended, the women outnumber the men.

In the main courtyard a group of Goddesses, the Navadurgā are carved into niches along the walls. Flowers and rice are strewn all about. The thick scent of incense fills the air. Red, orange, and yellow powder stains my fingers and is smeared on my face from brushing my hair back every time I kneel down to rest my head on a deity's smeared crimson feet. A vibrant array of colors and offerings are all over the ground and cover every deity and divine icon along the way.

Even though I am not Hindu[1], I am allowed inside. The inner sanctum is dark, moist, pungent with smells of the many offerings to Goddess. After placing my head on Bhagawatī/Durgā's stained red feet and giving Her my offerings and prayers, I go back outside to light a butter lamp, light incense, and ring a bell as a means of communicating with the Divine. Such gestures signal our devotion and reverence, as well as our acknowledgement of being in sacred space. I stand there in prayer for a few moments, complete these offerings, then turn to see a middle-aged Nepalese woman warmly smiling at me. Her eyes meet mine, "Jai Mā, Victory to the Mother" she whispers to me as she touches my hand. I am so moved, so grateful for this opportunity to be in Nepal and to express my reverence to Durgā, so honored by this woman's recognition of my love for and devotion to Goddess that I begin to cry.

Later as I am wandering along the banks of the river soaking in the sights, smells, and sounds, I am given a kalaśa that was abandoned on a bench beside the river. A strong young mother who lives in a tiny hut near the river motions for me to take it. I am ecstatic—my very own kalaśa! I remember how before my wedding I had prayed to find a kalaśa for my wedding altar because it is symbolic of abundance, creativity, fertility, and sacred sexuality. Goddess is answering my prayer, but instead of it being for my wedding, I come to Nepal and receive a kalaśa during my first pūjā experience. For a brief moment I wonder whether this means I am marrying Durgā? The kalaśa in my arms is not something that has been created for tourists, but is a sacred relic, an authentic Mother Vessel made from Her body, the mud of the riverbanks. I am deeply moved. I return to the hotel and show our dance teacher, Rajendra. He is surprised and amazed that I, a Westerner, had been given a real kalaśa. "Do you know what this means?" he asks. "Mother is taking care of you. She considers you one of Her own. This is a truly a gift, but it is more than a gift for it is Durgā Herself. Durgā is in this vessel, Laura. She IS the vessel." Since it is empty, Rajendra tells me I need to put something inside it: a coin, water, some kind of offering. Instinctively, I fill it with flowers, incense, red bangles, and other gifts I receive throughout the festival. Later, I learn that Nepalese women are given many gifts from their husband and relatives during Durgā Pūjā, all of which they store in the sacred kalaśa until the festival is over.

Despite Saraswatī's presence during the first three days of the Durgā Pūjā and Her direct relationship to all forms of creative expression, the undeniable connection between our creative and sexual power is overlooked, if not denied in many of these orthodox rites. Within the Tantric tradition, it is understood that we are more than our physical body. We have an energetic body, a bliss body and other energy bodies that form a sheath around our physical forms. We perform practices to clear these energy fields and to activate certain energetic centers or cakras. Although we have hundreds of cakras in our energy bodies, seven main cakras located along our spine correspond to various emotional, physical and spiritual experiences. Our second cakra, located a few inches below our navel, houses both our sexual and our creativity energy. As a generative Goddess, Saraswatī is inevitably tied to the sexual processes within the natural world. And as we see in Her attributes of being a Goddess of the Arts, She is also the creative impulse and inspiration behind all expression. However, despite Her direct association with creation in any form, the brahmanized[2] Saraswatī lacks full agency as an empowered female model. Her nature is glorified as silent, calming and purifying. While these are essential qualities, they are restrictive in that Saraswatī is not allowed to unleash any real emotion. Creativity and sex are not necessarily silent endeavors. By having been reduced to an expression solely of calm and tranquility, Saraswatī is not allowed to present the full possibility of creative and sexual expression. In many respects She takes on the patriarchy's ideal woman who is meek, quiet, and stands by to nurture.

In most of the myths where we find Saraswatī, Her sexual nature only appears in its relation to patriarchal male beings. As we will see, Saraswatī's sexuality becomes something that is to be possessed by male gods or demon kings. In these brahmanic myths Saraswatī expresses only one side of Her multifaceted nature—that of the quiet and obedient woman. Yes, She is Wisdom, but She is given more of a transcendental rather than embodied presence. Saraswatī's ancient origin as an untamable and wild Goddess is forgotten—for the patriarchal beings we encounter in Her myths all are bent on possessing and controlling Her.

Mahāsaraswatī and Her Teachings from the Devī Māhātmya[3]

In the Saraswatī carita (chapter) of the Devī Māhātmya text, Mahāsaraswatī is featured; however, she is also referred to as Ambikā (little Mother of the Universe), Mahādevī, Durgā and other names. Throughout the chapter various epithets are used to refer to Her—indicating Her all-pervading nature and Her ability to approach any task in the divine form that is most appropriate. While there are many layers of interpretation of this section of the greater myth, it is interesting that Saraswatī is sexually objectified and threatened with force by a male (demon) that desires Her and erroneously thinks he can possess Her. In this section of the text, the demon king in his form as Śumbha sends two of his nastiest generals Caṇḍa and Muṇḍa to abduct Her and bring Her to him for wedlock. These demons have decided that this Goddess is the "jewel among women" and the demon king is determined to have Her at any cost. Does She have a choice in the matter? Well, not in their minds. If She resists, they will beat Her, they will rape Her, they will do whatever it takes to force Her to submit to male desire. Here is patriarchy at its misogynistic worst.

Śumbha's demon generals arrogantly approach Goddess and make crude, insulting remarks. Durgā stares them down, unfazed. They mistake Her composure for fear. Their egos swell and pride overcomes them as they get lost in visions of the grandeur that awaits them once they conquer this Goddess. However, they are forgetting who She is. As Mahāmāyā (Great Illusion), the all powerful Goddess outwits the demons by influencing their minds to think they can overcome the Divine. She immediately knows, through Her omniscience, that these demons are clouded by ignorance. As they advance toward Her She lets out a sigh, which is the mantra Hūm. Like Her earlier epithet Vāc, Saraswatī is the power of sound, a power which can create and destroy. As Her divine utterance reverberates out across the cosmos, She points Her finger at them and the demons are destroyed. When the demon king learns he has not only lost his two favorite generals, but has lost them to a woman, he is outraged. He calls Her duṣṭā, which means "that vile woman," "wicked woman," "wretch of a woman," "shrew" and "whore."[4] How sadly familiar is such a scenario in this day and age? How often is a woman who refuses or says no to the patriarchal male, cursed at and threatened with physical violence? Fortunately, Mother Durgā is always ready to take on the demons. Here in this appearance, Goddess speaks to the power of a woman who refuses to submit to patriarchy's demands.

Saraswatī, Goddess of Independence and Sexual Autonomy

Margaret "Saraswatī" Kruszewska is a Yoginī and scholar of South Asian studies. She received her spiritual name in India at the Sivananda ashram in 1990. Before this initiation she did not know who the goddess Saraswatī was, but has since spent the past twenty years as a devotee, yoga practitioner, and Goddess scholar. Kruszewska calls Saraswatī "Goddess of no husband, no child" an apt description of this ancient pre-Vedic goddess who is wild, fierce, and the source of all creation in Her early myths.[5] Kruszewska's fascinating research gives Saraswatī Her rightful autonomous and fiercely empowered place in the pantheon of Hindu deities. Contrary to brahmanic attempts to pacify and domesticate Her, Kruszewska's research proves that Saraswatī is originally a matriarchal Goddess. In fact, she writes "the origins of most Indic Goddesses, including the later brahmanical Goddesses, show them to have been happily unattached to husbands or children." She goes on to say that Saraswatī can be "reread as proof of resistances to the Aryan patriarchal systems of marriage and control of female sexuality."[6]

Kruzewska poses a crucial question: "Are all women, including goddesses, to be judged primarily in their capacities as mothers and wives?" Women are often defined by our relationship to other. Although it is slowly changing in some parts of the West, for centuries one of the most pressing questions about a woman is whether or not she is married (or in a heterosexual relationship). In the spring 2009 issue of Ascent magazine the executive publisher Vanessa Reid shares similar sentiments in her editorial. She notes that while traveling in India "I was unsettled by the questions that came like a mantra each time I met someone new: From where are you coming? Are you married? Are you Christian? *Who are you?* they asked."[7] There seems to be a universal and conditioned, yet unconscious, need of placing woman into neat categories—*is she married, is she is a mother*? If a woman is not a mother and/or a wife, then what and who is she? There are many of us who want to be able to live outside of patriarchal expectations and conditions. To have *both* this *and* that, which is modeled within the non-dualistic Tantra tradition, is structurally prevented through the visible and invisible restrictions placed on women. However, many of us do not want to be *either* the mother *or* the wife, yet if independent from men then a woman is virginal or called a whore. With each of these roles, unless we choose to reframe and recreate how we express being mother and wife, we still lack agency in patriarchal society. We need other choices, and we must not be limited to them alone. Women need to be seen outside their roles as mother or wife, and to be accepted whether or not they make that choice.

In Western culture, there is no notion of a woman constantly becoming: rather, her identity is static, fixed, pinned to one aspect of existence. For example, mothers are often stripped of their sexiness and their sensuality. Independent women are accused of not being nurturing, or are perceived as seductresses who threaten to take the husband away. No matter how we act as women in this world, the patriarchy insists on tying us to one expression of reality. Perhaps in this way we are easier to tame. But, at the essence of the Tantra, Śākta and Kaula tradition are ritual and meditative opportunities for both women and men to explore the very question, *who am I,* outside of patriarchal constructs. Then, in consideration of who we are, another question inevitably arises: *Am I Divine*?

Goddess Saraswatī, like Durgā and Bhagawatī, is not defined by Her relationship to a husband or child. In fact, in one of the Purāṇic myths we find a disturbing narration of the incestuous violations Her father, the god Brahmā imposes on Her. Saraswatī's father lusts after Her and attempts to force Her into wedlock. But Saraswatī is strong, outspoken, willful, and courageous. She refuses to submit to Brahmā's incestuous and abusive demands and, consequently, she is exiled and disinherited. Since Saraswatī does not fit into the wife or subservient mother model we find in these later myths, a few other Purāṇic[8] myths still present a debilitated picture of Her. Saraswatī is placed in a competitive and jealous position against Goddess Lakṣmī. There are tales about them both pining for the love and attention of the god Viṣṇu, and others that describe how Lakṣmī (wealth and prosperity) wants nothing to do with Saraswatī (creativity and the arts) because of some squabble they have had over winning the attention of a god. I believe that such stories, on an energetic level, perpetuate realities around the starving artist, or the spiritual practitioner who struggles with material success. In some respects, myth is lived reality. Such myths imply that those who are creative will not be able to take care of themselves physically. They suggest that a woman without a man or child has to be seething with jealousy and will do anything she can to be in relationship—even if he is another woman's husband. This mindset is obviously not empowering to women or men and is based on fear and feelings of disconnection and scarcity.

Aside from the few myths that speak to this competition for Viṣṇu between Lakṣmī and Saraswatī, we do not find other myths that describe Saraswatī as pining for the love of a father or husband. In fact, she has no need for them and stands alone with much dignity and integrity. Saraswatī may have been exiled and disinherited for refusing to obey, but Her exile is self-imposed.[9] Saraswatī consciously challenges the patriarchal demands and purposely alienates Herself from that system. Instead of Her creative energies being siphoned off into placating Her husband or father, or even having to defend Herself from him, She is able to use Her Śakti for Her own endeavors. Nevertheless Hers is not always an easy path. Often She is made to wander alone. And yet this solitude feeds Her. I am reminded of great writers like Virginia Woolf who wrote about woman's need for *A Room of One's Own*, or Alice Walker who has shared her own felt necessity for solitude in order to write. A woman who aligns herself with Saraswatī must create uninterrupted time and space to manifest her creative projects. The pain of past betrayals, her anger at injustice and her sense of alienation become transformative and can be the very stuff from which her artistic projects are made. Saraswatī is the muse of the creative female whose art threatens to shake up the status quo. The Goddess of Creativity, Learning and the Arts contains a self-determined and fearless independence as well as inner strength and freedom. A woman blessed with Saraswatī's grace must stand up for herself and for her creative ideas and manifestations. She must also learn to use Saraswatī's silence or her voice as a weapon of self-protection. She must not be afraid to express her emotions about any form of injustice. In order to experience the creative freedom that Saraswatī offers, a woman must be willing to face all memories she has not made peace with, and transmute them with Saraswatī's fierce wisdom, serenity and composure.

Saraswatī reminds us of the importance of discipline and detachment in revisiting difficult memories. We cannot deny or ignore certain experiences in our lives. If our minds will not remember, our bodies will—and sickness and/or discomfort may come to help us remember. From our pain, we can and must create, thereby sharing our uniquely female perspective rather than having our lives defined for us. And we must allow ourselves to be angry. Saraswatī is no meek Goddess. Her sharp tongue lashes out to destroy injustice. Her anger is righteous. She is the power of women to forcefully speak our truth. It is crucial that Her anger be expressed constructively rather than self-destructively.

Saraswatī is memory. She is intuition, inner knowing, and the flow of ideas. Saraswatī is precognitive thought, embodied knowing, and critical thinking. She is the spoken and written word. She is the sound that dances off our tongues and is comprehensible as speech. She is the power to comprehend. Saraswatī teaches us to transcend the limitations of the phenomenal world. Saraswatī, as Her name dictates, teaches us to flow with our thoughts, to follow our intuition, to listen to the inner voice that is asking us to do or say something. The more we listen to Her the louder and more confident our Saraswatī voice will be. She may urge us to do or say something that feels threatening or alienating—that will shake "consensus reality." But Saraswatī does not care about convention. Peace of mind, integrity to self, honesty, and inner wisdom are of utmost importance to Her.

The Saraswatī River dried up centuries ago, but some still believe the Saraswatī River flows underground and converges with Saraswatī's two river sisters: Gaṇgā and Jamunā at the sacred confluence in Allahabad. Perhaps Saraswatī's original essence disappeared when She went underground—and perhaps Her exile was ultimately Her own *choice*. Instead of being forced into patriarchal reality, maybe Saraswatī took Her power underground and is waiting to re-emerge at a time like the present.

The wild force of rivers is Saraswatī's true nature. She can flow gently or uncontrollably. She loves to meander and forge new paths. As River Goddess She is the Source of Life and Death for all who live along Her banks. She carries the calmness and gentleness we find in some rivers, and She also carries a ferocious and untamable nature. We should never underestimate the fierce power of Saraswatī. After all, She is the sound and vibration that brings the manifest world into being—all civilization comes from Her. As the kalaśa or sacred vessel, She is the womb of all existence. And as Goddess of Creativity, She is unequivocally a Goddess of Fierce Independence and Sexual Power. In many respects, the peaceful demure Saraswatī who does not really speak is the Saraswatī that patriarchy has passed on to us today. To find Saraswatī's true nature, we must return to the river and its fertile banks which have served as a place of creative inspiration and meditative contemplation for artists and spiritual practitioners for millennia.

Notes

1. Mrinal Pande, *Devi: Tales of the Goddess in Our Time* (New Delhi: Penguin, 1996), 48.
2. Brahmanized: The process of changing, adopting, and converting indigenous customs, rituals, traditions to suit the ideologies of the elite higher caste.
3. The *Devī Māhātmya* or *Śri Śri Chandi* was written in the fifth century by one or more authors. Scholars Thomas Coburn and Devadatta Kālī provide the most comprehensive English translation of the text. However, retellings of the order of the caritas or chapters and various aspects of the battle vary. In his book, *Devī Māhātmya: The Crystallization of the Goddess Tradition*, Coburn discusses the various earlier texts that relate similar

stories of the Goddess's battles with demons. (Mahabharata, Rig Veda) Although the Saraswatī carita is the third in Kālī and Coburn's translations, I refer to it as it pertains to my own understanding of Saraswatī.

4. Devadatta Kālī, trans., *In Praise of the Goddess. The Devī Māhātmya and Its Meaning. A New Translation* (Berwick, Maine: Nicolas Hayes, Inc., 2003), 124.

5. Margaret Kruszewska does not use capitalization in her epithet for Saraswatī, so I have kept her original spelling.

6. Margaret Kruszewska, "Saraswati: Goddess of no husband/no child" in *The Constant and Changing Faces of The Goddess: The Goddess Traditions in Asia* (Newcastle upon Tyne: Cambridge Scholars Press, 2008).

7. Vanessa Reid, "Supernova Editorial," *Ascent Magazine: Yoga For an Inspired Life*. Issue 41 Union, (2009), 6.

8. Purāṇic: From Purāṇas. Refers to a genre of texts that emerged in the fourth and fifth centuries C.E. "The word *purāṇa* means "ancient" and the texts characteristically present a highly mythologized history of the universe through successive cosmic cycles." (Devadatta Kālī, *In Praise of the Goddess*, 12). They marked an ongoing process of assimilation of indigenous, non-Aryan cultures within the nomadic Aryan pastoral takeover.

9. Pande, *Devi: Tales of the Goddess in Our Time*, 63.

day two
the kumari: living virgin goddess

The second day of my pilgrimage in 2000 brought an encounter with the Kumārī. I have described how, when I first visited Nepal in 1998, I was intuitively drawn to Her, the Living Virgin Goddess of the Kathmandu Valley. The Kumārī shares qualities with Saraswatī such as a love for knowledge, wisdom and creative expression. Both are associated with the peacock, the majestic male bird whose colorful plume is a physical expression of the transmutation of poisons the bird has consumed. These Goddesses in their Tantric appearance have much to teach us about transmuting what is toxic in our lives. As the pure virginal essence of creation, the Kumārī and Saraswatī are indeed linked. Legends around the Great Goddess deciding to take human form in the body of a young girl to prevent unwanted sexual advances tell yet another all too familiar tale of patriarchal man sexually objectifying the female sex. In one particular story a medieval king could not take his eyes off of Goddess Durgā's body. He was so focused on Her sexuality alone, that the Goddess became enraged and declared that She would only take the body of a young girl whenever he invoked Her aid—so as to prevent his unwanted advances. The fierce Goddess from then on appears in the living body of a virgin girl.

The nature of the Kumārī is paradoxical, for although Her virginity and purity is emphasized, She is directly related to woman's blood mysteries. Despite the Kumārī's youthful appearance, some of the mythology and rituals around Her center on Her menstrual blood. Women who suffer from any menstrual disorder visit the Kumārī to pray for healing assistance. In fact, this is one of Her special domains of healing. Given that my own life has involved issues of disempowerment stemming from childhood abuse and reproductive illnesses around my menstrual cycle, it is interesting that it was this virginal form of Goddess Durgā who drew me into the complex and mysterious Śākta Tantric world. When I first learned in 1998 who Goddess Durgā was, that She was a "slayer of demons," I knew I had come home. I had even used that specific language for years—that I had had "to slay demons" that had plagued me since I was very young.

The Kumārī has become an important model and guide in the years I have been conscious of Her existence. In fact before the festival in 2000 even began, our group was greeted by the Pañca or five Kumārīs[1] as we got off the plane. The

Pañca Kumārī are a group of five young girls, believed to carry heightened states of Goddess energy. This collective form of Goddess, the Pañca Kumārī, appears for dignitaries and notables. Although we were unaware of who they had come to greet as our group disembarked the plane on that autumn morning, seeing the Pañca Kumārī upon my arrival to the Kathmandu Valley felt like an auspicious omen of what was to come.

Encountering the Kumārī, September 30, 2000

On my second day of being back in Nepal, Ranju, our self-described feminist guide explains that she is taking us to see the Kumārī, The Virgin Goddess of Kathmandu. The thirteen of us on the pilgrimage go to the center of Kathmandu, Durbar Square, where throngs of people are going from temple to temple to give offerings to the Gods and Goddesses. Ranju tells us we are going to a special temple for Ganeśa, and then we will visit a young living Goddess. But along the way three of us get separated from the group and find ourselves in front of Kumārī Chowk, the courtyard of the Kumārī's palace. The rest of the group has disappeared into the colorful, bustling crowd. We feel called, pulled into the courtyard as if it were a vortex of powerful energies waiting to spin us into an alternate reality. Space and time shifts as I enter the courtyard of the Kumārī to wait for the rest of the group. Suddenly, I feel like I am in a dream. I remember reading that the Living Goddess will only come to the window if she is asked by a guide. We have come at a perfect time, there is another group waiting to see her too. "No photos! No photos!" I hear their guide saying nervously, and then. . .

The Kumārī comes to the window. Her eyes are huge: the whites are so pure and her dark irises seem like magnetic pools or portals to the Divine. Her face is stern and serious for a little girl. Her darśan is penetrating. . . . Our eyes meet for a split second and I begin to shake, then cry. This is really darśan—to see and be seen by the deity. Waves of gratitude wash over me. Over and over I chant to myself, "I am home." Then, moments later, this time without a guide calling Her to the window and only the three of us in the courtyard, out She comes again! I am looking at Śiva's feet that are on a short pedestal shrine in the ground, when I feel Her stare on the back of my neck. It is hair-raising. I look up and there She is. I notice the elaborate eye make-up and heavy gold jewelry on such a young body, but it does not seem out of place for the power that emanates from Her and makes Her seem larger than life.

Within a blink of an eye, She is gone again. I feel all fear that I had experienced that morning dissipating. I have a sense that I am being prepared. I stand there shaking, my eyes transfixed between the elaborately carved wooden window frame through which She appeared. One of the other pilgrimage participants offers me an oracle of Goddess pendants. I reach in and pull Saraswatī, Saraswatī whose blessing and guidance I had asked for yesterday morning. I am struck by the synchronicities.

Ranju comes with the rest of the group and gives me one of Her knowing smiles. I am speechless. I just received darśan twice from a living Goddess. This is why I am here. This is what I have come for, to experience Her Śakti, to pay homage to Her, to thank Her for making my wish to come and see Her again come true.

Ranju asks one of the Kumārī's attendants for Her to come to the window again. She is having lunch and we must wait. And wait. The tension builds. Other groups come and go, many of the visitors chattering away, and their irreverent entrance feels like an intrusion on the space. Encapsulated in the courtyard of the Kumārī, the Living Goddess, beyond the bounds of time, I turn my gaze to Her window in great anticipation. And then, after what feels like hours, but has only been about 15 minutes, She appears again and I catch Her eye for the third time. This is my second day in Nepal and already I have received darśan from the Pañca Kumārī, and now, the royal Kumārī three times.

Fortunately, the magic and mystery of female power did not end with the Kumārī's darśan that afternoon. As we were waiting for the Kumārī to appear for the third time, we were blessed by yet another living Goddess. In the stillness of our anticipation I hardly noticed the beautiful older woman who passed through the courtyard, greeted Ranju, and then entered the house to pay her respects to the Kumārī.

"Did you see that woman?" Ranju asked us. "She is also a living Goddess. She is Ajimā." Ajimā means grandmother and is one of the most ancient manifestations of Goddess in the Valley. She calls her over and this woman says a chant for us, then gives a pranam or blessing by joining the palms together and taking a slight bow. Ranju tells us that we are very lucky to have seen this Ajimā. Many Nepalese go to her before they undertake a long journey to receive her blessings. She is also known as a great healer.

Living Goddesses are common throughout the Kathmandu Valley. In fact, all women have the potential of awakening the Goddess' energy within. All women are Śakti. A woman's Śakti can be activated by being in the presence of a realized Goddess or at a Goddess shrine where she has come to pray. Goddess shrines all over the subcontinent, particularly those that are associated with some part of the natural landscape have been in continuous worship for hundreds if not thousands of years. Attending these sacred sites can trigger latent Śakti energies within the devotee and open her to healing and psychic powers that she may never have utilized before. Yet, some, like the Kumārī, must go through an intensive initiation process. Powers that are inherent in every woman, that can naturally be invoked and utilized for personal empowerment, have become controlled by orthodox practice. Nevertheless the vibrant reality of female spiritual power that was once available to all women remains evident when looking more closely at the living Kumārī. In this young girl's life and lore the patriarchal dismantling of female power is juxtaposed against the strength of female Śakti power.

Legends of the Kumārī's Origin

The origin of the Kumārī warrants some attention, although viewpoints among scholars differ. Some texts document her initial institution during the Malla period (fifteenth-seventeenth centuries), while others trace Her to the sixth century.[2] Local legend around the Living Goddess provides more insight. "King Trailokymall of Bhaktapur, or so one of the legends claims, used to play games of dice with Durgā. Overwhelmed by her beauty and feminine appeal, he found it increasingly more difficult to concentrate on the game. Perceiving the king's amorous thoughts, the goddess took offense, telling him that never again would he see her in her form as a goddess, but in the body of a virgin girl of the Śākya caste."[3] This legend leaves much to be explained. In this day and age, the body of a young girl does not stop men's sexual objectification of the female sex no matter what age she is. The legend indicates an uncontrollable male desire for the female body that is no longer rooted in respect and even recognition of the sacrality of the female body. In order for patriarchal man to deal with male desire, the female is seen as the problem. To deal with the male ego, female erotic power must be subdued and Goddess is made only accessible through the body of a "pure" virgin girl.

Another version of the story tells of the King playing dice with an extraordinarily beautiful woman. "Even the most casual of observers would notice that she is not only far too beautiful to be an ordinary mortal, but that she had an intense and penetrating third eye in the centre of her forehead."[4] During their nightly games, he asks for Her advice on certain affairs of the state. One night the door suddenly bursts open and a very jealous Queen comes in and accuses him of infidelity. The Goddess stands, waving Her ten arms furiously in all directions. Several other enraged faces emerge from the beautiful face of Goddess, showing Her multi-headed manifestation as the royal Goddess Taleju, a tutelary and wrathful form of Durgā. Taleju is outraged and declares She will no longer assist the King because of such human frailties as his wife's jealousy. He is bereft at the lost of this divine advisor and companion and blames his wife for making Her disappear. For days he performs pūjās until he wins back Taleju's affection. But Taleju will only return to him in the body of a young girl so as to prevent future outbreaks of jealousy.[5] Once again we read how the female is to blame. Although the king is in a monogamous marriage, his wife the Queen should not react to finding her husband playing games with a gorgeous woman in the middle of the night? How disturbingly familiar is this tale? How often has men's infidelity been blamed on women's jealousy and insecurity? We see how the female is either sexually objectified as in the first story, or blamed and accused of being jealous and insecure as in the second. Female qualities of erotic power and beauty are to blame. We learn from both versions of this legend that the full expression of female power must be tamed, toned down, and purified. From now on Taleju, a fierce emanation of Durgā will only appear in the body of a virgin girl, a Kumārī.

Kumārī: The Living Virgin Goddess

The Kumārī or Living Goddess is a virgin form of Durgā. In Nepal, the word *Kumārī* or virgin means prepubescent girl. Therefore, all premenarchal girls are Kumārīs. There is also a special institution of the Kumārī, three of whom preside over the three medieval kingdoms of Bhaktapur, Kathmandu, and Patan. In the case of the Kathmandu Kumārī, a young girl is chosen from the Buddhist Śākya caste, but is worshipped by both Newar Buddhists[6] and Hindus alike. The process to choose the young girl who will become a vehicle for Devī is a demanding one. The selection process is similar to that of finding reincarnated Tibetan lamas. Hundreds of Śākya girls from the Newari caste between the ages of three and five are interviewed and examined for thirty-two auspicious marks on their body. The Śākya caste is one of the highest-ranking Buddhist castes. They are "mostly metal workers and temple custodians, (and they) claim direct descent from the ancient Śākya clan that gave birth to Śākyamuni Buddha over 2,500 years ago."[7] The final candidates who fit the requirements are then placed inside the Taleju temple on the eighth night, Astami, of Dashain—Durgā Pūjā. In a darkened courtyard the children are surrounded by the heads of 108 freshly slaughtered buffaloes while men wearing the masks of the Mother Goddesses, Matṛkās, dance around them trying to frighten them, for hours on end. The candidate who shows no fear, who can identify possessions of the previous Kumārī, and whose astrological natal chart does not conflict with the king's, becomes the next Kumārī.[8] Her status is equal to if not higher than the king. Indeed, this young Goddess holds powers "associated with women's sexuality and women's blood (which) were consistent with, and equivalent to, the divine power in gods, goddesses, forces of nature, animals, warriors and kings."[9] Through such severe tests, the Kumārī has to prove that she indeed embodies the fierce, terrific, fearless qualities of Durgā.

Once in office the Kumārī is worshiped throughout the year at various festivals, but primarily She is visited by women with menstrual disorders and mothers who come to Her with problems around their children's health.[10] For the most part the Kumārī leads a very sheltered life. She is not schooled,[11] does not play with other children, is waited on hand and foot by Her various attendants, and carried from place to place so Her feet do not touch the "polluted" ground. If she loses a tooth, cuts Herself, or starts Her period the Brahmans believe the Goddess will leave Her body and a ritual must be done to de-install the Goddess. It is interesting that a Goddess who demands bloody sacrifice for Her propitiation will leave Her vehicle at the first sign of blood.[12] This is a likely inversion of earlier rites that honored the potency of menstrual blood and centered their practices around its monthly arrival—in particular on a girl's menarche or first menstruation, a highly regarded initiatory rite of passage from girlhood to womanhood.

Sanskritization has transformed the spiritual significance of menstrual blood into something that is considered polluting, whereas in early cultures and in some cultures today, menstrual blood is honored for its power. However, this power does not come without danger. In her essay, "Menstruating Women/Menstruating Goddesses" Dianne Jenett points out the connection between young girls or Kumārīs and menstruation and draws from Savithri de Tourreil's[13] firsthand experience. Jenett writes:

> A female embodied the Goddess—became the Goddess, in a certain sense. Each female had to be prepared, entitled, properly readied, ritually, to receive the onrush of power, to become the vessel who contained the goddess "necessary for the proper unfolding of female auspiciousness, fertility and prosperity."[14]

Interestingly, the Nayars of South India and Newars of the Kathmandu Valley share several common beliefs and practices. Both groups are likely descendents from early tribal cultures and "are unorthodox in their attitudes towards sex and marriage; and they accord a high status to women."[15] Considering that the Kumārī in the Kathmandu Valley must come from the Newar population, but nevertheless participates within the brahmanic fold of religious practices, it seems evident that the fear around the Kumārī losing blood, especially menstrual blood, is a sanskritic overlay onto earlier menstrual seclusion rites. Again citing de Tourreil, Jenett writes:

> de Tourreil argues that proscriptions against menstruating females exist not because they are "polluting," but because they are "too pure" and thus dangerous. "The whole thrust and texture of menarchal ritual demonstrate unambiguously that the notorious menstrual taboos make sense only as a mechanism for the protection of both the sacred female and the non-sacred categories of persons."[16]

Let us examine concepts of purity/pollution, and auspiciousness/inauspiciousness within the sanskritized practices. Women are deemed less pure than men due to their involvement in natural life processes of menstruation, childbirth, and lactation. The Kumārī is chosen from the Śākya caste because it is believed to be a "pure" rank of people due to their "minimal involvement in life processes, especially those of a disintegrative or decomposing kind, but also including the positive forces of growth, expansion, accumulation,"[17] For a Śākya and Brahmin alike, dealing with menstrual blood, urine, feces, and dead bodies is relegated to the untouchable castes. These "higher" castes, hierarchical and patriarchal at their core, believe that women and sexuality inhibit the male sex from achieving salvation—a sphere that is transcendent, beyond this material existence. Practices include celibacy, and an overall renunciation of participation in any "impure" rituals around birth and death. Ironically, these processes, so inherent to our existence are totally feared and controlled through restrictive practices and ultimate avoidance. In this respect, the higher castes can only worship the virgin form of Goddess in the body of a young girl, but once she begins menstruating, her "dangerous power" threatens them with loss of control. Furthermore, "male members of a caste are in large measure dependent for their status rating on the purity of their women—primarily on that of their daughters and sisters whom they give in marriage, and secondarily on that of the women they take in as wives,"[18] Thus, marriage serves as a way of keeping women in line.

It is interesting to note the tension that plays out in the institution of the Kumārī and speaks to the confrontation of two distinct worldviews within the brahmanic orthodox tradition. On the one hand, there is an emphasis on renouncing life and an overvaluing of marriage, celibacy and monasticism. On the other, life-affirming practices that center on the "positive erotic, reproductive and ritual values of sexuality" are feared and must be denied or controlled.[19] Marguerite Rigoglioso's groundbreaking research on parthenogenesis and the cult of divine birth in ancient Greece emphasizes the role of the virgin in ritual practices.[20] She conjectures that through specific practices, these young women in the ancient world were able to conceive a child without sperm. She turns to the myths as historical reference and describes practices of pubescent girls who immaculately conceived in ritual and then gave birth to a deity or heroine. Her fascinating book outlines various categories of priestesses who engaged in these practices. She shows how the shift into patriarchy did not stop these practices. Instead they were utilized to perpetuate the patriarchal agenda of dominance and control by conceiving male leaders, specifically male gods. Rigoglioso posits that equating virginity with purity is a patriarchal concept. In fact, virginity (here defined as girls not having engaged in intercourse with a man), was crucial to these highly esoteric and powerful practices. Rigoglioso describes priestesshoods, collectives of women who came together to perform such practices. Her research is not based on new age notions of sex but is grounded in sound research from primary and secondary sources. Furthermore, her theories do not seem outlandish if we consider how divine birth is at the base of Western religion and civilization.[21] The Kumārī seems to have retained many of the priestess powers Rigoglioso describes, except that when she reaches puberty, she is thrown out of the temple. The patriarchal and brahmanic concepts of purity and impurity play out in the status of the Kumārī, as do the three philosophical gunas or qualities of existence that were previously discussed: sattva, purity/white; rajas, passion/red; tamas, inertia/black. Despite the overemphasis on the dire necessity of the Kumārī's purified status, she most strongly embodies and represents the rajastic qualities that are indicative of early female-centered and agriculturally based rituals. In fact, this energy described as rajas is what patriarchal culture most fears because it carries sexual and creative power and is the natural birthright of all women.

Rajas is red. In Hindu tradition, married women who are in their childbearing years often wear red clothes as well as a red stripe in the part of their hair and on their foreheads to signify the potency of their fertility. Synchronously, during Navarātri or Durgā Pūjā, the second set of days are devoted to Lakṣmī, Goddess of fertility, prosperity, and abundance—all rajastic qualities. Although the Kumārīs are virgins, instead of the sattvic white color that would be expected in their appearance, the girls are dressed in rich reds. Their foreheads are fully painted red with the third eye, a symbol of their divine status placed between their eyebrows. The placement of the third eye is directly over the hypothalamus and pituitary gland, which is known in both Chinese and Ayurvedic medicine to regulate the menstrual cycle. Meditative practices from Tantric and Chinese traditions that concentrate attention on the hypothalamus can induce or inhibit the menstrual flow. Furthermore, the Kumārī is not propitiated to aid Her devotees within sattvic spheres of existence, but for rajastic qualities: She rules over menstruation and childbirth, aspects integral to worldly existence—and to female experience.

Men come to Her specifically to aid them in issues of gaining, maintaining, or forestalling the loss of power.[22] In this respect, the Kumārī has even more power than the king, and is propitiated to keep him in office. Allen notes:

> in the case of the royal Kumārī, her chief worshiper is the king of Nepal. He comes to her residence once a year at the climax of a popular festival during which she is dragged around the city in a huge chariot for public worship. After bowing down and kissing the girl's feet he then accepts her blessing (prasād) in the form of a tikā.[23]

The tikā is the red mark placed between the eyes of women and men. Nowadays, the tikā is given by priests after a pūjā is performed. It is a potent blessing from Goddess. I contend the red tikā, which is made out of red vermilion powder, rice and curd, is symbolic of menstrual blood (rajas par excellence!), especially when we consider its placement over the menstrual regulating pituitary gland.

Another interesting symbol associated with menstruation and the Kumārī is a special nāga (serpent) necklace that she wears for the most important rituals. The serpent has long been associated with female power, specifically menstrual power as the shedding of snake skin is comparable to the monthly release of our uterine lining while we are in our menstruating years. One former Kumārī notes a distinct difference in the power she felt when she put on this special ritual necklace: "I am not sure at what age I first began to notice feeling different whenever the nāga necklace was put on, but wearing it I suddenly felt myself to be in some way apart from and superior to the people around me, and I never felt like talking to anyone."[24] The powers of this necklace induced a trancelike state and seemed to deepen the feeling of possession within.

It is interesting to consider the altered state experiences that some women experience when menstruating.

When the Kumārī menstruates, the orthodox tradition states that the power of Goddess leaves her. I disagree. When the Kumārī menstruates she comes fully into her power without the need of male institutionalized rituals to "install" the Goddess. In a matriarchal system, her bleeding would signify her readiness to participate in erotic rites, and perhaps practice parthenogenetic birth as Rigoglioso has posited in her work. In South Asia, once she bleeds, the Kumārī like other menstruating women becomes uncontainable, untamable, and uncontrollable. Like Saraswatī, the self-empowered young Goddess becomes marginalized, peripheralized, yet still held in awe and fear. Her powers of fertility, sexuality and destruction threaten to upset the male-dominated status quo, and therefore the Kumārī and Saraswatī are relegated to a specific sphere outside the ordered sanskritized world. As "Virgin" Goddesses, they are an undeniable force of nature, of our worldly existence and as such are propitiated. They are included in the festival, in part, to keep potentially explosive, rajasic qualities under lock and key. Menstrual blood and its association with Goddess is deemed impure and dangerous to those in the orthodox world. As Jenett points out:

> "Danger" is unpredictability, the direct engagement with the power of the deity through the body of women and the unknowable nature of what will be required/acquired as a result. There is risk and high reward in the ancient method of engaging the life force on behalf of the community. We can also see that in the matrilinieal context the "dangerous" power of women is not contained by faithfulness to a husband and is not based on their literal virginity but rather on their autonomy, their freedom from subordination to a single man and their own internal preparation and self-discipline.[25]

In patriarchal culture the virgin is the unmarked, not-yet-possessed female. She is an object of male desire and greed. Irigaray notes how the virgin "is not yet made woman by and for them (men). Not yet imprinted with their sex, their language. Not yet penetrated, possessed by them."[26] Irigaray asserts, "Patriarchy is founded upon the theft and violations of the daughter's virginity and the use of her virginity for commerce between men, including religious commerce."[27] Not only is virginity a prized possession of patriarchal men, but ancient law dating back to the second century CE ensures a young girl's virginity by imposing child marriage. According to the restrictive Laws of Manu, girls had to be married off before their menarche. A prepubescent girl who was not married before her menarche "is thought to endanger the purity of all (the household's) residents, especially males. Hence, the prepubescent marriage of girls must be understood as an institutionalized response to the dangers believed to be associated with female reproductive sexuality outside of the confines of marriage."[28]

As we shall see in the chapter on Day Nine, the worship of groups of girls as Kumārīs regardless of caste, class or ethnic origin is a common ritual in the Kathmandu Valley. However, not all girls were subjected to child marriage. In part, as a likely response against the orthodox Hindu practice of child marriage, young Newar Buddhist girls undergo a special marriage ceremony, called *ihi*, before their first menarche where they are married to the fruit of the wood-apple tree.[29] The tree represents a god, either Viṣṇu or Nārāyaṇa or Kumāra, the son of Śiva. Virgin girls are protected by the energies of the tree, and even in the case of their later human husband's death they do not have the ill-fated status of widowhood, which used to imply either a death sentence or ostracization. Women married to this special tree retained their married status even after their husband's death and did not have to perform the inhumane (and now illegal) orthodox Hindu practice of self-immolation on his funerary pyre. Furthermore, these women's relationship with the tree gives them the authority to divorce.[30] The alignment of girls with a tree that is considered an incarnation of a god is very significant. While virginity is something that is fiercely protected in orthodox society, widowhood is a status that is ostracized and demonized as inauspicious in orthodox culture. As long as the Newari girl is married, her virginal status is, in a sense, protected. The potential for the chaotic forces that are unleashed with menarche is tamed and controlled. The powerful and protective relationship between girls and trees is intriguing, especially because trees tend to fall into the classification of elemental deities and nature spirits who are unpredictable and chaotic. These are likely matrifocal remnants, even alternative solutions to the enforcement of marriage imposed by the dominant orthodox culture. Instead of these Newari Kumārīs being the possession of their fathers or husbands, through their marriage to Nature, they are protected throughout their lifetime and remain virgins in the original sense of the word: *whole unto herself.*

The Contemporary Kumārī

Today, being a Kumārī does seem to serve some of the women who have held this position in positive, even empowering ways. Rashmila Shakya, the royal Kumārī in Kathmandu from 1984 to 1991, reflects on her time as Kumārī in the book, *From Goddess to Mortal.* Shakya notes that she rarely if ever cried while the power was within her. She never doubted her power to heal or her ability to help political leaders make decisions that on a human level she could not even comprehend.[31] Moreover, she states, "I had a self-confidence almost unheard of in a child my age and never had any worries or fears the entire time I lived in Kumārī che. They would come later."[32] Shakya is able to recognize how as Kumārī, she was over-pampered and got very used to bossing others around.[33] However, even as indulged as she was, she did find ways to exert her independence within the palace temple.[34] Shakya describes how she was not properly prepared for the transition back into her birth family's home when Goddess left her. Despite the difficulties of adjusting to a more mundane existence, she does not have any regrets of being a Kumārī. For Shakya, the only thing she would change is that education is provided for the girls while in office.[35] When she returned to her parent's home, she was illiterate; making her acculturation and acclimatization even more difficult. But aside from having lacked education, the rest of her experience was empowering.

Today the institution of the Kumārī is being challenged and questioned by human rights groups in Nepal and abroad. Despite legitimate concerns around education and socialization, there are aspects of this maiden ritual that have a powerful effect on a girl's self-esteem, sense of self-worth and self-image. I cannot help but wonder what a culture would be like that would continuously honor not one but all girls (and boys) as Divine.

Notes

1. The Pañca Kumārī are five young girls chosen by the King to represent the country. They are most likely associated with the five elements. Other esoteric Tantric practices make up their worship. They appear whenever dignitaries and court officials arrive in public places.

2. Michael Allen, *The Cult of the Kumari: Virgin Worship in Nepal* (Kathmandu: Mandala Book Point, 1996), 14.

3. Ibid., 79.

4. Rashmila Shakya, trans. Scott Berry, *From Goddess to Mortal: The True Life Story of a Former Royal Kumari* (Kathmandu, Nepal: Vajra Publications, 2005), 7.

5. Ibid., 7-9.

6. Newar culture is very ancient and "its earliest immigrants into the valley were predominantly tribal in social structure and shamanistic in religion"(Allen, The Cult of the Kumari, 5). The Newar population is essentially an urban people whose economy is largely based on rice cultivation (Ibid., 5). The Newar and Hindu Brahmanic priesthood have lived in the Kathmandu Valley for over 2000 years and seem to have assimilated both Hindu and Buddhist practices into their religious beliefs and practices. Newar Buddhism shares similarities with Vajrayana Buddhism but is distinguished by "the total replacement of the usual Buddhist monastic and celibate religious virtuosi with a hereditary married priesthood"(Ibid., 6). Although the Newar use Buddhist texts, symbols and worship Buddhist deities, they also participate in the yearly Durgā Festival and worship Durgā, Taleju and other fierce emanations of Hindu deities—especially in the body of a young girl from one of the highest Newar castes, the Śākya. The Newar and brahmanic priesthoods both perform rituals and follow practices concerned with purity and pollution. Like the brahmins, the Newar also employ a complex caste structure. However, Newar women have more freedom and agency than Hindu women. Other

matrifocal and matrilineal elements of this ethnic group are evident and connect them to the matriarchal Nayar of South India. See Goettner-Abendroth, *Das Matriarchat II, 2: Stammesgesellschaften in Amerika, Indien, Afrika* (Stuttgart: Kohlhammer, 2000).

7. Allen, *The Cult of the Kumari*, 7.
8. Anthroplogist Michael Allen, who wrote the classic work on the Kumārī, describes these gruesome, fear-inspiring elements of the selection process. However, in recent years, locking the young girls in a room with slaughtered buffalo heads apparently does not always occur. Rashmila Shakya says that this was not her own experience when she served as the Kumārī, in Kathmandu from 1984-1991. Shakya and Berry, *From Goddess to Mortal* (Kathmandu: Vajra, 2005), 142.
9. Dianne E. Jenett, "Menstruating Women/Menstruating Goddesses: Sites of Sacred Power in South India," in *Menstruation: A Cultural History*, ed. Andrew Shail and Gillian Howie (New York: Palgrave MacMillan, 2005), 177.
10. Ibid., 11.
11. Apparently, education for the Kumārī, while in office, is becoming more available. See Rashmila Shakya and Scott Berry's *From Goddess to Mortal*, 2005.
12. Ibid., 26.
13. A scholar from the matrilineal Nayar community in southern India.
14. Dianne E. Jenett, "Menstruating Women/Menstruating Goddesses: Sites of Sacred Power in South India," in *Menstruation: A Cultural History*, eds. Andrew Shail and Gillian Howie (New York: Palgrave MacMillan, 2005), 182, quoting Savithri de Tourreil, "Nayars in a South Indian Matrix: A Study based on Female-centered Ritual," PhD diss. (Concordia University, 1996), 15.
15. Allen, *The Cult of the Kumari*,123.
16. Dianne E. Jenett, "Menstruating Women/Menstruating Goddesses," 182, quoting Savithri deTourreil, "Nayars in a South Indian Matrix," 23.
17. Allen, *The Cult of the Kumari*, 7.
18. Ibid., 8.
19. Ibid., 9.
20. Marguerite Rigoglioso, *The Cult of Divine Birth in Ancient Greece* (New York: Palgrave MacMillan, 2009).
21. See Rigoglioso regarding immaculate conception in Christianity (Ann giving birth to Mary, Mary to Jesus, Elizabeth to John the Baptist) and in Judaism (Sarah giving birth to Isaac).
22. Allen, *The Cult of the Kumari*, 11.
23. Ibid.
24. Shakya, Rashmila and Scott Berry. *From Goddess to Mortal*, 37-38.

25. Jenett, "Menstruating Women/Menstruating Goddesses," 185-186. Italics mine.
26. Luce Irigaray, *This Sex Which Is Not One*, trans., Catherine Porter (Ithaca, New York: Cornell University, 1985), 211.
27. Luce Irigaray, "The Forgotten Mystery of Female Ancestry," in *French Feminists on Religion: A Reader*, eds. Morna Joy, Kathleen O'Grady and Judith Poxon (London and New York: Routledge, 2002), 75.
28. Ibid., 101.
29. Allen, *The Cult of the Kumari*, 100-113.
30. Ibid., 111.
31. Shakya, Rashmila, and Scott Berry. *From Goddess to Mortal*, 21.
32. Shakya, Rashmila, and Scott Berry. *From Goddess to Mortal*, 63-64.
33. Ibid., 145.
34. Ibid., 64.
35. Ibid., 144.

day three
mai, ajima: ancient mother, ancient grandmother

On the third day of the festival in 2006 I find myself at the Māīthan Temple in Kathmandu. Inside the small square temple with an ornately carved and gilded pagoda style roof is a circle of stones that represent various Mother Goddesses. A line of devotees pours from the entrance and winds its way around the building. It is drizzling and the air is ripe with the smells of rain mixed with incense and the smog from the busy streets surrounding the site. A large tree smeared with red and yellow is a central shrine in the small cobblestone courtyard. Devotees gather round leaving offerings of incense, apples, oranges and red flowers. I wait in line with other devotees and then approach the central altar that houses a half circle of stones. Each stone contains the spirit of a different Mother Goddess. It does not matter if we call Her Durgā or Saraswatī, this temple is the place of the Mother, and it is the Mother Spirit that I revere. Since I intend to visit a Living Goddess in the afternoon, paying homage to one of the most ancient Mother forms at this temple before I go to see the Kusali Devī feels appropriate. In the Valley, the main deities who spiritually "possess" a woman are the fierce, indigenous Goddesses: Ajimā, Māī, Mātṛkās, and Bhagawatī.

Hours and many Goddess temples later I find my way through the laundry district to the home of "Kusali Devī." This woman is known to possess the Mother (Māī,) and Grandmother (Ajimā) spirit. She is a shaman and performs Tantric rituals to the deities including embodying 108 different forms of the Mother on one of the nights of the Durgā Festival. China Galland first introduced Kusali Devī to westerners in her wonderful book, The Bonds Between Women. *Although this woman is a Living Goddess, she leads a simple life. She lives on the third and fourth floors of an apartment building and many of the rooms are connected by an open hall. Females that seem to span at least four generations wander in and out of the apartment's rooms carrying babies and toddlers, books, pūjā items, and household wares. The rituals take place in her home. Pilgrims come from all around the Valley to ask for healing, protection and blessings. Devotees are ushered into a living/shrine room and motioned to wait. Along the longest wall in the room are two large altars with statues and pictures of various deities. Between these altars is the Goddess' Nāga (serpent) throne—a very regal chair with Śakti red cushions and the heads of about ten serpents rising up behind it. When it is time to begin, this living Goddess takes Her seat on the throne, rings a bell, then begins to chant invocations to Ganeśa and various Mother Goddesses. She performs a pūjā and gives attendance to all who come seeking blessings—whether it be a healing or darśan.*

In 2006 when I call her by the name Kusali Devī, one of her granddaughters tells me that this is not her grandmother's real name. Kusali refers to the place that she lives in—the laundry district. Her real name is Ratna Māyā Devī Mātā. And still the fact that Ratna Māyā Devī Mātā also is known by her relationship to a specific place, just as so many other Goddesses in South Asia are, shows how this ancient understanding of Goddess being deeply connected to the land and her surroundings has carried into contemporary consciousness.

I first met Ratna Māyā Devī Mātā on my pilgrimage in 2000 when she did a special blessing ritual for everyone in the group. Later I returned by myself and she performed a fire pūjā for me. The endometriosis had come back, and I was in quite a lot of pain. At the end of the ritual Devī had me lie down in front of her grand multi-headed Nāga throne while she chanted and rubbed sacred ash into my belly. While antibiotics and other Western treatments had been unsuccessful in treating my condition, with this shamanic healing, the severe pain and infection cleared up within days. She told me the same thing that other healers had told me. "You do not know your own power, you do not accept your power as a woman and as a teacher and healer, and you invite this pain back." This has always been a very difficult lesson for me. On an intellectual level I understand what she is saying, I have examined my fears, my anger, my suffering. I know my yoni is crying out for me to remember who I am—that I come from a kula, a spiritual lineage of powerful and divine women and that I must learn to be fully embodied, fully conscious in my female body without fear. And yet on a cellular level the memories of severe abuse in this lifetime—as well as in all likelihood countless others—return as the asuras or demons that I, like Durgā, must slay. In my agony, I have cried for Mā thousands of times. I have needed the fierce protection and guidance of the Mother, protection and guidance my biological mother was not able to give me. Here in the Valley, home to hundreds if not thousands of Goddesses and Gods, I find myself being taken care of by a Living Goddess. Under Ratna Māyā Devī's shamanic care, I feel I have come home. I have a deep understanding that every single being on this planet has one Mother. I call Her Durgā , Saraswatī, Ratna Māyā Devī, and countless other names. To others She is Inanna, Pele, Mary, Aphrodite, Demeter, Sekhmet, Yemoja, Gaia, Isis, Nut, Mami Wata, Changing Woman, names as numerous as there are women in this world. Goddess is every shape, form, preference and color. She is Mother, Sister, Grandmother, Daughter,

Lover, Mittini (soul sister, friend). She does not discriminate: She loves all her children equally. She will always protect us. And when we turn to Her we will realize She has always been there.

Durgā Pūjā and Matriarchy

Durgā Pūjā is at its roots a matriarchal celebration. The root of the word *matriarchy* means "beginning with the mother" and refers to a social, cultural, political and religious system that is structured on and around the female.[1] Within a matriarchal system, women hold positions of power and are accorded not only societal status, but also agency. Women have social, political, and religious or spiritual authority. Despite the positions of power available to women, matriarchy promotes gender equality, rather than female rule. As far as we can determine from archaeological records of these ancient civilizations, matriarchal societies are typically peaceful and just. Contrary to patriarchal culture, matriarchal culture is not hierarchical and domination does not exist. Instead, there is a focus on balance and equality between genders, generations, nature and humans. Difference is not viewed as threatening but as a complementary energy where tension between polarities, for example, is understood to actually create and perpetuate life. Matriarchal cultures tend to embrace a *both/and* rather than *either/or* paradigm. Nothing is exclusively good or bad, right or wrong. Matriarchal values allow for fluidity and the recognition that life brings both painful and joyful experiences. Males and females are not pitted against each other, but are respected for their inherent differences which can serve and enhance the societal structure as a whole.[2]

In contrast to matriarchy, *patriarchy* means "*rule* of the father."[3] "Patriarchy has been defined as the social arrangement in which men possess structural power by monopolizing high status positions in important social, economic, legal and religious institutions."[4] Patriarchy is a system of male domination centered on war, violence and capitalism that pervades every level of society. Within the capitalist market commodities are given a value and are exchanged. Within this system, women and their children are, according to European philosopher Luce Irigaray, *sacrificed*.[5] Much of women's work goes unpaid and women are essentially "forced" to raise a child who could be called to war. Irigaray describes how life is not valued under patriarchy except in the way it can be used and exploited to uphold the dominant paradigm. Therefore, any child born under patriarchy could ultimately be "captured" within the patriarchal system and (unconsciously) forced to perpetuate the patriarchal agenda on numerous levels.[6] Capitalist patriarchal beliefs and practices pose a threat to life. They are based on destructive, ego-centered and competitive values. On the contrary, matriarchal tenets are at their core life affirming and celebrate the abundance that Earth provides; while patriarchy thrives on a fear-based and scarcity model of consciousness.

Heide Goettner Abendroth, the founder and director of *Hagia: Center for Matriarchal Studies* in Germany, posits that matriarchy was humanity's original social structure and that it has persisted into contemporary time in various pockets around the world, albeit in many cases today with patriarchal, patrilineal and patrilocal overlays. However, we can learn to recognize remnants of matriarchal cultures in present day and past societies through examining a culture's rituals and practices, familial structures and relations, building structures, and also by examining whether or not a particular culture was/is an agriculturally-based society. Vicki Noble has also done research on female-centered and matriarchal cultures around the globe for decades. She explains the difference between patriarchal and matriarchal families:

> In ancient times, during the Neolithic (agricultural) period of human cultural development. . . families were different then, not "nuclear" with a husband, wife, and kids living in a little house together, isolated from the rest of the community. Families were extended and matriarchal, made up of mothers, daughters, granddaughters, and their blood kin. People had sex, obviously, but biological fatherhood (although fully understood) was not important. It was brothers who participated in raising their sisters' children, and all children belonged equally to the family—none could be "illegitimate." There would also have been no domestic violence.[7]

Matriarchy is a complex and diverse system that has several different components. Some cultures can carry certain matriarchal elements, yet still operate under patriarchal codes and rules. While others may be predominately patriarchal with only hints of what was long ago a female-centered society. No matter how much or how little matriarchal evidence remains, I would argue that an ancient society that revered and understood earth and the cosmos as Mother and/or Goddess lies at the root of every culture around the globe. Could it be that the earliest origins of culture are *matriarchal* at their core? Cultures with matriarchal values and elements have always existed—in fact they predate patriarchy by about 25 to 30,000 years. They offer an alternative social paradigm that may help to bring peace to the planet.

The power of the female lineage is a central aspect of worship within the Śākta Tantra tradition. The Durgā Pūjā is at its core a reunion of women. Daughters who have been married off to distant villagers return home once a year and are reunited with their mothers, grandmothers, aunts, sisters, and female cousins for the ten days of the festival. Rituals centered on food, flowers, song, dance, and young girls are central to every day of the festival. And all Śākta sites carry Māī (Mother Spirit). The inexorable presence of the Divine Female in the sacred geography, village, and city life shows how the Durgā Pūjā is a wonderful social and cultural example of veneration for the powers of ancient earth and cosmic Goddesses over millennia.

Infinite Names of the Goddess

Durgā's diverse origins are reflected in Her multitude of pacifying and terrifying manifestations and names. In her peaceful aspect She is known as Pārvatī, Umā, Gaurī, Bhavānī, Lakṣmī, Saraswatī, Kumārī, or simply, Devī (Goddess). In Her fierce or "terrible" aspect she is venerated as Kālī, Bhagawatī, Cāmundā, Taleju, the Māīs and Ajimās, Dākinīs, Matṛkās, and Yoginīs.[8] During the pilgrimage I encountered several Living Goddesses who played a significant role in the festival. They all are identified as Ajimā or Grandmother Goddess as well as other manifestations of Durgā suggesting that historically Durgā's motherline can be traced back to indigenous mother and grandmother divinities known as the Māīs and Ajimās. The various epithets of this Goddess reflect the localization of deities whose names changed over time to become the Goddess more popularly known as Durgā.

Since my first formal introduction to Durgā occurred in the Kathmandu Valley of Nepal, I have looked to the history of the Valley to trace the origins of this all-powerful Goddess. However, over the years I have experienced Durgā in Her various forms throughout South and Southeast Asia, Europe, and California. What has interested me about the Valley is that the Himālayas have protected the inhabitants from outside influence for millennia—and until about forty years ago Nepal had very little exposure to the West. It seems that the natural environment has allowed for ancient traditions to be preserved. A persistence of devotion for Goddesses that embody both the fierce and serene aspects of existence has survived millennia Therefore, it is important to look at the enduring presence of the Māī and Ajimā (mother and grandmother) spirit in the land, living women, and in the deities that are worshiped in the thousands of shrines and temples throughout Nepal. The prominence of the Māīs and Ajimās at the core of both the Hindu and Buddhist traditions, suggests a matrilineal social structure from earliest times.

As we have seen, the word *kula* also refers to matrilineality in that it denotes a female clan. It also points to the power of female fluids (menstrual and birthing blood as well as sexual fluids). Thankfully, respect for this aspect of the feminine, which has ties in ancestor worship, has survived in such a basic form. No fancy epithet is needed. We all come from the female body of a Mother, who has come from a mother, our grandmother, and by recognizing this ancient female spirit to which we are ALL connected, we are reminded of our own matrilineal roots.

Animism and the Ancient Mother

Animists believe that all things have spirit: trees, animals, rocks, the mountains, rivers, and every aspect of the land. Animism has been an important aspect of the socioreligious life in the Valley since remotest time. Amita Ray explains the importance of the animist spirit in *Art of Nepal*: "This live spirit is indeed the fertile force which makes the land yield corn, roots and flowers, the herds to multiply and women to bring forth offspring. The Nepalese know this force as 'Māī or 'Ajimā.'"[9] Māī and Ajimā are two of the oldest names for the goddess in Nepal, meaning mother and grandmother respectively.[10] There are many places in Nepal, which are called *māīthan* or the place of the mother, thus affirming the ancients' relationship with the Earth as Mother. The aboriginals used the art of magic and spells to seek Her aid in avoiding and curing disease, inducing human or vegetative fertility, and invoking Her protection against enemies, destructive natural elements, death, and malevolent spirits. Such religious practices symbolized their participation in the mythic drama of the agricultural season. The essence and development of Hinduism, Śaktism, and Tantrism can be found in animism, ancestor and Mother worship. Today the practice of reciting mantras (chants) can be understood as a kind of spell. Through the recitation of words of power, we focus our intention on manifesting certain qualities or desires. Mudrās (hand gestures) are also used to invoke a desired result. Today, these ancient practices have become more stylized in some circles, however, no matter how elitist and theoretical, we can always trace their origin back to the land—and back to the spirit of the Mother.

According to Mary Slusser's study of the Kathmandu Valley's diverse languages and ethnic inhabitants, specific vocabulary has survived from the ancient, presumably earth-based cultures:

> Although written in Sanskrit, they rely on a heavy non-Sanskrit vocabulary for many administrative terms, personal names, and more than eighty percent of the place names. The latter include hamlets, towns, rivers, ponds, and other physiographical features. These names have often survived to present times with little change, frequently as alternate names employed exclusively by Newari speakers.[11]

People who live in such close contact with the earth, as the aboriginal Valley people did, would have naturally come up with language that expressed their surroundings. Indigenous names associated with the local geography indicate the longevity of the aboriginal's connection to these places. It is not uncommon to hear the Nepalese describe the landscape of the Valley by the names of Goddesses. "To the Nepalese each Himālayan peak is a Goddess who protects the people and surrounding lands."[12]

The Ancient Mother in Village and Ritual Life

Who were the ancient dwellers of this land, whose history was not recorded in literary form? It is likely that Durgā, in Her collective form as the Mātṛkās, evolved from aboriginal earth-centered cultures of the prehistoric world. She remains a powerful model of female authority. Looking at contemporary village and ritual life provides possible clues about ancestral beliefs and practices. One can substitute *South Asian* for *Indian* in the following statement:

> To trace the survival of the life patterns of another age, and to witness their transformation and operation within village societies today, is to grasp the true significance of the [Indian] scene. There is perhaps no other country where those prehistoric elements are so clearly discernible or so important, and nowhere is this as apparent as in the art and ritual of village and tribe.[13]

The lives of contemporary villagers most likely mirror the beliefs of their ancestors. In her book, *The Earth Mother,* Pupul Jayakar writes:

Rural arts include the arts of these people whose religion gives every instant of their life a sense of mysterious sacredness; people potent with magic, with knowledge of incantation and ritual, with an intense awareness born of (human's) concern to combat and propitiate the unseen, the terrible; people with power over and intimate kinship with animals, with trees, with stones, and with water; people with a central concern for fertility, with their ears close to the earth who whispers to them her secrets.[14] Based on this observation, the lives of people in antiquity can be seen as attuned to cyclical rhythms of the earth and the cosmos. Life was centered around their dependence on the earth for sustenance. All was imbued with the Sacred and the belief that the earth is a Great Mother. Goddess has been worshipped in aniconic form at crossroads, rivers, the sea, and mountains for centuries. These ancient people's deep reverence for the earth is evident in the folk tales and epics describing pīthas, holy places of Goddess such as forests, mountains, rivers, crossroads, the sea[15] that are still relevant today. Jayakar suggests "The sacredness of sites survives the changing of the gods. A primordial sense of the sanctity of place, of the sthalā, and an ancient knowing of the living, pervading essence of the Divinity of the Earth Mother, establishes her worship at crossroads and in aniconic stones."[16]

Donna Jordan, an independent scholar who wrote a brilliant dissertation on the fierce Śakti of South Asia, asserts that their extreme antiquity is proven by the fact that they originally had neither images in iconic form nor a male consort, rather, many are "still represented by numerous shapeless little stones daubed with minium (red lead powder), or by red marks on the sides of a tank, or on a rock, or on a tree by the water."[17] The Goddess' various manifestations in aniconic form represent variations of the local Goddesses. These aniconic forms symbolize the Divine that is imbued in the landscape—the Motherland and the body of Goddess. As is found in tribal villages today, Goddesses have various spheres of responsibility and fall into categories according to their functions and modes of production. In his book,

The Indian Mother Goddess, N. N. Bhattacharya groups them as Mothers of Earth and Corn; Children; Cities; Animals; Disease; War; Mountains, Lakes and Rivers; and the tribal Bloodthirsty *Ugra* (Fierce) Goddess.[18] Donna Jordan adds two more genres of Goddesses, one of which is the Mātṛkās. She writes:

> The genre of the Mātṛkās subsumes not only one of Kosambi's important Goddess Genres, the Goddesses of the Crossroads, but also the Śmāsanā (cremation-ground) Goddesses as well as the Goddess of Mountains, Lakes, and Rivers. Although all Indian goddesses may be called Mātṛkās, the term is used in this section to distinguish those virgin mothers whose fierce, victorious nature was required by Aryan gods to slay demons. In this context, the massive earth Mātṛkās share form and function with war and bloodthirsty goddesses.[19]

In Her wrathful warrior manifestation, Goddess protects from that which threatens to destroy the equilibrium of Her earthly domain. As we have seen, Goddess is deeply embedded in the land. Aniconic representations of the Earth Mother exist all over the Valley and are often propitiated and worshipped with offerings of rice, flowers, red vermillion paste, and/or blood. The sight and experience of the sacred places of Goddess remind us that the earth is indeed Her body and demands respect.

Shift into the Sanskritic and Brahmanic Order in the Valley

By the fifth century C.E., the early indigenous people of the Kathmandu Valley (the Kirāta) had become absorbed by the new ruling dynasty known as the Licchavi. The Licchavi are responsible for sanskritizing religion in the Valley and blending rituals and beliefs of the ancient religion with Hinduism.[20] The Licchavi greatly influenced the epics, and the story of Durgā's triumphant battle in the *Devī Māhātmya* scripture can be traced to this era. According to one scholar, the people became "strongly united" and lived in relative peace under the Licchavi dynasty.[21] Although Amatya Saphalya suggests these diverse ethnic groups of people lived in peace, it is evident that he is reporting the history of the ruling brahmanic class. Without written records or iconography from the aboriginal people during this period, we can only speculate on what occurred. In fact, some argue that the myth of Durgā's battle is based on historic confrontations between aboriginal and nomadic peoples.

The transition from food-gathering to food-production is crucial in understanding how the introduction of a new ethnic group, the Indo-Aryans, affected the Valley; however, it is a complex issue. Bhattacharya writes: "Archaeological explorations and excavations have revealed that in India the transition from food-gathering to food-production and that from rural settlements to urbanization did not follow a uniform and orderly sequence of events."[22]

Were the indigenous Valley people still hunting and gathering their food supply, or were they already part of agricultural communities? Pupul Jayakar and Donna Jordan suggest that the indigenous communities of the Indian subcontinent were already agriculturally-based when the Aryans arrived. In the assimilation that occurred with the shift in the mode of production between the pastoral Aryans and the agricultural aboriginals, the Aryans co-opted the local inhabitants' beliefs in order to subordinate and brahmanize them.[23] Jayakar explains: "Cataclysmic changes were inevitable when the cattle-rearing Aryans met and fused with the autochthonous agricultural communities. Myth and epic legend reveal subtleties and nuances with which the ancient races absorbed and negated the power with the invader."[24]

When the Aryans came into the Valley they didn't completely destroy the diverse indigenous cultures that had inhabited the land for hundreds of years. The Indo-Aryan infiltration presumably pushed some of the indigenous people into the dense Himālayan rainforests, while others stayed and their beliefs were assimilated with those of the Indo-Aryans. The pastoral Aryans influenced the indigenous lifestyle and tried to usurp the supreme power of the Earth Mother by replacing Her with their own male gods of sky, earth, wind, water, sex, sun, and fire. Nevertheless, in order to suit the masses, the native earth deities, spirits, and demons were permitted to coexist with these Vedic gods through the agricultural rites and ceremonies of the indigenous people who remained in the Valley.

The survival of indigenous beliefs that are evident on a substratum level in myth and ritual today also much depended on the great retreats and migrations into the mountain forests and the hinterlands, which helped them to maintain the roots of their rituals and beliefs.[25] The mountainous terrain of Mother Earth became the indigenous people's protection and many ethnic groups continued to thrive untouched. Perhaps the Goddess names of the Himālayas can be traced back to the period before the Indo-Aryan influence. Even the Mātṛkās, descendents of the early earth Goddesses and collective manifestation of Durgā, still assume an important tutelary role all over the Valley today.

The influences of multiple worldviews that transformed the local pantheons over time is evident in the puranic scripture of the Devī Māhātmya, the text on which Durgā Pūjā is based. The Aryans used the Purāṇas to spread their views and beliefs. Myths of collective Goddesses such as the Mahāvidyās, the Sapta (seven) and Aṣṭa (eight) Mātṛkās, and Navadurgās (nine Durgās) reflects a syncretism of the various indigenous Goddesses with brahmanic Goddesses that occurred.[26]

The Spirit of the Mother and Grandmother

When I think of Nepal I remember the women who carry this spirit of Māī and Ajimā and who I experience as living embodiments of Goddess Durgā in all Her forms. These women, whose lives are by no means easy, mirror my own love and devotion towards Goddess. Watching them pray and speak to Durgā , Lakṣmī, Saraswatī, Kālī,

Vajrayoginī, the Mātṛkās, Navadurgās and other countless Goddesses affirms that what I am feeling is *real, mysterious* and *profound.* At each temple, at each roadside shrine, at each stone that has been worshiped for thousands of years as Goddess throughout the Valley, I encountered women dressed in vibrant red hues—cherry, hibiscus, crimson, ruby, pomegranate. Women on their knees in prayer, their eyes closed in deep devotion, their lips trembling slightly as they ask for Her blessing. Women feeding the Goddess—offering rice, chapatis, lentil-based sweets, fruit, and coconut. Women honoring Her light with ghee lamp flames burning from cotton wicks that they themselves had grown and so carefully and mindfully twisted while sitting on a doorstep chatting with their neighbors about life's trials and joys. Women waving incense and teaching their young daughters how to hold the incense sticks and wave them in a circular movement to please the Goddess, the wisps of smoke wafting through the womblike inner sanctum filling the air with sandalwood and jasmine scents. Women carrying plates piled with orange and yellow marigolds and red hibiscus, tucking the blossoms into every available crevice of the Goddess' majestic stone form, especially at Her feet and on Her head. Women reciting the sacred texts, muttering chants (mantras), whispering their fears and desires to the Goddess of their heart. Women bowing their heads to the deity's wet and sticky red feet and breasts, Goddess' now blood-red body lovingly smeared with red vermillion powder and coconut milk by thousands of devotees. Countless women—young and old, light and dark-skinned, poor, middle class, rich, Buddhist and Hindu—all pressing their red-marked foreheads to the Goddess' brow expressing their deep devotion and love and asking for Her grace.

In the Valley the presence of the Māī and Ajimā is undeniable. The Śākta Tantra texts state that all women are inherently Śakti, so one might hope that today women in twenty-first century Nepal are still perceived as living embodiments of Goddess. However, for the most part, the Nepalese, Newari, Tibetan and ethnic minority women I encountered were sadly not treated as Goddesses. Suffering, abuse, sex trafficking, poverty, debilitating illness are too often the horrifying reality of life for them, yet despite the abuses and injustice, the women remain devoted to Goddess. Life is hard in the Valley, but women's relationship to the Divine is what carries them through. It is Goddess who assuages their sorrow over losing a child; their worries about not having enough food to feed their families. It is She who listens to their fears about their health and the difficulties and pain they experience in their marriages or daily lives. It is Goddess who protects and embraces them. It is Goddess who smiles when they relate tales of love and caring, who pats them on the back when they share their successes and accomplishments, who inspires them to dance, laugh, play and make love. It is Devī whose shoulder and breast they can cry on, whose four to eighteen arms hold and caress them as they weep their sorrows about sickness, death, and poverty. It is Goddess who is everything to them:

a listener, a guide, a mother, a lover, a friend. The Māī and Ajimā in Her myriad forms bestows Her blessings in an endless, countless flow and women worship Her with deep gratitude and appreciation as they have done for millennia.

Notes

1. Heide Goettner Abendroth, "Matriarchal Societies and Modern Research on Matriarchies" (paper presented at the Second World Congress on Matriarchal Studies, San Antonio, Texas, September 2004). www.second-congress-matriarchal-studies.com
2. Summarized from three days of presentations on Matriarchy from various scholars at the Second World Congress on Matriarchal Studies in San Antonio, Texas, 2004. www.second-congress-matriarchal-studies.com
3. http://encarta.msn.com/encyclopedia_761589423/patriarchy.html (accessed September 19, 2009).
4. Joan Marler, "The Beginnings of Patriarchy in Europe: Reflections on the Kurgan Theory of Marija Gimbutas," in *The Rule of Mars: Readings on the Origins, History and Impact of Patriarchy*, ed. Cristina Biaggi (Manchester, CT: Knowledge, Ideas & Trends, 2005), 53.
5. Luce Irigaray, "Women, The Sacred, Money," in *Sexes and Genealogies*, trans.Gillian C. Gill (New York, Columbia University Press, 1993), 75-88.
6. Irigaray,*Women, the Sacred, Money*, 84.
7. Vicki Noble, "Dakini: The Goddess who Takes Form as a Woman." in *Goddesses in World Culture. Vol. 1: Africa, Asia, Australia and the Pacific.*, ed. Patricia Monaghan (Santa Barbara, California: Praeger (an imprint of Houghton-Mifflin), Spring 2010.
8. Mary Slusser, *Nepal Mandala: A Cultural Study of the Kathmandu Valley*, vol 1 of 2: Text (Princeton: Princeton University Press, 1982), 309.
9. Amita Ray, *Art of Nepal* (New Delhi: Indian Council for Cultural Relations, 1973), 67.
10. Slusser, *Nepal Mandala*, 307.
11. Ibid., *Nepal Mandala*, 10.
12. Mary Anderson, *The Festivals of Nepal* (New Delhi: Rupa & Co, 1988), 10.
13. Pupul Jayakar, *The Earth Mother* (New York: Harper and Row, 1989), 3.
14. Ibid.
15. Ibid., 1.
16. Ibid.
17. Donna Jordan, "A Post-Orientalist History of the Fierce Śakti of the Subaltern Domain" (PhD diss., California Institute of Integral Studies, 1999), 83.
18. Narenda Nath Bhattacharya, *The Indian Mother Goddess* (Delhi: Manohar, 1977), 278.
19. Jordan, "Fierce Śakti of the Subaltern Domain," 83.

20. Jayakar, *The Earth Mother*, 14.
21. Saphalya Amatya, *Art and Culture of Nepal: An Attempt Toward Preservation* (New Delhi: Niral Publications, 1991), 19.
22. N.N. Bhattacharya, *History of the Śākta Religion* (Delhi: Munshiram Manoharial, 1996), 9.
23. Jordan, "Fierce Śakti of the Subaltern Domain," 78.
24. Jayakar, *The Earth Mother*, 14.
25. Amatya, *Art and Culture of Nepal*, 12.
26. Jordan, "Fierce Śakti of the Subaltern Domain," 79.

day four
Lakṣmī: Goddess of Abundance

Goddess Lakṣmī appears to us wearing a pomegranate red sari holding pink lotuses in Her two upper arms and offering gold coins from Her right and blessings from Her left lower ones. Elephants showering water from their trunks flank Her sides. Sometimes an owl, Her animal vehicle for Her Tantric, Kaula or Śākta worshipers, is perched near Her feet. Verdant leafy plants, plates laden with coconuts, flowers, and fruits and pots filled with teeming vegetative life often surround Her suggesting not only Her fertile and abundant nature, but Her earthy roots in the ancient agrarian past and contemporary agricultural rituals. As a Goddess of fruition and perseverance, Lakṣmī is an elemental force, much like the spirit of the Māī or Ajimā. She is the power to animate the fields and produce fruit, legumes, seeds, nuts and vegetables for our nourishment. Today, Lakṣmī's vegetative role in the cosmic order is virtually lost outside of the festival. Instead of being a wild and elemental force as Her earliest origins suggest, Lakṣmī is most known and worshiped as a Goddess of material wealth and marital harmony. Lakṣmī remains one of the favorite Goddesses within the Hindu pantheon today, however, the reasons for Her popularity are not necessarily in the spirit of Her earthy essence. I will address Lakṣmī's shift in cultural status shortly, but first let's look at Her appearance during the Durgā festival and in one of the greatest battles of the Durgā myth.

Lakṣmī and the Durgā Festival

During the second three days of the Durgā Festival, Mother Lakṣmī is celebrated. While the generative principle of the universe is honored during the first three days, the preservative and growth aspect of existence is expressed and worshipped on the days devoted to Lakṣmī. Lakṣmī is a Goddess of Abundance, Prosperity, Harmony and Love—qualities that inspire and bring pleasure and also give us the spiritual strength to maintain. She is the embodiment and expression of the infinite generosity of the Universe. Lakṣmī is rajas (sexual and creative passion or juice). Lakṣmī's essence is enlivening, fertile and deeply sensual. Lakṣmī *is* the nectar of life. She is the sexually mature woman, the ripeness of fruit, the fall harvest, and the rain that nourishes the land.

On these second three days that Lakṣmī is actively worshiped, the sprouts of barley seeds planted only a few days before first appear. Some say the green blades that poke through the earth are Durgā's swords. During these days the daily ritual bath at a certain tīrtha still takes place in the predawn darkness, and circumambulations are made at the various temple complexes. Candles, incense, fruit, music, and the touch of the devotees' hand or forehead to the deity invoke the five elements and reconnect the practitioner with these elements' governing spheres of existence. Every morning Māhālakṣmī's name is invoked, Her carita is read and Her fierce aspect as Durgā continues to be worshiped. Nothing is dualistic in these practices. When one worships Lakṣmī, they worship Durgā. These Goddesses are not separate, but varied faces of the Divine. In fact, it is on these days that one of the most significant of the mythic battles related to Durgā takes place.

Mahalakṣmī and Her Teachings from the *Devī Māhātmyā*

If Saraswatī is the river and mind, Lakṣmī is the earth and physical body. Some retellings of the myth in this chapter of the *Devī Māhātmyā* honoring Lakṣmī describe what some define as the actual *birth* of Durgā. However, such versions of this epic story that declare that Durgā was created from the gods are slightly off the mark. The gods call the Supreme Mother Goddess to their aid, for they are impotent in their attempts to stop the demon and his minions from destroying all the planes of existence. The gods ask for Durgā's assistance, and She appears. Each god hands Her their tool, weapon, or some attribute—Śiva, his trident, Viṣṇu his discus, and so forth. They give their tejas or heat, which has a creative and sexual essence to it. On one level this speaks to the merging of male and female energies and what can be created from such a union. Finally She holds all the aspects of the gods and is ready to go into battle. However, as D. Kālī points out, an actual birth from the gods is impossible. Durgā is certainly not born from them. "The tejas that emerges from the bodies of the gods is not their creation but the Devī's already indwelling presence. . . note that in no instance is the tejas that forms any part of Her anatomy said to be born of the gods themselves, but only of their tejas."[1] Each god lends Ambikā/Durgā a tool or weapon, but it is essential that the gods are ultimately agents of *Her* power. These male gods do not give birth to Her, they do not create Her, they only call on Her, and lend their energies.

In this second part of the epic myth, we find Durgā as Māhālakṣmī battling the demon Mahiṣāsuramardinī. Sweet, demure Lakṣmī—the orthodox tradition's ideal model of traditional "femininity," wifedom, and motherhood—engaging in battle? Well, yes, but as we shall see, Lakṣmī has a much greater presence than what we have been led to believe. This chapter metaphorically describes some of the more earthly struggles we have in our physical lives. Whereas the first carita of the myth focuses more on Durgā's transcendent and cosmic nature, for example in Her role as Mahāmāyā, the Great Illusion, this chapter shows what a palpable and formidable force she is in the physical realm.

The Goddess' victory over the Mahiṣāsuramardinī or buffalo-headed demon is one of the most ubiquitous images of Goddess throughout the Hindu world. As Durgā and the demon engage in battle, the demon king continually takes different forms. Durgā (who is now referred to as Caṇḍīkā, the angry one) does not decide to slay the demon until this elusive beast shows his true form. All throughout the battle, Durgā sees right through his ever-shifting forms and knows that under all these ego-ic displays, the divinity of this creature does indeed lie. The battle is Her līlā or play. As Mahiṣāsura appears to Durgā in the form of a buffalo, She steps on his neck, pinning him down. She then pierces his heart with Her spear and decapitates him with Her sword. With this act, the demon can no longer evade Her and disguise his true and ultimately divine form through shape-shifting into different creatures. On a psychological and behavioral level, we can see this demon and the various forms he changes into as the many ways we act irrationally, or repeat the same bad habits and behaviors over and over. Just as Durgā pins down the demon and demands he show his true nature, we must focus on what is at the core of any issue we are struggling with. On a spiritual level, Durgā's sword brings penetrating wisdom right into this creature's heart, and She chops off his head thereby destroying his ego. It is significant that She completes this act with the utmost composure. We always have a choice about whether we will respond or react to any situation.

We can read this myth as a guide for what is needed in confronting the demons in our own lives. Whether they are external and appear in our community and families or rise in our own minds as addictions, memories of injustice or past abuses, we must find ways to subdue them, to temper and transmute their violent actions. We must stop negative thoughts before they manifest and harm others or ourselves. We must ensure that they do not trap and inhibit us on our journey through life. We must find that place of calm deep within and take action from our center. Durgā's spear pierces the heart reminding us that the wisdom of the heart is always victorious in destroying what most threatens us. And Lakṣmī embodies all the qualities of the heart. We must learn to listen to our hearts rather than only acting from our minds/egos. By severing the head of the demon, Durgā cuts the power that the ego mind has had over the heart. As D. Kālī notes, "Durgā's decapitating sword of knowledge allows us to discern between what appears as finite and fleeting and what is infinite and abiding. In practical terms, it distinguishes between selfish, harmful impulse and the noble selflessness that promotes harmony and points toward unity."[2]

Today Lakṣmī in orthodox culture does not have the formidable nature that would help one defeat the great demon of all the worlds. In many respects She has become a model of submission and obedience. Painted as the ideal mother and wife, Lakṣmī's embodiment of harmony within orthodox tradition is not the one that guides one towards the divine unity metaphorically described in the epic text. Instead, Lakṣmī has been used to uphold patriarchal notions of female submissiveness, selflessness, and an ever generous nature. Lakṣmī's dissatisfaction with the ways Her energies are controlled and prohibited is expressed in Her manifestation as Chanchallā, the Restless One. Lakṣmī is said to have a fickle nature. She is described as capricious, but perhaps it is an intolerance for adversity and discomfort. Śakti is always in a process of becoming. It is only natural for some of us to feel fickle, to vacillate between decisions, even opinions. It is important that we do find a way to commit, to stay with one idea or experience; however, we must learn to make our decisions from a deep place of self-assuredness and certainty. We must discard our fears of what others will think and act from our own volition. We must try to remain unattached to outcome, and yet open to the possibility of material and spiritual abundance. Lakṣmī embodies the blissful and abundant energies of the universe. This is what the original Lakṣmī has to teach. She does not tolerate disharmony or any form of oppression. Her gifts of beauty, high status, fame, wealth, and earthly success are all impermanent. She may grant us certain desires, but eventually She will take them away. We must learn to not become attached to them and not to become complacent and irreverent. She teaches us about endless abundance. There is always enough if we call on Lakṣmī and honor Her as Source. She teaches us to be self-sufficient and resourceful like the ocean from which She comes. When I think of the Lakṣmī presented to us today I wonder how such a Goddess could really be passive or meek if She came from the sea?

One of Lakṣmī's most popular myths tells of Her rising from the sea of milk. The demons and the gods are engaged in the great challenge of churning the sea to produce the sacred ambrosia. At first only poisons spew out, and Śiva steps in to drink them and hold them in his throat—thereafter being known as Nīlakaṇṭha, Blue Throated One. The churning produces monstrous waves, until suddenly they pass and the waters become calm. At this moment the resplendent Goddess Lakṣmī emerges from the water and offers the golden pot of sublime nectar to the gods. It is a sacred elixir of immortality. She comes bearing riches of spiritual wealth and enlightenment as symbolized by Her vessel of ambrosia.

The myth is a potent allegory for the meditative journey. When we meditate the "demons" of our mind are churned out like poisons. Our thoughts may become like the tumultuous waves of a stormy sea, but eventually, these waves or thoughts will run their course. Everything has its cycle. The oceanic waters are stirred by the churning of the demons and deities, but eventually, once all their energies have expended, the waters return to a calm mirrorlike essence. This profound state of calm after the storm is Durgā's essence. In Tantric meditations, Śiva or our receptive, quiescent, all pervading consciousness absorbs the turmoil and poisons, and the ambrosia or Śakti of creativity then rises and inspires the fruits of our practice. The nectar of immortality is ultimately the divine consciousness that flows through us all. Ultimately our meditation practice brings stillness to our mind, calmness to our heart and an all-pervading sense of interconnection.

Goddess of Flowers, Fruit, Trees, and All Vegetation

In Bengal and other parts of India, nine different plants or fruits are worshiped as embodiments of the Goddess during the festival. We will return to the list of these plants in the chapter, *Day Nine: The Nine Durgā.* This connection between different plants and a Goddess suggests that this ritual is rooted in earlier agrarian cultures that viewed the vegetative world as animate. The iconography of vegetation as sacred is consistent throughout ritual and temple art over the ages. Vegetative deities express an interconnection between humans and the natural world.

Lakṣmī, Goddess of Fertility, Growth, and Life leads us to examine the relationship between women's bodies and the earth, in particular the agricultural cycle. One of Lakṣmī's most common epithets, Śrī, connects Her to Her Vedic vegetative roots. Śrī has etymological connections with the word, *Ceres*, the Roman Goddess of Grain. The Indian Śrī also presides over grain. Etymologically, Śrī has many layers of meaning. Śrī means auspiciousness and suggests general well-being in terms of physical health, material prosperity, bodily beauty, and ruling majesty.[3] It was a common name for the Earth Goddess in the Vedas (1000-500 B.C.E.).[4] Śrī is the indwelling radiant presence of the divinity.[5] In the Vedic texts Śrī "suggests capability, power and advantageous skills. As an external quality Śrī suggests beauty, luster, glory and high rank. The term is especially used in later Vedic literature to refer to ruling power, dominion and mastery of kings."[6] Śrī has royal significance. It also refers to a seat of power. The cushion that a king sits on is sometimes called Śrī. As Śrī evolved into Lakṣmī, Her essence was maintained in its use as a prefix. Placing "Śrī" before any name enhances it with auspiciousness and grace. Śrī's direct relationship with the harvest and royalty has not been completely lost over time, Lakṣmī has always been a popular Goddess with royalty. With royal power comes an obligation to uphold the dharma or code/duty and the belief that what happens in the cosmic spheres is reflected on earth.[7] However, with the royal tradition also come hierarchy and systems of dominance and control. Lakṣmī was not always as fettered as She became in the later mythology. Her abundant nature is limitless and ultimately cannot be contained for Lakṣmī governs both cosmos and earth. Let's now consider where She came from.

Yakṣīs

The evolution of Lakṣmī's nature cannot be separated from the tree spirits or Yakṣīs. Yakṣīs and the male Yakṣas have elemental natures (fiery, watery, airy, woody, and ethereal) and are often found in groups. The earliest images of the Yakṣīs date to 1 B.C.E. Texts describe how a Yakṣīs's touch could cause a tree to blossom or produce fruit.[8] The Yakṣīs are the fairies or sprites of the Celtic tradition. They represent the innocence, trust and spontaneity of childhood that too often gets lost and broken in adulthood. They contain the essence of the fool. Inseparable from instinct and intuition, they teach us to trust our deepest self. They are mediators between humans and the natural world. Yakṣīs express trickster energies, (they are known to be mischievous), and they also offer protection. In Nepal it is common to find Yakṣīs and Yakṣas carved into temple struts and at the base of pillars. The Yakṣīs have a minor yet very supportive function in maintaining the cosmic and earthly order. Their presence and power cannot be denied. Yakṣīs carry a kula (clan) spirit. And as we shall see, they later evolved into groups of elemental Goddesses like the Matṛkās, Navadurgā, and the Yoginīs. These early vegetative deities may not have had the supreme power over cosmos and earth as Lakṣmī, Durgā, and Saraswatī do, but they have an important place in the schema of existence. It was believed that the Yakṣīs would grant their devotees all their desires.[9]

In the Kaula tradition, Yakṣīs and Goddesses were worshiped in the form of trees in order to conceive children. Blood offerings, preferably menstrual blood, were given. One finds tree shrines all over the Kathmandu Valley and India. Some have their own local following of devotees. Their names are many: Śītalā, Harītī, Kubjikā, and Śrī. Worshiping trees as Goddesses is an important practice within Tantric and Kaula circles. In many traditions the tree is a life-force symbol. It is an image used in some meditative practices and is a common symbol of spiritual connection between earth and sky. In the Kaula and Tantric traditions, trees also can take on a distinctly female nature. Often villages will worship a tree as the presiding Goddess of the village. Usually, this Grama Devī or Village Goddess is worshiped in the center or on the edge of the village. Elinor Gadon, founding mother of the Women's Spirituality Graduate Program at the California Institute of Integral Studies, has done extensive research on the phenomenon of the Grama Devī. She has explored Her significance and presence in her forthcoming book on the Village Goddess in India. These Goddesses are central figures in ritual worship and are consulted for protection, fertility, a successful harvest, health, and prosperity. They are Mother Spirits, who like the more anthropomorphized and philosophically developed Lakṣmī, bestow grace through life experiences involving the full cycle of life, death and rebirth. Their mythology also connects them to living women who have died prematurely.[10] These are fierce Goddesses of death, justice and protection.

Often the triangular openings of trees look yoni-like and are smeared with red vermillion powder and blood—emulating the vulvic opening of a woman's yoni. The banyan tree, for example, with its winding tentacle-like roots has a triangular formation near its base that opens to a womblike cavern within the tree. The ubiquitous banyan trees can be found throughout South Asia. There are many mythological stories of Goddesses, Gods and banyan trees as well as Yoginīs, Yogis and Buddhas who gained enlightenment meditating at the base of such trees. This tree becomes not only metaphorically, but in actuality, a site where one's consciousness can expand. Whether one refers to the tree as Grama Devī, Yakṣī or Lakṣmī, what each of these deities has in common is the power of bestowing liberating transmissions. Lakṣmī's original nature shares many elements with the tree spirits. "Other Hindu deities with possible Yakṣa or Yakṣī roots include Gaṇeśa, the elephant-headed god and protector against malevolent forces and Śrī, the female guardian of wealth and treasures associated with the Yakṣas' god Kubera."[11] As a Goddess of all forms of vegetation, it is not surprising that the tree and other natural symbols associated with Lakṣmī such as the lotus, owl, elephant and cowry shell also express union with the Divine and the possibility of mokṣa or enlightenment.

Lakṣmī and the Lotus as a Symbol of Our Spiritual Journey to Enlightenment

The lotus is a powerful symbol of spiritual transformation. It symbolizes fertility, growth and authority. In Hindu and Buddhist traditions it represents the journey from darkness or ignorance into light or awakened consciousness. Often seen as the seat of Tantric deities or the mandalic background of devotional art, the lotus is also a potent metaphor for the sādhaka or practitioner. Its roots grow out of the dark mud and push their way up through murky water. Finally, they pierce through the water's surface into the light and blossom into a multi-petaled pink flower that rests serene and unsoiled on the surface. The growth and blossoming of the lotus is a potent metaphor for the spiritual transformation we are called to undergo again and again. Lakṣmī is the fruit that ripens out of a dark night of the soul. The symbolism of the lotus connotes the mental and emotional journey we can experience in our meditations, and even life experiences. We may be led through difficult passages, we may encounter despair and suffering, but it is not without reason. While the reasons may not be logical to the rational mind, and while we may never even fully understand why we had to endure what we did, the process of our consciousness unfolding will eventually blossom. The pain of loss, death, illness, and despair may feel as if it could destroy us, in actuality it is destroying our ego mind, breaking through restrictive thoughts and emotions that separate us from realizing that we are one with Spirit, with Goddess, with the Universe. We are not victims, but co-participants and while the answers to our questions may not be evident, we can be assured that we will rise from the wreckage stronger and wiser and certainly more conscious than we were before.

Lakṣmī and Sexuality

Lakṣmī's connection to the lotus not only reflects the journey of the spiritual initiate, but also expresses Her unbridled sexuality. The lotus is often a symbol of a woman's yoni. White explains: "The identification of the body of a woman (or a goddess) with a flower or tree, her anatomy with the plant and flower anatomy, human reproduction with plant reproduction, and female sexual emissions with plant or flower essences are developed at every level in these traditions."[12] The word *padma* is used interchangeably with a woman's yoni and the lotus flower. In the Tantras women are affectionately called "lotus-vulva-ed."[13] In erotic Tantric texts the ideal lover is called *Padmini*—a term of endearment that plays on the word padma (yoni). Lakṣmī is rajas—the nectar of the lotus, the blood and sexual juices of the yoni. Rajas is also a name for pollen,[14] recalling the connection of the Bee Goddess, Brahmārī and the yoni at Kāmākhyā. Bees, flowers, nectar, women all have been used poetically, ritualistically, and philosophically as references to female sexuality. Some Kaula texts have created classifications of women, types of sexual fluids and ten types of flowers.[15] Semen too plays a role, for in Tantra, rituals are always about unifying opposites. White and red flowers not only represent the male (semen) and female (menstrual blood), but these bodily substances are used in the rituals.

One cannot speak of the lotus without considering the maṇḍala which refers to both kulas of deities, and also certain cities and places. Often these sacred sites[16] are said to have been generated from a lotus. Furthermore, "a central element of Tantric theory and practice, the maṇḍala is the mesocosmic template through which the Tantric practitioner transacts with and appropriates the myriad energies that course through every level of the cosmos. . . . Tantric maṇḍalas (are) graphic representations of the universe as a clan (kula) of interrelated beings, as an 'embodied cosmos.'" And the yoni too becomes a maṇḍala and portal of sacred energies during sexual rituals. In Tantric texts there is a complex and profound understanding of female anatomy. The *Cakrasamvara Maṇḍala*, a Tantric Buddhist text states how names of the eight female door guardians of this maṇḍala share their names with those of the eight principal veins that radiate outward from the vaginal nerve center.[17] When we consider how the yoni is the focus and locus of patriarchal dominance, fear, loathing, and control, it is not too surprising to see how female sexual anatomy is at the heart of unorthodox and ancient religion. The female body and sexuality obviously has tremendous power. One of Lakṣmī's symbols is the cowry shell because it resembles a woman's yoni. The rounded part of the shell has been likened to a pregnant belly, and the opening on the other side as the vulva. The cowry also has been used as a form of currency in various cultures since earliest times. Perhaps this in part explains Lakṣmī's association to commerce and the market. She is not only a creator of resources but also one who controls them with great authority.

Lakṣmī is a Goddess in full sexual maturity whose rajas alters consciousness in ways that have direct implications on the physical plane. Sexual practices are a crucial aspect of Tantric practice for the advanced sādhaka and the energies that are generated through such rites can be used to help the practitioner break through oppressive experiences. Tantric rites also can inspire one to create. It is interesting to note that while Lakṣmī is widely worshiped as a Mother Goddess, She, like Saraswatī and Durgā, is not a Mother of Her own children. Perhaps one could say She is the Mother of *all* children. Lakṣmī is the very essence of creative sexual power—plentiful, stimulating, and prolific.

Pande claims "Laxmi[18] reflects the system as it originally was."[19] Her origins are rooted in prepatriarchal times, where love and sex could not be harnessed into a tradition that was limiting to either sex. Unbound by financial and business obligations, lovers did not live together, but visited each other and the rajas or passion of their courtship perhaps was able to embody and express more Lakṣmī-esque values: love, passion, harmony, bliss. In some tales, the king of the Yakṣas was the god Kubera. Kubera was one of Lakṣmī's lovers for a time. As lovers Lakṣmī and Kubera contain the unbridled passion that is so intricately integral to this concept of rajas that Lakṣmī embodies and imparts.

The Tantric Lakṣmī that we know from the Śākta tradition maintains Lakṣmī's original free and limitless nature. When we worship Lakṣmī with Viṣṇu from the Tantric perspective we see Viṣṇu and Lakṣmī as inseparable. Viṣṇu is *being* and Lakṣmī is *becoming*. The God is the ground of being, the foundation of our consciousness, while Goddess is the dynamic state of always evolving and becoming new and ever new again. The pairings of Goddesses and Gods within the Tantric traditions speaks to the union of energies. When a man can show up with his consciousness merged in Viṣṇu, he allows his partner to radiate her Śakti/Lakṣmī energies back. The Union of Goddess and God within the Tantric tradition presents different ways of describing non-dual reality. The energies the deities create *together* allow the world to exist. Their sacred dance of creation and destruction is their līlā (divine play). Viṣṇu upholds the universe, and Lakṣmī enacts Divine Will.[20] Whatever Lakṣmī offers, whether it is love, harmony, and/or abundance, Viṣṇu maintains. In the Tantric sense, theirs is a partnership that complements one another. As equals, each has a crucial role in the creation, sustenance and destruction of existence.

The Elephant and the Owl

Elephants are often depicted with Mother Lakṣmī. The elephant is an animal that is closely associated to royalty. We see in divine images as well as paintings that Lakṣmī was grandly worshiped on palanquins flanked by elephants. Medieval Kingdoms co-opted the powers of Goddess for military pursuits, especially the acquisition of land. As Goddess of the Earth, Her assistance ensured the attainment of desired territories as well as the successful harvest of crops. Elephants also connect Her to rain clouds. Dark voluminous clouds in the monsoon sky sometimes appear as elephants. Lakṣmī's association with elephants and clouds expresses Her power over the crop cycle. She is earth and rain.

Sometimes Lakṣmī is accompanied by an owl. The owl is a creature of the night that can see through the darkness. Symbolically, this power animal of Lakṣmī's, with its 360 degree vision, guides us in seeing through ignorance and deceit.

Lakṣmī's association with elephants and owls is shamanic at its core. When we understand the significance of Lakṣmī's accoutrements, symbols, and companions, a fuller energetic reality of the Goddess emerges and we learn that the subservient Lakṣmī we often find today is not the Mahālakṣmī we are celebrating as the all-pervading Śakti/life force energy during the Durgā Festival. We have a lot to learn from Lakṣmī, whose domain is very much the earthly realm. How do we find the sacred in the physical? How do we understand Nature and any living body as Divine? What are the origins of this Goddess, who today is the ideal model of marital harmony and material wealth? Who is this very passionate and wild Goddess, who at Her essence defies all orthodoxy and patriarchal conditioning? And what happened? How did such an all-powerful Goddess lose some of Her freedom and power?

The Domestification of Lakṣmī

By late epic period 400 CE Lakṣmī had lost most of Her original self-authority and independence and was depicted as Viṣṇu's devoted wife. "As the beloved of Viṣṇu, Viṣṇupriya, she slowly relegates all responsibility and turns placid, calm and loyal, displaying a disturbing obedience to all the social mores that had begun by then to control the lives and energies of women married to successful men."[21]

Around 200 CE the Laws of Manu came into effect and have endured. *Manusmṛti* is a manual that stripped women of all rights and enforced a code of obedience and male-based morality that affected the social, religious and cultural mores of the Hindu world. Fierce Goddesses of the Kaula and Śākta traditions like Durgā, Kālī, the Matṛkās and Navadurgā were relegated to the margins of orthodox society—although they still remained central and supreme in certain kulas or clans and communities. Nevertheless, at the core of the orthodox practices was a denial and fear of female sexual power. Within the orthodox Hindu tradition women were excluded from positions of authority, and relegated to a domestic role outside the sphere of spiritual authority.

The Goddess Lakṣmī became the model wife: obedient, sweet, and beautiful. Although She is the Great Mother, She is not the mother of children in any of Her myths. Nevertheless the imposed expectation for Lakṣmī to be selfless and ever nurturing paints Her as the ideal mother. "When women are blessed with the words '*Be like Laxmi*,' it implies that they shall be warm, generous, home-loving, but passive and obedient."[22] The idea is that women stay subdued and maintain the orthodox order—preferably by providing sons to the male lines. The Kaula Lakṣmī with Her association with elephants (a matriarchal symbol of female power, majesty and authority), was a fierce and loving Mother Goddess who lost Her power when She was married into the patriarchal tradition. Pande notes,

> Lakṣmī's old spirit, when it appears at all, reveals itself as a sharp-tongued and fractious wife, who is always quarrelling for her conjugal rights and nagging her lord when he awakens. Or else she acts petulant and jealous of independent women. We see her worrying endlessly about female competition for her 'ever-flirtatious' lord—in this way she is defanged. Men need not fear her. She is a safe model.[23]

We find that Lakṣmī's place in the orthodox Hindu world today is primarily one of passivity, subservience, and as grantor of material wealth. Her primal erotic nature, with its wild vegetative roots and multi-faceted desires has been eclipsed, but fortunately not lost or entirely forgotten.

Lakṣmī Temple, Patan, Nepal, 2005

I have traveled to Nepal with one of my soul mates. It is difficult to explain my connection to this woman in my life. I call her Ajima[24] *or Puntu Māīju, the name the Ratna Māyā Devī Mātā gave her. Daughter of Māī. She is my friend, my sister, my spiritual mother, my anam cara (soul friend), and a midwife of my soul. Once when she asked a healer what it was about our profound connection, the healer said "You have been everything to each other over the ages: mother/daughter/lover/ partner/ friend/ healer/wife/husband. You have spent lifetimes together. You really are like one soul." Both she and I know this is so.*

And so here we are together in Nepal for Durgā Pūjā in the fall of 2005. As we move from shrine to temple to shrine, I watch this woman becoming Devī. She has always carried Lakṣmī qualities: the way she has been a devoted mother to her two beautiful and free-spirited daughters; the way she has mothered literally thousands of emotionally and mentally exceptional children; even in her distaste for poor manners (at the dinner table especially) and dirt and dust (I remember her wiping down the door handles at one of my apartments during one her visits); the way she loves arranging flowers; her healing touch; the way she enjoys cooking and preparing exquisite feasts; her appreciation for art and beauty, particularly in the home; the way she cried and felt the pain in her own body when the trees in her yard were mistakenly cut too far back; the way she lives life with such grace. But I sense her consciousness awakening and expanding in greater ways. I see Lakṣmī's light blazing forth. I remember the experiences I had during the festival in 2000 and am amazed by the similarities. She has that Śakti fever. Literally and figuratively. She spends several days in bed, with fever and purging. She is being shaken to her core. And as it was for me with Durgā, I witness how my friend's unfolding consciousness is directly related to Lakṣmī: issues around relationship, marriage, harmony and disharmony in the home. She is remembering abuses she suffered in her first marriage. She cries to me about the injustice, about the powerlessness she felt, about how she was stuck for years. And she joyously shares how she got out!

In the Lakṣmī Tantra *Lakṣmī tells Viṣṇu:*

> Remember, my son, that when I first manifested myself in perceptible form, I deliberately chose to appear in a female body. . . . Therefore a person devoted to a spiritual practice should never, ever, abuse a woman, not physically, not verbally, not even in thought. I am inherent in all women and in the material universe itself. Therefore anyone who disdains women disdains me, while anyone who honors women simultaneously loves and praises the entire cosmos. The devotee who loves and respects women, never thinking an evil thought about them, is very close to me. Since women are my direct embodiments, yogis should revere and worship them. . . . Men who wish to become enlightened should show the highest respect toward women, regarding every woman they meet as their mother and as my human emanation.[25]

Each night at dinner I am privy to the sexiest and most fabulous of stories from a woman who has passionately explored her sexuality with numerous lovers over her lifetime. We drink wine (another form of Lakṣmī's rajas!), we feast on dahl bhaat and other Nepalese specialties. Her eyes sparkle and she looks like she is 20 years old as she tells me stories about the musician, the writer, the asshole, and another younger lover who at the moment is dying of cancer and wants to see her again. We laugh and we cry. As I listen to these stories one theme in particular dominates my consciousness: Men must respect women and honor our divinity. And women must respect the primal divinity in men. Lakṣmī's mythological history connects Her to a multitude of gods—Kubera, Śiva, Rāma, Kṛṣṇa—suggesting early matriarchal roots of this Goddess. In a matriarchy, marriage, as the institution we know it today, did not exist. One might have one partner, or many, and yet a social structure existed that equally supports the ways women and men related to each other.

My companion has married again and tells of the ways she feels restless, the ways she still does not feel seen or heard, how she longs for that juicy, free life. There are two parts of her self pulling at her heart—the free-spirited primal nature of Lakṣmī, and the conventionalized Lakṣmī that was conditioned into women born in the 1930s.

I think of how Durgā must fearlessly confront the shape-shifting demon. Ajima sometimes has a hard time with the more painful memories—like Lakṣmī she prefers not to dwell long on any unpleasantness. Nevertheless, the pain, the wounding, the heartbreak is there; and it is not surprising that these "demons" would appear in Ajima's consciousness during the Durgā festival. You do not make a pilgrimage to the Mother who removes Difficulty and Fear, the Great Mother who brings Justice and Equanimity without having to confront the hauntings of your past. She has been called here to make peace with her past. And to do this work, must confront these haunted memories—she must stare them in the face and through witnessing their true nature, she will be able to transmute their negative charge.

As I consider Ajima's process of continual awakening and her attachment to joy and harmony, I see how I, on the other hand, tend to be fixated on the suffering of existence. Having lived there for so long from a childhood of physical, sexual, mental and emotional abuse to a decade of dis-ease and incessant pain to drama after painful drama and heartbreak in many of my romantic relationships—I am more "comfortable" with the underworld for it is familiar terrain. It has been hard for me to trust the bliss, the joy, the love. Here in Nepal, with my copilgrim, a living Lakṣmī, we are both mirroring what is missing for the other. She cannot hold only light at all times, I cannot only be cloaked in darkness. We are both the light and the dark. Lakṣmī's bliss and joy are as equally mine, as Durgā's resilience and Kālī's rage are equally my friend's.

On the first day dedicated to Lakṣmī, we go to the temple in Patan and I watch Ajima being transformed. . . she enters the temple and bows to Lakṣmī's aniconic form—three stones smeared with blood, rice, flower petals and sticky coconut juice. Her body convulses, she stands dazed and can hardly walk to the door. I hold her hand and accompany her to a seat beneath a banyan tree. Tears stream down her face. She is muttering to Lakṣmī. I explain I cannot hear her, she looks at me with the most serene expression I have ever seen on her face, and tells me how grateful she is to Lakṣmī. How different she feels. How she always had felt this love for Lakṣmī, but now it's all making perfect sense. During these three days of the festival she is getting an empowerment. This is the Śākta Kaula tradition at its core. No heady philosophical practices are needed, no highly sophisticated Sanskrit mantras need to be recited, only love for the Mother—only Mā Mā Mā. Only reverence. Only gratitude and acceptance. She only asks that we understand that we are Divine, inseparable from Her. We must learn to find balance within ourselves as life swings us from joy to sorrow, celebration to mourning. We need not know the history, we need not sit for hours at a pūjā led by a Brahmin priest. By the very nature of our female body, we are Mā. We contain the pain and the sorrow as well as the bliss and ecstasy. My precious Ajima wishes to make more offerings. "Can we buy more flowers for Lakṣmī?" *she asks. Unaware of her request, our guide suddenly appears and hands a plate of flowers to Ajima.* "These are for you, Lakṣmī Mā," *he says, and smiles reverently. She has done the work, she has begun to face her demons, and Lakṣmī is blazing through her.*

Notes

1. Devadatta Kālī, trans., *In Praise of the Goddess. The Devī Māhātmya and Its Meaning. A New Translation* (Berwick, Maine: Nicolas Hayes, Inc., 2003), 71.

2. Ibid., 81.
3. David Kinsley, *Hindu Goddesses: Visions of the Divine Feminine in the Hindu Religious Tradition* (Berkeley: University of California Press, 1986), 20.
4. Vasudha Naryanan, "Brimming with *Bhakti*, Embodiments of *Shakti*: Devotees, Deities, Performers, Reformers, and Other Women of Power in the Hindu Tradition," in *Feminism and World Religions*, eds. Arvind Sharma and Katherine K. Young (Albany: State University of New York Press. 1999), 88.
5. Kālī, *In Praise of the Goddess. The Devī Māhātmya and Its Meaning*, 88
6. Kinsley, *Hindu Goddesses*, 19.
7. Kālī, *In Praise of the Goddess. The Devī Māhātmya and Its Meaning*, 71.
8. Vidya Dehejia, *Yogini Cult and Temples* (New Delhi: National Museum, 1986), 36.
9. Ibid.
10. Corinne Dempsey, "Double Take: Through the Eyes of Yakṣīs, Yakṣass and Yoginīs," in *Journal of the American Academy of Religion* (March 2005, vol. 73, No. 1), 5.
11. Ibid.
12. David Gordon White, *Kiss of the Yoginī: "Tantric Sex" in Its South Asian Context* (University of Chicago Press, Chicago, 2003), 115.
13. Ibid.
14. White, *Kiss of the Yoginī*, 20.
15. Ibid.
16. For example, Nepal Maṇḍala and the Kathmandu Valley, the city of Bhaktapur, and Madurai in Tamil Nadu. White, *Kiss of the Yoginī*, 136.
17. Ibid., 96.
18. Laxmi is an alternate spelling to Lakṣmī.
19. Mrinal Pande, *Devi: Tales of the Goddess in Our Time* (New Delhi: Penguin, 1996), 70.
20. Linda Johnsen, *The Living Goddess: Reclaiming the Tradition of the Mother of the Universe* (St. Paul, Minnesota: Yes Publishers, 1999), 71.
21. Pande, Devi: Tales of the Goddess in Our Time, 71.
22. Ibid., 70.
23. Ibid., 71.
24. I purposely do not use a diacritic here to distinguish my friend, Ajima, from my references to the Grandmother Spirit of the Kathmandu Valley, Ajimā.
25. Johnsen, *The Living Goddess*, 69.

day five
the eight matrkas:
the power of women in groups

In 2006 I visit the Mātṛkās or Mother Goddess shrines around the city of Bhaktapur. First my companion and I go to Indrāyaṇī's open air temple. Within a one foot high brick and stone wall is a semicircle of 13 stones, all different Goddesses, while a separate shrine to Kumārī occupies the space in front of one side of the temple enclosure. These aniconic Goddesses embody the following deities: Bagalāmukhī[1] and Bhairavī, two of the ten Tantric wisdom Goddesses, Bhairava, a fierce form of Śiva, Ganeṣa, a Māī and the eight Mātṛkās. The Mātṛkā Indrāyaṇī is the largest rock in the center. The majestic presence of an ancient banyan tree with mirrors nestled into the twisted knotted trunk overlooks the site from one corner. Rows of butter lamps are placed before the stone aniconic forms of Mother. The site is abuzz with mostly women and children who first pay homage to the Goddess of the banyan tree and recite mantras with a young male pujari or priest. After completing this preliminary ritual, they sit before one or more deities of the stone council in prayer. The Mātṛkās are the protectors of children and I notice how there seem to be more children at this ancient boundary shrine than in most of the temples I have visited.

After making our own offerings and prayers, we make our way to the Mātṛkās temple to Kālī in Her fierce form as Cāmuṇḍā. We must climb a narrow stairway to the temple compound. Several large banyan trees decorated with colorful katas (scarves used as offerings), prayer flags, garlands, and red and yellow markings greet us. Cāmuṇḍā's shrine is behind these trees at the compound entrance on the top of a hill that has had other shrines, small temples, and housing built all over it. Her open-air main altar rests at the top of the hill and remains enclosed, protected by natural boundaries and shrines in each direction. Although this is a Mātṛkā site to Cāmuṇḍā, any name of the terrifying Mother, especially Kālī, is used interchangeably to refer to the presiding Goddess. Each of the eight Mātṛkās has Her own niche in the surrounding walls as do the ninth Durgā as well as the Mahāvidyā or Tantric Wisdom Goddess Tripurāsundarī, and a mūrti of a bhūt—a ghost or spirit often of a woman who has died in childbirth that must be appeased. While I am permitted to take as many photos of deities as I like, it is interesting to note that the only being I am not allowed to take a photo of is bhūt. This is out of respect for the spirit who lost her life unexpectedly. Such a tragic death can often disorient and agitate the soul—sometimes to the extent of her getting stuck in between worlds. As Goddesses of liminal realms, especially pregnancy and birth, the Mātṛkās take on a protective role for both mother and child, who during childbirth stand at the threshold between death and life. The presence of the bhūt reminds me of the fragility of existence, and how closely interconnected life is with death. It also is a reminder that this waking reality is not the only realm in this universe. Kālī is the Great Mother of Death and Transformation, and it is no wonder that the Kālī/Cāmuṇḍā temple honors the death aspect of existence more visibly than other Mātṛkā shrines.

The central shrine has an open brass canopy demarcating the sacred space. Clusters of stones expand across the earthen altar and mūrti of Goddesses stand vigilant behind them. Elaborately carved designs decorate the posts of the canopy: flowers and skulls are a dominant theme. Two skeletons carved into posts in a classic Yoginī pose with one leg raised and knee bent, flank the sides. A woman and her two young daughters are working in the shrine. But even while performing her duties I see the mother, whose name is Gaurī, making offerings and praying. She kneels with water hose in one hand, bucket in the other, cleaning out consecrated and now decaying offerings. Rotting fruit, flowers, and rice soaked in blood is cleared away. Gaurī removes the old prasād that have been placed on Cāmuṇḍā's mouth to feed Her. She then showers Her with water from her hose and she lovingly dries Her just as a mother bathes her child. All the while she sings to the Mother. She calls out Her favorite names with no particular tune. Yet her devotion, her service, her respect and her love make this one of the most beautiful songs I have ever heard. "Jai Durgāy Mātā Bhavanī Kālīkay Kālī Mātā Jai Durgāy! Ambe! Ambe! Durgāy! Mātā Bhavanī Jai Durgāy Kālīkay Kālī Mātā Mahāranī Bhagawatī Mātā Kālī Mātā! Jai Durgāy! Mātā Bhavanī!" Gaurī sings her heart out for about five minutes, and I am able to record her on my voice recorder. She moves from mūrti to mūrti washing the Goddesses' faces and bodies, and clearing the earthen altar before each of them. There is a five-foot-tall sword that stands erect in the center of a small circle of stones at one end of the shrine. Gaurī wipes it clean then places her hands in prayer position or anjali mudrā at her forehead and bows to the sword. "Kālī always protects you," she turns to tell me, and then continues singing to Mā.

Later as we are sipping chai under the banyan trees near the entrance, Gaurī and our translator are talking, and she tells him she must clean the entire temple grounds to prepare for the rituals that will take place for Kālī in the coming nights. She complains that the devotees do not leave the space clean, that there is even more filth and "untouchable" offerings leftover from their rituals. And she is the only one who cleans it away. She is a living Mātaṅgī, I think to myself. Mātaṅgī is one of the Mahāvidyās who is offered leftovers and all that is deemed taboo in orthodox culture. Despite her outspoken annoyance, She seems to have resigned herself to her duties at this temple to Mā. I want to know about the rituals and the people who come here. "They have parties each night." My translator tells me. "Parties?! What kind of parties? Can anyone participate?"I ask. Neither of them answers me. I wonder if these parties are actually Tantric rituals where wine and other substances are used in sexual rites.

We sit in silence for some time. I feel the fierce stillness of Kālī. My companion tells me she feels completely possessed by Kālī. I ask her how it feels being at this Kālī shrine compared to the numerous other sites we have visited. "I saw Kālī's eyes see me. . . . Kālī saw me. I mean, She saw my soul. That is the difference." She tells me. She is describing darśan. To see and be seen by the deity. Although she is not aware of this concept, she has fully experienced it. She feels changed. She tells me she asked Kālī for protection and blessings for her friends. She said she whispered the name of each of them for Kālī. "I can ask Her to protect, serve and guide these women. And Her eyes told me She will."

The Power and Significance of Female Collectives

Groups of women bonding together over a cause, purpose, or passion have always existed. Women's councils, caucuses, organizations most often focus on providing care, compassion and workable solutions to the injustice and violence that riddle this world. The Śakti that builds within such female communities magnifies the creative potential women have on an individual level. Today, more and more people are recognizing the need not only for Divine Female wisdom but also the participation and knowledge of women working together to help us find alternative solutions to the political, economic, humanitarian and environmental crises on this planet.

In looking for new models of female power, we can turn to the past as well as unorthodox practices that still take place in the East today. The power of the female group is a central aspect of worship within Kaula and Śākta Tantra traditions. The earliest roots on the Indian subcontinent point to circles of stones that have been coated with vermilion paste, blood, or red fruit juice. These places are called māīthan, place of the spirit of Māī, the mother. They are also associated with the Mātṛkās or Mother Goddesses. Often these Goddess stones are found at crossroads or some other geographically auspicious place that holds millennia of Mother worship energy.

Worshiping Goddess in aniconic forms as a tree or stone is an ancient practice and demonstrates the longevity of the place. The rajasic or passionate sexual nature of Goddess is also worshiped at single stones embedded in city streets. Reverence has been given to these stones for millennia. In the Kathmandu Valley they are called *dhokas* or gateway, suggesting their connection with the yoni as sacred gateway of life and death. The Mātṛkās, Māīs, Ajimās, and Tantric Goddess Mātaṅgī are all propitiated at these stones with offerings of menstrual blood, birthing blood and anything that is deemed polluting within orthodox culture. Mātaṅgī is one of the ten Mahāvidyās or Tantric Goddesses of spiritual liberation. She is an ancient elephant-headed Goddess who is the likely antecedent of the now masculinized deity Ganeṣa. The dhokasas well as crossroads serve as focal points of worship of these Goddesses. In the Kathmandu Valley one will often find a triangular hole marked with red—symbolic of the yoni[2]—carved into the nearest wall next to the dhoka ever reminding us of the female sexual force behind all existence.

Honoring the female sexual and creative force is continuously evident in collectives of female Goddesses. The Sapta and Aṣṭa Mātṛkās (seven and eight Mother Goddesses) are aspects of the Great Goddess Durgā and come to Her aid in the battle against the demons. They are feared and respected for their elemental natures and life-giving and death-wielding powers. They appear to us in groups of both seven and eight. The number seven is a sacred and significant number in many ancient and spiritual traditions. It is a way of ordering the universe: seven musical notes, seven colors, seven days of the week, seven cakras (energy centers), seven-hundred verses of the *Devī Māhātmya* and so on. Eight is another important numerological symbol. It relates to the union of sky and earth, the cosmological concept of above and below, and also the four cardinal directions and intermediary points. Whether the Mātṛkās are worshiped in a collective of seven or eight varies from region to region. Katherine Anne Harper's book, *The Iconography of the Saptamatrikas: Seven Hindu Goddesses of Spiritual Transformation,* traces their origin to the Pleiades, a constellation of seven stars known as seven sisters, that perhaps influenced beliefs around the agricultural cycle and its relationship to the female in the Saraswati Valley Civilization.[3]

During certain rites of the festival, some will say the eight Mātṛkās are being worshiped, while others will refer to this collective of Goddesses as the nine Durgās or Navadurgās. This is because the Mātṛkās are sometimes worshiped interchangeably with the Navadurgās. We will look closely at the legend and function of the nine Durgās in Day Nine. Why these Goddesses are often conflated perhaps speaks to the syncretism of localized Goddesses into brahmanized ones that occurred over the ages. It also reflects the inhabitants' understanding of the inseparable nature of the Divine from functions of time, space, and protection as these Goddesses rule these realms.

There are eight Mātṛkās shrines, one in each of the cardinal directions and intermediary direction points surrounding the city of Bhaktapur, just outside a former city wall. While one finds shrines to the Mātṛkās at major and minor Goddess temples throughout the city of Bhaktapur and the Kathmandu Valley, Durgā's tutelary role is again emphasized in the placement of the Mātṛkās' shrines around Bhaktapur. Bhaktapur is a world heritage site, which has allowed for remnants of earlier cultural and religious practices and worship to remain relatively undisturbed. Nevertheless, do the eight Mātṛkā shrines that surround the medieval valley city of Bhaktapur in Nepal predate the development of this medieval city itself? Or, was the city built within the invisible boundaries that they protect? Is the natural aniconic presence of Goddesses at these sites evidence of thousands of years of worship and devotion?

When I visited each of the Mātṛkā shrines on my pilgrimage in 2006, I noticed how each site has either some or several of the following characteristics in common with ancient Goddess sites throughout South Asia: a tree or trees as a focal site of worship, a location near a river or stream or small body of water, single or multiple stones that the locals call Goddesses, a location on a hilltop and/or at the edge of the agricultural field or forest, or at a cremation ground. Whether these Goddesses' peripheral location is indicative of their history, or is a response to their antinomian nature is not clear. If we take the Tantric perspective, it is probably both. While the Mātṛkās are especially significant to Tantric rites in general and seem to be more "accepted" as part of the complex Hindu and Buddhist pantheon of deities in the Valley by the masses during the Durgā Festival, they are mostly propitiated and tolerated by orthodox society as an untamable elemental force that deserves recognition. Only such wrathful and terrifying Goddesses have the power to keep untamable supernatural and elemental forces that threaten the stability of the city inhabitants at bay. Let's turn now to the nature, characteristics, and function of the Mātṛkās and explore how and why they have been embedded in the Valley's sacred landscape for millennia.

The Mātṛkās

The Mātṛkās are said to dwell in trees, open spaces, crossroads, caves, cemeteries, mountains and waterfalls. All the natural places where they are believed to reside represent the unbridled powers of Mother Nature. Within villages, towns and cities, the peripheral location of the Mātṛkās' outer shrines emphasizes their role in representing and protecting that which "borders on the outside."[4] The Mātṛkās represent the chaotic, wild, and dangerous forces of nature that lie beyond the city's borders and threaten its survival, yet are vital aspects of cyclical existence. Although these Goddesses can be wrathful and destructive, they also offer protection. Perhaps most significantly they portray the "hinterland of moral community,"[5] and serve as a representation of the forces of the universe that threaten moral order. For this reason, they rule over all that is considered polluting within orthodox traditions: blood from pregnancy or menstruation, extramarital sex, excrement, urine, sexual body fluids, and death. Yet, because these powers and forces are real, they cannot be totally subdued, so practices in which attempts are made to subdue and propitiate these Goddesses take place.

One must ask why such vital expressions of human experience have been demonized as polluted and forbidden. Is it because many of these "pollutants" are related to inherent natural female power? How is it that in this day and age they are feared and believed to upset the moral established *patrilineal* order? It is curious that one of the Kaula epithets of Goddess is Kulāgamā, "She whose issue of blood gives rise to the clan."[6] In Bhaktapur, an important medieval and Tantric city in the Kathmandu Valley, the urban layout has been divided into districts that are organized according to one's clan.[7] These districts are called *twa,* which means branch of a tree and figuratively refers to the female clan lineage. The term *mātwa* is used for the larger districts.[8] Trees embody the Yakṣī spirits or Grāma Devīs, elemental Goddesses that are related to the Mātṛkās and Yoginīs. It is interesting that the larger areas are referred to as *mā*-twa. Perhaps in earlier times the clans were matrilineal, as seems possible due this connection of twa and Śākta ideology.

In the center of the community is the Goddess Tripurāsundarī, a manifestation of Durgā in Her playful, sexual and blissful form. This Goddess embodies all the other Goddesses. Other Goddesses are said to be aspects of Her, and Tripurāsundarī, like Durgā, is known as the one and the many. In some villages, such as Bhaktapur, the houses and placement of shrines and other ancient Mother sites geographically form a maṇḍala, a sacred geometric diagram that is expressive of the cosmic whole. According to Nandu Menon, in ancient matriarchal India a different Mātṛkā was worshiped in each individual house. The eight Mātṛkās governed the eight sections of the house in the Vastu tradition.[9] Vastu is the Indian expression of Feng Shui. It consists of aligning the energies of certain elements within the physical realm with the unseen forces that govern that psychic space. By working with certain energetic principles and techniques which pacify the tension between opposites, Vastu and the Mātṛkās bring harmony to the home. It is a way to maintain a "balanced relationship between the different spheres, human and superhuman or godly. It is believed that this relationship needs to be continuously cultivated and not taken for granted or, worse yet, spoiled with the possibility of rectification."[10] The consecration of the dwelling space is one of many microcosmic expressions of Durgā pacifying the demons on earth and providing protection.

By looking at the spatial layout of the city of Bhaktapur and the location of the Mātṛkā and other Goddess shrines, ones sees a pattern that is mirrored in other references to the physical and subtle realities of the community. Much of the language and references refer to the city or village as lotus, and therefore yoni—because lotus is often synonymous with yoni. In the ancient past the village itself was abstractly conceived as the yoni of Goddess. However, why has this consciousness not remained? In a personal conversation with Amarananda Bhairavan, author of *Kālī's Odiyya*, Bhairavan provides one possible reason for the shift. As nomadic peoples entered the village, they were brought into the system of Goddess worship through various means. The family rituals and devotion to such Goddesses were carried out of the home and into the village. As new patrilineal practices began to take over and replace the old matrilineal ones, the Mātṛkās moved to the periphery of the village in order to keep wild and chaotic forces at bay.

To the citizens of Bhaktapur and other cities and villages, these untamable "demons" inhabit the world outside their structured boundaries. They are the uninvited forces of nature: natural catastrophes such as storms, floods, hurricanes, etc. as well as various illnesses that afflict their "clan" and steal the life force from them. However, protection from such life experiences had always been one of the Mātṛkās' functions. In fact, in the ancient worldview, these Goddesses *brought* the disease or disaster, *were* the disease or disaster, and *removed* the disease or disaster. They were inseparable from these natural experiences. As elemental forces indispensable to this existence, the new patrilineal order knew that these Goddesses would not completely disappear. They needed to be placated, invoked during various rites and passages, and honored for the domains of existence over which they rule. The Mātṛkās speak to a primal reality of our existence and represent all that the orthodox and puritanical traditions consider taboo or threatening to civil order. They would not simply go away, and practitioners still familiar with more ancient forms of worship recognized the power of these Goddesses that can be utilized to achieve various means.

> A particular Tantric way of making use of this world for supramundane ends is the ritual and soteriological use of things that are normally forbidden, that is the transgression of norms. The main reason for this antinomian behavior appears to be the wish, by so doing, to participate in the dark, chaotic, undisciplined, and very powerful forces that are normally repressed and kept outside the pure, orderly circumscribed world of the Brahmin. . . . Such transgressive practices include the transgressive use of sex.[11]

Under the brahmanic sanskritized systems, male lines were centralized and maintained, while women's status and inherent powers were relegated to the periphery. Through ritual practices around these Goddesses the vices of the city inhabitants or their participation in so-called "polluting" activities is reconciled and absolved. These forces are dangerous and fearsome because they threaten to upset the contained "order" of the city, yet they are also viewed as vital. Natural processes such as birth, sex, menstruation, and pregnancy are integral aspects of the natural cycle of existence, yet the potential "polluting" power they contain must be subdued by the patriarchal order. While women were the bearers of these "polluting" experiences, the Mātṛkās were the unseen female forces that ruled these realms. Thus, the female on both the physical and spiritual plane contains elemental powers that must be subdued and contained within patriarchal structures in order for patriarchy to exist.

The worship of these Goddesses, especially as it is still expressed in contemporary village festivals, cannot be separated from these Goddesses' responsibilities around pregnant women, childbirth, and protection of new life. Therefore, many village rituals, particularly during the Durgā Pūjā, emulate this relationship between the nine lunar months of pregnancy and the nine-month agricultural and monsoonal cycles.

As Goddesses of the Elements, the Mātṛkās have a direct relationship with rain. Dancing to bring on rain has long been an important ritual in many Native American and indigenous people's cultures, and is one of the central features during Durgā's main festival, Navrātrī or Durgā Pūjā. Shamans are known to change or invoke certain weather, and these Goddesses share this capability.

The Dance of the Mātṛkās

The dynamic nightly invocation of the Mātṛkās in Bhaktapur reveals another important aspect of these Goddesses' function. There is considerable overlap between the functions and rituals of the fierce Mātṛkās, or Mother Goddesses, and the Nine Durgās in the Kathmandu Valley. In addition to their governance over health and disease and birth and death, they serve to demarcate the boundaries of space and time as well as between order and chaos. Rituals summoning and celebrating these Goddesses' tutelary governance take place throughout the year, but perhaps the most significant rituals are the sacred dances that begin during the Durgā Pūjā. The ritual dances of these Goddesses recall the art of ritual dance and possession that is a common aspect of village life in many parts of Asia and also of "groups of shamans of the hill tribes of Nepal."[12] Many vestiges of shamanic ritual are still evident in the Dashain festival, as it is known in Kathmandu, and Mohani as it is called in neighboring Bhaktapur. For example, trance possession of the deity; the use of masks; healing herbs and intoxicating substances in the rituals; rattles, horns and bells to attract and ward off spirits; and the aid of power animals or the spirit of the animal's vehicle that each Mātṛkās is associated with. In fact, many of the social and spiritual characteristics of the class of men (guthi) who invoke the Goddesses during the Pūjā "irresistibly reminds us of the groups of shamans of the hill tribes of Nepal."[13]

On each day during the festival one of the Mother Goddesses is worshipped. Historian Robert Levy writes, "The mandalic pīthas are required foci of attention and worship for families during important rites of passage, and of the city as a whole during Dashain." On the first day of the festival the male dancers are expected to shave their heads bald, purify their bodies through a bathing ritual, then go to the shrine of the Mātṛkā they are going to dance to ask for Her blessing. Before the performances begin, the dancers must invoke the deity at Her shrine to come and dance through them. Trance possession is central to Tantric practices. The dancers recite mantras at their respective Mātṛkā's shrine to ask for Her permission to dance

Her energy. Transgressive rites, such as alcohol consumption, animal sacrifice, and perhaps even sexual practices all lead to spirit possession and are part of the preparatory rites at the shrines. In performing such specialized and antinomian rituals at the shrine of the Goddess, the dancer becomes possessed with Her energy. These dances begin with much shaking, yelling, and frenzied movements, which signifies to the inhabitants of the city that the bodies of these men are housing the elemental forces of the Goddesses.

Every night in Durbar, or the main square of Bhaktapur and another medieval Valley city, Patan, the masked Mātṛkās dance is held close to midnight. The following twelve deities are represented by the masks: Mahakālī or Cāmuṇḍā, Kaumārī, Vārāhī, Brāhmanī, Vaiṣṇavī, Indrānī, Maheśvarī, Bhairavī, Seto, Simā, Ganeśa, and Dumā. The latter five extra deities are protective deities that accompany the group during the nightly ritual. They are unique to Nepal. Throughout India, many of the names will vary reflecting regional differences; however, the essence of this group, especially as qualities of the evolution of our consciousness through life experience, is evident in the following brief descriptions of a more generalized collective of these Goddesses.

Brāhmanī, Mātṛkā of the East carries a mala or rosary, and a sacred pot. In addition to Her accoutrements and goose animal mount, Brāhmanī shares many attributes with Saraswatī. Her puranic name associates Her with the god Brahmā. Brāhmanī is a generative Goddess. She is worshiped on the first day of the festival as Brāhmanī or Her Navadurgā form, Brahmāyaṇī. She has three faces that remind us of the integration of mind, body, and spirit, past, present and future. She is the immeasurable power that gives birth to all creation.

Maheśvarī, Mātṛkā of the Southeast, is worshiped on the second day of the festival. Like Śiva or Maheśvara, who is Her namesake, Maheśvarī holds a three-pronged trident—each prong holds the essence of a different guna (sattva, rajas, tamas). She also carries a drum and beats the rhythms of destruction and creation. She rides a bull, the vehicle of Lord Śiva, and is invoked for steadfastness and security. Maheśvarī carries the powers to unite and dissolve all oppositions.

Kaumārī is the guardian of the South. Her name relates Her to the Kumārī, and Kaumārī Herself is sometimes conceived as a Virgin Goddess. She carries a javelin and spear that pierce the veil of ignorance and delusion. She cuts through the māya (illusion) of this reality and helps us to come back to our virginal natures in that the original meaning of virgin is whole unto oneself. Kaumārī rides a peacock, whose many colored feather eyes symbolize the beauty that is inherent even in what is most poisonous. The vibrant eyes on a peacock's feathers come from the poisons that this bird transmutes. Kaumārī teaches honesty and perseverance.

Vaiṣṇavī, Mātṛkā of the Southwest comes riding on Her garuḍa (mythological birdlike creature) reminding us of the lived reality of myth. Connected to Viṣṇu,

God of Maintenance and Preservation, Vaiṣṇavī governs the earth. She carries a conch and discus. She embodies sustainability and nurturance and as protector of the earth and physical body, reminds us of our inner greatness and beauty.

The boar-headed Vārāhī presides over the West. She also takes Her place in each of the four directions on the boundaries of the Kathmandu Valley (where She is known as the four Vārāhīs). She also has Her own cult following both as Vārāhī and Vajravārāhī. She has a forest temple on the greater outskirts of Patan and is worshiped in other temples within the various Valley cities and in Orissa, India. As Goddess of Justice and Protection She grants loyalty, discrimination, and passion. She wears a garland of skulls as a reminder to always align with our divine self.

Indrānī is a Mātṛkā of the Northwest She appears on Her elephant and like the God Indra is associated with rain clouds. She is a purifying and transformative force. She carries a whip that removes false perceptions. She teaches how to overcome all forms of betrayal and deception. She is endurance, compassion, and flexibility.

Cāmuṇḍā, fierce Mātṛkā of the North, has an emaciated and withering form that reminds us of the transience of life. Her piercing stare instills fear and awe. She promises freedom from all that binds us once we allow ourselves to detach from that which does not nourish us. This Mother of disintegration and transformation grants liberation from our pain and suffering. She rides the owl of death, creature of the night that sees in the dark and has 360 degree perception. Cāmuṇḍā has Her own following and can be found on hundreds, if not thousands of temples in India and Nepal. As one of the fiercest forms of Kālī, She plays a significant role in the Durgā myth and festival rituals.

Mahālakṣmī in Her Mātṛkā form in Nepal protects the Northeast. She grants abundance, brilliance, vibrancy, sweetness, and love. She eases troubled minds and hearts with Her love, grace and peace. Her lotus reminds us of the spiritual gifts She bestows when one taps into Her powers to grow out of the darkest and murkiest places.

These are eight of the forms of Goddess Durgā in the Kathmandu Valley. And on several nights during the festival, they are invoked and danced. In 2000 I was present for one of the midnight dances in Patan.

Before the dances the presiding priests offer a goat sacrifice to Bhairava, the fierce form of Durgā's consort, Śiva. The dancers gather round to witness the ritual although many of them cannot stand on their own and are held up by attendants. The combination of the weight of enormous clay masks, accoutrements specific to each Mātṛkā, and the ritual substances and practices that have altered their consciousness since dawn make it difficult to stand on their own—until they go more fully into the bhava (mood) of the Goddess. Each dancer is dressed in a long black cotton gown with draping sleeves and wears a striped apron across his midline. The masks have been painted a different color depending on which Goddess they embody—yellow for Brāhmanī, red for Kaumārī, black for Cāmuṇḍā. As we witness the preliminary rituals, some of the masks must be more securely fastened to the dancers' necks and shoulders for they swing precariously with every movement the dancers make. The attendants take on this duty in addition to keeping the men on their feet. These larger-than-life and quite frightening masks tower over the puppetlike bodies of the dancers giving them a formidable, supernatural appearance. Each mask is decorated with geometric Tantric symbols: concentric circles, triangles and mysterious squiggly lines that when meditated upon are said to induce any practitioner into a deeper state of consciousness. As Tantric priests chant and recite prayers, some of the participants ring bells or bang drums so that the dancers will enter more deeply into a trancelike state.

After all the pushing and shoving to get as close to the center where they will perform as possible, it is surprising that the crowd of about one hundred people barely moves nor breathes as they wait for the men to become fully possessed by the Mātṛkās. I watch the dancers quiver and shake, each of them taking their turn in the center. They call out mantras and groan, growl, and cry out. They stomp their feet and twirl in circles. Some imbibe substances, others smoke pipes and still others blow conch shells. Each act pulls them deeper into the bhava (mood) of the Mātṛkā they are invoking. As each dancer becomes more entranced with the Goddess' energy, the Śakti rises throughout the complex. The energy of the courtyard is electric! The fervent devotion and faith of the Nepali people is palpable. The presence of these mysterious forces is awe-inspiringly real and tangible. The dancers move with wild and chaotic gestures and dance steps. I watch as the dancers move around the circle, sometimes scaring those nearest to them and causing them to back up and cry out. A mixture of fear and awe is in the air. Their presence is far from gentle and soothing, but I, like the others, stand captivated by this unpredictable and intense performance of fierce Goddess energies.

When I first witnessed the Mātṛkā dances in the Kathmandu Valley, I wondered why men would be dancing as Mother Goddesses. Men dressing as Goddesses seemed to be a transgressive act. Could it be that men are the main participants in this part of the ritual because they want to invoke and embody the power of the Goddess? Or, was this yet another female tradition that has been co-opted by men? If women naturally possess Śakti, then perhaps these men take part in the ritual in order to invoke the Goddess into themselves? How does the presence of male dancers embodying the Mother Goddess affect the community, particularly in a culture that today is influenced by the patriarchy?

Cross-dressing is not an unusual occurrence in tribal communities. Anthropological studies describe numerous cultures where gender roles transcend the traditional boundaries of femininity and masculinity.[14] Citing Marjorie Garber's theories on gender fluidity as outlined in her book, *Vested Interests: Cross-Dressing and Cultural Anxiety*, Vicki Noble notes the liminal nature of such cultural figures "who inhabit and incarnate the margin."[15] The power of such figures "disrupt(s), expose(s), and challenge(s), by showing the boundaries or borders to be permeable."[16] Therefore, the role of the transvestite, in some ways, is similar to the contemporary marginality and transgressive nature of the Mātṛkās and other untamable collectives of Goddesses like them. Curiously, in Nepal it is men who take on the elemental, paradoxical nature of Goddess within the more orthodox context of ritual. As Barbara Tedlock describes in *The Woman in the Shaman's Body*: "shamanic transvestitism offers some clues to beliefs. . . about shamans, animal spirits, and the manipulation of their energies."[17] In such cultures there seem to be more fluid notions around gender than there are in the West, or even other parts of the modern world. Tedlock notes that "some researchers have suggested that a shaman is neither masculine nor feminine but rather a mediator between the sexes."[18] She goes on to say that "it is not membership within any one of these gender categories per se that is directly linked to shamanic practice but rather the transformation of gender or the frequent gender switching, bending, blending, or reversing that is important and that enables shamans to manipulate potent cosmic powers during rituals."[19]

Although the Mātṛkā dancers are male, trance possession is quite common to women and is a viable sphere of female power and authority. While possession can occur spontaneously or at will, some women become charged with Goddess then act as the oracle for the community. They become possessed by a Māī or Ajimā or specific Mātṛkā or other Goddesses. It is in this function as healer and oracle that women receive status and respect. They are viewed as a mediator between worlds. In a culture that still recognizes the potency and influence of unseen beings, some women, albeit very few, are able to have agency. These women's non-rational ways of relating to the world, of knowing the deeper, often hidden meanings behind illness and other life events and experiences has a power that is no longer afforded women, especially in the West. It is interesting to consider that women never become possessed by the spirit of a male god.

According to Angela Dietrich in her study on Tantric healing in Kathmandu, the phenomenon of possession or trance was noted to be more frequent amongst chiefly female Parvatiyas, than among any other group. These lower caste women are afforded more status and spiritual authority than their higher caste sisters. Accessing elemental energies and experiencing the enlightenment these Goddesses offer is open to them and "the importance of the human body (is recognized) as the principle instrument for liberation, rather than an impediment as propounded by other traditions."[20] In her book, *Pure Lust, Elemental Feminist Philosophy*, Mary Daly examines how women's elemental "principalities and powers" get tamed. It is not only men who are the perpetrators, but also women who have become victims of the male agenda. Daly purports that:

> to be actively potent is to realize/release that which is most dreadful to the impotent priests, the prurient patriarchs-our participation in Be-ing. This is Dreadful also to women who have not yet Realized their own powers. Since no one has fully Realized her potency, emergence of our own powers is terrifying to all women. In this situation, it is predictable the priestly predators will attempt to use fear-filled women as powers holding down Elemental female powers.[21]

Daly describes "lusty" women as erratic in the original sense of the word: "having no fixed course, wandering." She writes that such women are wanderlusty and are known for "our resistance to being fixed."[22] If more women tapped into these natural powers that the Mātṛkās exemplify, if more women recognized the potency of their intuition as expressed through their bodies and dream life, what kind of impact would this kind of knowing have on our own lives, and the world?

Iconographical representations and mythical narrations of the Mātṛkās almost always depict them in a group with their distinguishing animal and bird mounts and faces. For example, the Mātṛkā Brāhmanī rides a goose; Indrānī, an elephant; Vārāhī has the head of a boar; Vaiṣṇavī, the garuda or mythological eagle, and so forth. These animal life forms the Mātṛkās are associated with are similar to the concept of power animals or totems in Native American and other indigenous traditions. The intrinsic energy of the plant, bird, or animal helps the deity to achieve whatever goal or task She is focused on. It may carry the deity between the worlds, or serve as a metaphor for some quality that needs to be transmuted or transformed.

Indeed, the forces that these Goddesses carry and the animals and birds that assist them can be considered shamanic. Relating with other life forms and opening to alternate modes of consciousness is instructive, mind expanding and life enriching. Furthermore, it provides a deeper, more integrative understanding of our own lives and our place within the universe. In all likelihood, the primal nature of these Goddesses was modeled on living women who did spiritual practices, performed healings, knew the medicinal properties of herbs and plants, communicated with nonhuman animals, and performed rituals around birth and death for their communities. The word *kula*, as well as being a concrete substance, namely, female menstrual blood and sexual fluids, also refers to groups of animals or human communities that descend through the female line. This makes sense when we consider how we all come through a woman's body and are conceived through an integration of female and male sexual fluids. Therefore, we find kulas in the collective forms of Durgā as the Mātṛkās which historically can be traced to the Kaula tradition which flourished from the 1st–5th centuries and evolved into the Śākta and later Tantric traditions. The ancient sexual rituals provide opportunities to change our consciousness. The eight Mātṛkās exemplify the varied nature of female experience. What would it be like to be part of an awakened female collective-a group of women who are conscious of the mysterious workings of Goddess throughout our lives? When we perform rituals that tap into Her cyclical nature and allow Her energies to flow through and shape our lives, a different consciousness emerges. A Śākta consciousness speaks to connection, understanding, and completion. It grants wisdom and bliss. It is a consciousness that is ancient and embedded in the cycles of earth and cosmos and has been revered as Goddess, Mother, or Grandmother for millennia.

Considering the prevalence of groupings of Goddesses throughout the Valley (the seven or eight Mātṛkās, the nine Durgās, the five Kumārīs and as we shall see in Day Six the 64 or 81Yoginis), perhaps these Goddesses have something to teach us about the power of women in groups, about the individual, yet collective female nature. The Mātṛkās are Goddesses who, to me, embody the full spectrum of the female psyche. They are fierce, yet beautiful, wrathful, yet compassionate, at times grotesque and even sensual. They do not fit into any prescribed notions of femaleness and embody a daring, radical, almost ruthless spirit—teaching us to go after what we want, how to confront any obstacle that appears on our path and how to leap with blissful abandon towards our deepest desires.

When women who are consciously doing Tantric or Śākta practices get together a very sacred and powerful energy begins to flow. It is primal in nature, fierce, seductive, invincible, and sensual. Women who are open in this way cannot tolerate the exploitation and severe abuse of women that is endemic to the majority of contemporary cultures on this planet. Nevertheless, there are not many of us who know we can take back our power of choice, especially spiritual choice. Women who live alternative lives, who remain authentic to our own desires are too often ostracized or even feared. We live peripheral lives on the fringes of society and like the Aṣṭa Mātṛkās within the orthodox Hindu tradition are marginalized because of our sexually empowered and formidable natures. Yet, despite the marginalization of female collectives, in the Tantric perspective there is always power to be found in what appears to be challenging and difficult. Ultimately these Goddesses offer us guidance and solace. They show us a path of female autonomy and self-determined sexuality.

Notes

1. One of the ten Mahāvidyās, Fierce Tantric Goddesses of Spiritual Transformation and Liberation. *Bagalāmukhī* is the crane-headed Goddess.

2. Gerhard Auer and Niels Gutschow, *Bhaktapur: Gestalt, Funktionen und Religiőse Symbolik Einer Nepalische Stadt Im Vorindustriellen Entwicklungsstadium* (Darmstadt: Technische Hochscule, 1974.

3. See Katherine Anne Harper, *The Iconography of the Saptamatrikas: Seven Hindu Goddesses of Spiritual Transformation* (Lewiston, New York: Edwin Mellin Press, 1989).

4. Robert I. Levy, *Mesocosm: Hinduism and the Organization of a Traditional Newar City in Nepal* (Delhi: Motilal Bandarsidass Publishers, 1990), 284.

5. Ibid., 157.

6. David Gordon White, *Kiss of the Yoginī: "Tantric Sex" in Its South Asian Context* (Chicago: University of Chicago Press, 2003), 79.

7. Levy, Mesocosm, 193.

8. Ibid., 182.

9. Nandu Menon, personal conversation with the author, January 1, 2006.

10. Angela Dietrich, *Tantric Healing in the Kathmandu Valley* (Delhi: Book Faith India, 1988), 44.

11. André Padoux, "What Do We Mean By Tantrism?" in *The Roots of Tantra, eds.*Katherine Anne Harper and Robert L. Brown (Albany: State University of New York Press, 2002), 21.

12. Gérard Toffin, "A Wild Goddess Cult in Nepal. The Navadurgā of Theco Village (Kathmandu Valley)," in *Wild Goddesses in India and Nepal: Proceedings of an International Symposium Berne and Zurich, November, 1994*. eds. Axel Michaels, Cornelia Vogelsanger, Annette Wilke (Bern: Peter Lang, 1994), 249.

13. Ibid.

14. Vicki Noble, *Double Goddess. Women Sharing Power* (Rochester, Vermont: Bear & Company, 2003), 225-227.

15. Ibid., 228.

16. Ibid.

17. Barbara Tedlock, *The Woman in the Shaman's Body: Reclaiming the Feminine in Religion and Medicine* (New York: Bantam, 2005), 250.

18. Ibid.

19. Ibid.

20. Robert Levy in Angela Dietrich, *Tantric Healing in the Kathmandu Valley* (Delhi: Book Faith India, 1988), 18.

21. Mary Daly, *Pure Lust: Elemental Feminist Philosophy* (Boston: Beacon Press, 1984), 188-189.

22. Ibid., x-xi.

day six
the yoginī: goddess and priestess of erotic arts and mysteries

As I have wandered along brick and dirt streets passing temple after shrine after temple, I have marveled at the decorative, natural and spiritual symbols that pervade every inch of the Valley. Much of my time has been spent in contemplation of these symbols' sacred relation to various rituals and accoutrements during the Durgā Pūjā. Sacred pots, garlands of red hibiscus, orange and yellow marigolds, ruby-colored bangles, combs, vegetative imagery, triangular openings painted red, holy cows and ravens, serpents, tigers, boars, and countless other animals and creatures, spirals, circles, stone yonis and lingams all emanate sacred wisdom. Every rock, creature, and physical structure whether for dwelling, work, or worship is imbued with Śakti. Each is an integral part of an enchanted world called Nepalmaṇḍala where the profane and the sacred commingle and merge.

I travel as a Yoginī, a devotee, practitioner and attendant of Goddess Durgā, who in some texts is called the Queen of the Yoginīs. In my pilgrimages to India, I have found myself drawn to Yoginī temples where the energy and depictions of the sacred female reminded me of the kulas of Goddesses I have encountered in Nepal. The powerful female images that abound in both the Kathmandu Valley and Yoginī sites in Orissa and Madhya Pradesh suggest a lineage of female-centered beliefs and practices on the South Asian subcontinent that are instructive to the contemporary woman and man. At these temples we find women and Goddesses who exude an aura of self-sovereignty, self-respect and authority. While these female figures present alternative role models for women in the West, they also have much to teach the male practitioner about the sacred power of the female sex and how millennia of misogyny have not only limited and oppressed their mothers, sisters, daughters, nieces, lovers and wives, but also prevented them from fully understanding their own "feminine" and "masculine" power in a balanced world. Traditional expectations and definitions of female and male-ness are ultimately limiting to both sexes.

In the Tantric tradition the most devoted practitioners are known as Yoginīs and Yogis.[1] For the *yogin* (male or female practitioner) every place, every experience, and every encounter provides an opportunity for expanding our consciousness and for understanding our place in the universal scheme of existence. Here in California, yoga in terms of the physical asana practice is a growing trend, and fortunately more and more teachers are incorporating other yogic practices such as prāṇayama (breath work), meditation and mantra into their practices. However, it is important to clarify that while yogic practitioners in the West may refer to themselves as yogis, not everyone who does a yoga practice is a Yogi or Yoginī in the devotional and esoteric sense I am referring to in this chapter. There is much complexity in the ritual practices and also much power that unfolds and expands in one's consciousness within esoteric circles of this tradition. This is not a path one can tread lightly. As true teachers know, certain practices that heighten awareness and stretch consciousness are not freely given out to anyone who joins the class or ritual. Because one can find details of the yogis' (male practitioner) experience in most of the Tantric and Yogic texts that have thus far been written or translated, and perhaps, more importantly because I identify with the Yoginī, this chapter will describe what I have come to know from experience and research about the path of the Yoginī. Hers is a life that demands fortitude, resilience, love and compassion.

The Yoginī

The path of the Yoginī is one of unconventionality. The Yoginī is the artist, the enchantress, and the autonomous woman, who enjoys being in relation to men, but does not necessarily seek marriage or partnership. The Yoginī is an alternative role model for women in the West, whether they decide to have children or not, but wish to live outside societal stereotypes and conventions. Yoginīs of past and present are women who choose a spiritual, social and cultural status that is outside the consensus patriarchal culture. Yoginīs are "women who dare to define themselves in relation to the metaphysical rather than the social."[2] A Yoginī is sexually and spiritually empowered. She is a shaman and a keeper of the mysteries of birth, menstruation, sex and death.

In one of the only and most comprehensive English works on the Yoginī, *Yoginī Cult and Temples*, Vidya Dehejia describes the various categories or definitions of the Yoginī. The Yoginī is Goddess Herself as well as practitioner, devotee and attendant of Goddess. Yoginīs cannot be pinned to one particular quality, rather, like the shaman, their natures are fluid. Yoginīs are wrathful and sensual, ferocious and seductive, furious and graceful. Each Yoginī is a universe unto her self. Most likely her attributes and iconography have been modeled after living women from the lineage. Yoginī practices obviously vary, but many carry a central theme of practitioners overcoming limitations within and around themselves in order to achieve a state of non-dual awareness and union with the Divine. In her article, "Probing the Mysteries of the Hirapur Yoginis," Elinor Gadon suggests, "Perhaps the key to the mysteries of the yoginis (at Hirapur) lives in the fierceness of the female whose body is the medium and the metaphor through which the power of life is transformed."[3]

Information on Yoginī cults and temples is difficult to find. According to Dehejia, "neither iconographers nor historians of Indian religion have paid any attention."[4] One must turn to manuscripts and the temple complexes and sculptures that remain. In the literature Yoginīs are sometimes described as human witches, or as Goddesses, or attendants of Goddess. There are also eight Yoginīs of astrology: Maṅgalā, Piṅgalā, Dhanyā, Brahmarī, Bhadrikā, Ulakā, Siddhidā, and Sankatā. Each is associated with one of the nine grahas, or planets. The stellar positions of these Yoginī-governed planets at birth gives specific details about the fate of the individual. Consulting the position of these stellar Yoginīs before a pilgrimage or any serious undertaking was common practice in the past and texts outline prayers, rituals and ways to appease these Goddesses.[5]

The Yoginī is sometimes perceived as a sorceress or a witch. Legends tell of her abilities to turn humans into animals. Several such stories speak of a magic thread that is tied around the Yoginī's lover's neck. He is then turned into a parrot or monkey and is forced to remain in that form until she sexually desires him and breaks the spell to make love to his human form.[6] Other tales tell of flying women (Dākinīs) or women who suddenly vanish in the night. The Yoginīs always meet in circles and sometimes do rituals with human corpses. The consumption of human flesh seems to be a common theme in the manuscripts and paintings of the Yoginīs between the ninth and sixteenth centuries. It is said to have given them supernatural powers.

Another grouping of Yoginīs is said to reside in our cakras. Their names are: Dākinī, Rākinī, Lākinī, Kākinī, Sākinī, Hākinī, Yākinī. Each of the seven cakras is presided over by one of these Yoginīs. They work with the subtle energies that travel through the iḍā, pingalā, and ṣushumṇā channels. They are involved in an energetic process of awakening kuṇḍalinī and inducing this energy, which is perceived as Goddess, to travel up our spines to the crown of our heads, where She unites with the Divine energy that is described as Śiva in many of the later Tantric texts.[7] The unification of polar energies is essential to reach a non-dual state of awareness. Moreover, each cakra hosts a specific Yoginī, so the practitioner can experience a kind of bliss and the siddhi or power associated with that Yoginī and cakra. Within Śākta circles, ritual practices invoking the Yoginīs as Goddesses within the stars, cakras, statues and the female body are known to increase Śakti as well as open one to the eight siddhis or special powers.[8] However, the aim of the Yoginī is not to get trapped at the various levels of consciousness along the way, but to reach toward overcoming all dualities and attachments. When Kuṇḍalinī reaches the crown, one's consciousness merges with Śakti and Śiva and a state of pure connection and bliss is experienced.

According to Dehejia, there are only about fourteen known temples to the Yoginīs throughout South Asia; however, there are other sites where worship of the Yoginī is still practiced. "The Kāmākhyā temple in Assam is one of the few Devī shrines where to this day, the daily worship of Devī Kāmākhyā includes the invocation of the 64 Yoginīs."[9] At the temple of the Goddess' yoni, practices including Yoginīs as well as participation by living Yoginīs still exist, suggesting at least 1200 years of continuous Yoginī worship. Given their unconventional status and the esoteric and culturally offensive practices that have been associated with the Yoginīs, one can assume that there are other sites where Yoginīs are and have been worshiped, which have been kept secret from the uninitiated.

Temples to the Yoginīs in India were built between the ninth and sixteenth centuries. Yoginī worship seems to have flourished between the ninth and twelfth centuries. "Royalty was closely connected with the Yoginī cult."[10] Rites were performed to gain territory, subdue one's enemies, expand dynasties, and for all militaristic adventures. These Goddesses were believed to bring fame and invincibility, strength and courage. In addition, they were also associated with all rites of sexual pleasure and love. Worshiping the Yoginīs in human form was important to the rituals. Music, dance, sexuality and the arts are the Yoginīs' domain.

All of the known Yoginī temples are circular, except for two, which are rectangular. I have visited the earliest known temple constructed to the Yoginīs in Khajaraho as well as one of the circular Yoginī temples most visited by Western feminist scholars in Hirapur. One common characteristic between all Yoginī temples is that they are hypaethral or without a roof. Perhaps the Yoginī temples are open to the sky to allow for the nightly ecstatic flights that the lore around the Yoginī cults described. Perhaps these women were divine beings who did fly, or perhaps they flew astrally; either through shifting their consciousness with prāṇayama practices, or through the use of sacred substances. Regardless, the openness of the temples allows for the expansion of energies and a merging of earthly energies with the cosmic energies of the sky.

The circular form of the temples denotes the demarcation of sacred space. Using circles has long been a means to separate mundane from sublime realms. We find other circular structures of the ancient world in the prehistoric stone circles of Avebury and Stonehenge—sites that are also known to have had strong female spiritual leadership. Feminist spirituality practitioners to this day still worship at these sites. Megalithic stone circles are also ancient astrological calendars. I wonder if the aniconic forms of the Matṛkās in the Kathmandu Valley, usually expressed in a full or semicircle could have been an earlier natural form that developed into the hypaethral circular temples we find today. The Matṛkās are each linked to a specific planet and mantra.[11] In Her nine Durgā form they are associated with the seven planets and two nodes of the moon.

Circles are known to be magically protected areas where energy is raised and does not dissipate. A circle symbolizes the sun, moon, eye, the zodiac, time, eternity, nothing and all. It is a shape that "expresses most effectively the complementary concepts of completeness and separateness: complete in itself and separated from everything outside of it. It is a symbol of the self as a self-contained whole."[12] Eight Maṭrkā shrines encircle the city of Bhaktapur in the Kathmandu Valley. The function of the Maṭrkās is to guard the space within the circle. The space within a city, village, Yoginī circle, or circular temple is a place where secret rites also must be protected.

Niches inhabited by Yoginīs in various postures and bhavas (moods or expressions of the divinity) line the inner temple walls and all bear witness to the central altar, which sometimes is inhabited by a fierce form of Śiva. However, the main and central deity of the temple is Durgā. Some of the Yoginīs stand in yogic asanas we practice today, for example: warrior, tree, and mountain pose; others are quite seductive and sensual and express an explicit sexual energy; and still others exude an aura of self-possession, mystery, fulfillment and contentment.

While the Yoginī temple at Hirapur appears circular, it has actually been constructed in the shape of the yoni lingam and the 64 internal shrines represent petals of a lotus, another symbol of the yoni. The structure of the temple walls emulates statues and diagrams of the cosmic stone yoni lingams found in smaller forms throughout the Kathmandu Valley and other Tantric Goddess sites. The round walls of the temple represent the labia of the yoni and the tall rectangular structure in the center of the temple represents the lingam. The circular design of the temple itself is emulated in the cakras or circles/wheels of practitioners both male and female. Circles can indicate movement, and in this context they represent the rajasic or dynamic quality of existence. This yoni-inspired space is as integral to the ritual as are the Yoginīs who come to worship and are worshiped within the temples. The Yogis who participate are called Bhairavas (a fierce form of Śiva). However, according to the texts, women have sexual preference over their consorts. Although each is considered equal, men may not approach the women.[13]

Various yogic practices can help the practitioners in accessing higher realms of awareness. This awareness is liberating and opens one to a very expansive and mystical reality. However, the ritual texts caution: "those who have the capacity for such cakra worship and yet do not perform this ritual will be destroyed by the Yoginīs."[14] Other texts warn that if a sādhaka (practitioner) insults a woman the Yoginīs will be angry. "He may not strike a woman even with a flower, and no matter what fault she may have, he must ignore it and speak only of her virtues."[15] Practices around the Yoginīs express a reverence for the female Divine and the sacred female body. They honor the tremendous power and potential of the female. The *Yoni Patala Tantra* holds women in very high esteem and states that "women are divinity, women are life, women are truly jewels."[16] In other Tantras this sentiment is echoed, "worship carefully a woman or maiden as she is Śakti, sheltered by the Kulas. One should never speak harshly to maidens or women."[17] They continue with statements against any form of violence against women, including threats, and insist that one view women as heaven, dharma, Buddha, Goddess, and the perfection of Wisdom.[18] Many of the Yoginī practices may seem to be a response to the fundamental repressive views around sex and life that the orthodox Hindus hold; however, most Tantric practices, especially the sexual rituals, originated in ancient cultures. Timing the rituals of union to different phases of the moon, the Kaulas would gather at secret locations which ultimately had some sacred relation to Goddess. Cremation grounds, remote temples, forest shrines, river banks, fields and caves all served as the sexual meeting place of Yoginī devotees and practitioners. "Yoginīs of the Kaula Tantric path do not live with any yogi on a permanent basis, but are called upon for ritual on holy days."[19]

The Yoginīs' rites focus on achieving union with the Divine. They involve practices which embrace and take one beyond the paradoxes of life into a state of bodily bliss and clear awareness. Many practices center on the divine union of the yoni and lingam—both through worship of statues of couples in maithuna or interlocked in sexual postures, stone yoni lingam, and the actual act of maithuna between the human Yoginīs and Yogis in the cakra or group. The Yoginī, through the beauty and sexual power of her body initiates males into the secret practices of the cult.[20]

In this tradition, the yoni and lingam symbolically embody complementary energies of existence: tensions such as female and male, death and life, joy and sorrow, wrath and gentleness are honored in the rituals and iconography. The Yoginīs and Yogis enacting the rituals become microcosmic representations of the macrocosmic whole—within the temple and beyond. The mūrti themselves also contain the microcosmic powers and expressions that are the essence of the entire universe. Sexual practices are part of the left-hand path. This is a path where anything considered taboo, threatening, or insulting to the orthodox order is worshiped and honored as Divine.

Left-hand Tantric rituals include doing practices involving the five M's or forbidden substances: *madya* liquor, *mudra* a grain (probably hallucinogenic), *maithuna* sex/sexual fluids, *matsya* fish, *mamsa* flesh/meat. The use of these forbidden substances has a transformative effect on the Yoginīs as it helps "overcome traditional notions of propriety."[21] Worshipping with "polluting" substances allows us to embrace negative conceptions of reality and transmute them into their elemental power. Intoxication is a cherished realm of the Goddess. One of Her epithets in Yoginī cakras is Kādambarī, She who is inordinately fond of wine. She does not judge or deem one reality less significant than the other. She cautions for moderation and balance and teaches that all levels of consciousness are aspects of Her Great Consciousness. The use of wine and sex in these rituals helps participants to recognize their Divinity and affinity with Śiva and Śakti.[22] Intoxicants bring a shift of consciousness that allow one to surrender to various realms of existence and divine states of awareness. Mantras are recited into cups of wine and offered to the Divinity within each human being. The texts state that "more advanced sādhakas (practitioners) may drink up to seven cups of wine, but on average five cups" is preferred.[23] The rite culminates when the Yoginī becomes an earthly embodiment of Goddess and receives "the male as an earthly equivalent of Śiva."[24] The use of intoxicants is not necessary for one to achieve these states, but they have been an important ritual practice for Yoginīs and other divine women throughout the ages. For thousands of years women have used substances to alter their consciousness and heighten their awareness. Brewing beer, fermenting wine or honeyed liquors has always been practiced by Yoginīs and other autonomous women in other parts of the world. Across the globe "women are recognized as the original brewers of fermented drinks from fruits, roots, leaves, bark, and grains."[25] Vicki Noble reports that "grains were fermented as early as ten-thousand years ago to make beer in Africa, Egypt, Iraq, and South America, the evidence suggests that honey was fermented long before grains, and in Africa bottle gourds were cultivated possibly as early as forty thousand years ago."[26] Mead, a red Celtic brew, as well as Greek red grape wines and Sumerian wheat and honey beers were imbibed as sacred elixirs in menstruation ceremonies and other rituals. The use of beer and other sacred substances enhances bleeding women's ability to have visions.[27] Menstruating women naturally experience an altered state of awareness. This slight shift from ordinary awareness deepens women's intuition and sense of connection.

Vicki Noble's research on priestesses of the Mediterranean during the Bronze Age (3000 to 1250 B.C.E.) considers a "legendary female shamanistic priesthood called *Maenads* ("wild women")."[28] Their iconography and legends point to groups of women who "handled snakes, domesticated wild bees, fermented a sacred honey beverage, and facilitated ecstatic rituals."[29] The Greek Melissae also made a "honey-brewed sacred beverage."[30] The Melissae were priestesses, wisewomen and performed similar rituals to the Yoginīs. Shamans, maenads, priestesses, Yoginīs—women of spiritual power around the globe drink wine, beer or some other altering libation and also utilize and worship menstrual blood and sexual fluids in their rituals.

Yoginī and other collective Goddess rituals express and celebrate a different perspective of the universe. Performing these rituals allows the practitioner to harness the unifying power behind creation and destruction. The purpose of these rites is to take one's consciousness beyond duality into a state of non-dual awareness. The Kaula, Śākta and Tantric practices are often transgressive by nature. The forbidden power that the culture has given certain experiences and substances is tapped and transformed by Yoginīs and Yogis. In addition to the use of intoxicants and participation in sexual rituals, most rituals involve spirit possession by the dead, demons, and female deities.[31] Yoginīs do practices that help them to open their consciousness to other realms of being and in doing so they are able to achieve supernatural powers or siddhis. These siddhis, however, can be a diversion from the spiritual path towards mokṣa (liberation). While some may take advantage of some of the powers that are gained along the path, each must eventually move beyond them in order to reach ultimate union with the Divine. The goal is for all limitations, frustrations, expectations to drop away so that one can experience a sense of dissolving and expanding into Oneness. Most important to the practice is freedom. However, achieving spiritual freedom requires transforming mental barriers. Amarananda Bhairavan notes,

> For spiritual freedom, a person needs to break away from this mechanical working of symbols, values, and labels into which awareness is fragmented and driven through life. . . . Liquidating these knots releases the energy of awareness bound in them. Collecting this awareness and rerouting it into your Self is the key to this freedom. When all these labels and tags are removed, the world of phenomena will not impose its perception on you anymore.[32]

A profound level of detachment and a very present and relaxed way of navigating through the world comes with these practices. The women who participate in these rites from past to present have semidivine status. Bhattacharya notes "originally the Yoginīs were probably human beings, women of flesh and blood, priestesses who were supposed to be possessed by the goddess, and later they were raised to the status of divinities."[33] They are members of the Kaula lineage and tradition and they worship the Yoginīs and Matṛkās as their principle deities. Through their reverence and ritual practices they acquire supernatural powers such as the ability to fly through the air.[34] Other powers include the ability to become minute in size and thus have absolute knowledge over the innermost workings of the universe; the ability to become gigantic and see beyond our solar system and universe; weightlessness and levitation as well as the ability to astral travel; excessive weightiness; irresistible will, hypnotic powers, the power of thought, and manifestation of one's thoughts; mind and body control over all living creatures; control over the natural elements: rain, drought, earthquakes, volcanoes; the fulfillment of one's desires.[35] Yoginīs are also said to be able to locate buried treasures, render people speechless, infatuate, stop destruction, fire, and subjugate through attraction.[36] Yoginīs were even said to cure lovesickness.[37] How would they have done that if they were not sexually independent, autonomous models of female authority?

The Yoginī sculptures portray a sexually autonomous and powerful expression of femaleness. The Yoginīs have voluptuous bodies, full round pendulous breasts, three to five folds in their bellies, curvaceous hips and earthy thighs. They are ornamented with necklaces, garlands, bracelets, armlets, bangles, anklets, earrings, and headdresses. They exude sexual authority. Passion. Grace. They smile enigmatically, some bearing fangs, others forked tongues. Their bodies emphasize their primal sensuality, their luscious femaleness. They are adorned with heavily ornamented girdles and sometimes headdresses. Many have animal heads pointing to the shamanic roots of the tradition: cat, serpent, lion, bear, buffalo, goat, cow, horse. These animals can be understood as companions or attendants of these Goddesses. The different plant or animal associated with each Yoginī offers her its powers and knowledge. The connection between them is primal, ancient, and wild. The plant or animal vehicle also represents the untameable, uncontrollable nature of elemental forces. Gadon notes, "The myths and legends about woman-animal hybrids reflect our fascination with the possibility of the animal nature of the female—still potent, raw, primal, fierce, instinctual, bodily, unrepressed."[38] She continues, "The hybrid human-animal nature of the yoginis, as well as their identification with their animal mounts suggests a holistic view of the life force that flows through all creatures. Perhaps this is a source of their magical power."[39]

The Yoginīs' names, tools and attributes vary from temple to temple, but their fiercely independent, yet sensual natures remain. Their Divinity is expressed through their weapons, haloes, and multiple arms. They carry skull cups, maces, clubs, tridents, books, flowers, spears, skull garlands, and curved knives. Their names include "Śrī Antakārī, She who destroys; Śrī Indrajālī, She who knows magic; and Śrī Phanendrī, She of the Serpents."[40] Durgā holds the central shrine at many of the Yoginī temples. In Khajaraho at the Chausath Yoginī temple the main shrine houses Durgā in Her Mahiṣāsuramardinī (slaying the buffalo demon) aspect. Also, she appears as one of the Yoginīs in this form at the Bheraghat temple in Madhya Pradesh. The Navadurgā are carved into nine niches on the outer temple wall of the Hirapur Yoginī temple. The Matṛkās are sometimes included in lists of the Yoginīs.

Sometimes temples to Yoginīs include the eight Matṛkās. Groups of eight Yoginīs at some of the 64 Yoginī temples are said to belong to the kula (clan or family) of the particular Matṛkā who heads their group. They are ordered by their elemental natures and relationship to the natural world and the cosmos. The Yoginīs and Matṛkās are descendants of the Yakṣīs or female elemental nature spirits.[41] An aspect of the Great Goddess Herself, the Yoginīs and Matṛkās are a "theological abstraction of the multiple tree, forest, and water goddesses of popular Indian religion—as well as the complex image of the Mothers in earlier traditions."[42] The interconnection between vegetative, animal, and divine human roles persists through the ages.

The Powers of 7, 8, 9

The number of Yoginīs varies between temples, although they all maintain certain numerological principles. Temples of 49 Yoginīs are based on seven groups of seven. 64 Yoginī temples are comprised of eight groups of eight. Similarly the 81 Yoginī temples are made of nine groups of nine. Seven, eight and nine are all esoterically significant numbers within Hindu philosophy. Seven stands for the order of the universe. Many aspects of Western existence have been compartmentalized into groupings of seven: seven musical notes, seven colors of the rainbow, seven days of the week and the seven cakras. Eight is a number of infinity, balance, and power. Eight also points to the four cardinal directions and four intermediary points of the compass, the eight siddhis or yogic powers the Yoginīs aspire to, the eight Matṛkās, eight types of metal, eight stages of yoga and eight primary mūdras. Nine represents culmination, completion, insight and wisdom. It is the number of the universal teacher and the healer.[43] Nine refers to the planets or grahas: Sun, Moon, Mars, Mercury, Jupiter, Venus, Earth and the ascending and descending nodes of the moon Rahu and Ketu. Nine also correlates to the nine nights of worship during the Durgā Pūjā, Navarātri, nine sacred plants, and nine precious gems. Temple floors were often based on 81 squares.[44]

The number 64 also carries great significance. In addition to the mystical properties associated with its division by 8, it is the number of the erotic arts of the Great Goddess. The Great Goddess *is* ultimately the 64 erotic arts, the 64 Yoginīs. There are also 64 schools of Tantra . Within Hindu cosmology and ideology, the entire universe is animated and in constant communication with us. Numerology and many other kinds of symbols, signs and omens are widely accepted as communications from other levels or forms of consciousness.

The Contemporary Yoginī

Today in India and Nepal we find living Yoginīs wandering temple and cremation grounds and living an ascetic life. They may be practitioners of yoga and other Tantric arts. Many live on alms and reside outdoors. Some have renounced the world and live on the margins of society. Survival is built on trust in the Universe which is most often understood as Goddess. But Yoginīs need not be wandering mendicants for there are many paths that the Yoginī can take. Some choose to be householders and keep such practices in private. Others choose to live creative, independent and autonomous lives. There are infinite ways of living as a Yoginī in this world. Most important to this path is a consciousness focused on service, devotion and autonomy, whether we are in a partnership or not. There is tremendous internal and spiritual power to be gained on such a conscious life path. Living outside the bounds of societal convention opens us to other, very mystical ways of being in the world.

Nevertheless, Yoginīs evoke a sense of awe and dread by people in India today. Dehejia reports "there is a widespread apprehension that one may be cursed by the Yoginīs for a whole host of reasons and it is believed that even approaching too close to their temples may have disastrous consequences."[45] This fear of the Yoginīs reflects the cultural fears within orthodox Hindu culture of female sexuality and power. In fact, it mimics the fears and judgments around sexually liberated women (courtesans, temple prostitutes, maenads, etc.) found around the globe since the beginning of the patriarchal era (circa 5000-7000 years ago). A Yoginī is threatening because she is NOT in relation to a man. She is not the model obedient mother or wife and cannot be owned. Her sexuality, her body, her mind and heart are her own.

It seems that the Yoginīs have always offered alternative forms of being female in this world. One of their most striking characteristics is that they represent sexual autonomy. Perhaps the medieval Yoginīs we find in the temple sculptures were modeled after living women who had the courage to live life in accordance with their wildest desires and a deep sense of freedom. Music and dance lie at the heart of sexuality. The Yoginī temples depict women and Goddesses dancing, playing instruments, and some include displays of sexual postures. The conspicuous statues exhibiting different forms of love may be referring to a ritualized sexual interaction between human beings. However, Tantric texts and teachers warn that the underlying message is not about lust, but Love for the Divine. Song, poetry, art, and sex all express a holy and creative communion with Goddess. Medieval manuscripts describe the poetry and love songs of lovers of the Divine: women such as the medieval poet mystics and Yoginīs, Mirabai and Lalla, and the devidasis or temple priestesses of Southern India. While some of these women expressed the art of love through their bodies, others directed their passion and devotion to the Divine through various expressions of their creativity. Music, poetry and dance have always provided a refuge for many women. Narayan notes how medieval women poets carved out a different space for themselves within marriage-dominated society.[46] In fact, such spheres of devotion are legitimate ways to liberation within the Hindu tradition and are seen as powerful religious and spiritual experiences. Poetry, dance and music are understood to express the deepest longing of the soul for the deity.[47] The connection between performing arts and religion in Hinduism is important not only as a means for communing with the Divine, but because it provides an opportunity for women to publicly express their devotion and spiritual longing.[48] Art is the medium of the Yoginī for it provides avenues of creative expression that helps us work through our struggles and suffering.

Let's consider an example of a contemporary Yoginī, who embodies the spirit of Goddess in all Her fierce, sensual, passionate and nurturing manifestations: the musician and artist Tori Amos. I must mention the music and divine artistry of Tori Amos as it has inspired, healed, and transformed me over the past seventeen years.

Amos' work investigates the biological, social, religious, and political roles and expressions of women under patriarchy. She sings about what has been ostracized, hidden, and repressed. She reminds us of the mysterious and invincible female force that is always waiting to be discovered. Amos addresses the transformative and empowering force of the Erotic and of the Sacred Female who stands up to religious, cultural and societal demands and expectations. Amos's ninth album, *American Doll Posse* explores the complex and diverse psychic landscape of five Greek Goddesses—all aspects of herself, and very relatable figures for many of us.

> What I'm trying to tell other women is they have their own version of the compartmentalized feminine which may have been repressed in each one of them. For many years I have been an image; that isn't necessarily who I am completely. I have made certain choices and that doesn't mean that those choices are the whole story. I think these women are showing me that I have not explored honest extensions of the self who are now as real as the redhead.[49]

Each of Amos' songs is a sonic landscape through which we traverse the mysterious, awe-inspiring and at times excruciating terrains of female consciousness. Through the perception of Goddesses and divinely female characters, Amos presents a wider spectrum of female experience—one that expresses our varied emotional, cultural, social and spiritual landscapes. Hers is a message of choice and self-exploration: how do we define our selves outside of patriarchal culture and religion?

In her latest album she sings of the tragic Ophelia, who we know from Shakespeare's Hamlet. She describes Ophelia as the woman who continues to choose destructive relationships and live her life as victim. She is the heart-and-soul-broken woman who has forgotten her Yoginī-ness, her Divinity. Sometimes Ophelia may see herself but she cannot quite get out of her conditioned thinking. In her visual vignette of the song, Amos depicts two women walking through a cemetery. These women represent the split in the female psyche. We see Ophelia being followed by a masked woman, who Amos says, holds the keys to the secrets of the universe. The woman behind the mask is the chaos we are trying to forget. She is the untapped power waiting to remind us to not get stuck in dead forms. She is the repressed part of our psyches that holds our erotic power. The masked woman's presence encourages Ophelia to "break the chain" of female oppression and conditioning that keeps us in a cycle of repeating harmful patterns. While change may be painful, it is in our best interest to confront what is holding us back and to send it off, "wishing it well."

Perhaps Amos's Ophelia has not entirely forgotten who she is. There is a part of her that is curious about the masked woman. We see Ophelia notice her alter ego darting between templelike grave stones. Through accepting pain and death,

Ophelia regains her memory. She shows us that through confronting that which scares us, we may find a way to liberate our selves. From a Tantric perspective, this song and visual vignette also reminds us we must draw from our Śakti, our internal power, rather than living a life that is defined for us by others. Śakti is the powerful female energy that "breaks the chains." It also energizes and inspires us. Amos asks:

> Where does sexuality and spirituality merge in women of today? Where and when is it still split? It seems as if the women I've run across in the last many years have had a real challenge trying to integrate their sexuality with their intellect or with their spirituality. It becomes this confusing triangle. It's almost a love triangle. Some women who choose intellect really look down upon the women that choose a more sexual way in expressing themselves and getting ahead in the world. Then, of course, your more spiritual women, I think, have a hard time balancing this hot, sensuous, raw passion that's very ancient that has been circumcised from the feminine when the patriarchy took over from the matriarchy thousands of years ago. You know, there wasn't shame in it.[50]

Like Tori Amos, we can see and express female consciousness through whichever cultural and spiritual lens we choose. Literal, visual and musical expressions of creativity offer sacred ways for us all to embrace and express our erotic, passionate and divine natures.

The Yoginī, Relationships and Love

While courtesans and temple prostitutes may be adept at wily practices specifically designed for seducing men, men are not necessarily the main focus of the Yoginī. The art of love is part of the Yoginī's repertoire; however, most important is her autonomy and her independence—whether or not she is involved in a sexual relationship. A Yoginī's primary relationship is with her self, as Goddess. We come into this world alone (all one) and we leave alone (all one). Cultivating our consciousness to be attuned with Divinity is the goal of the Yoginī. Sacred embodiment and sacred pleasures are integral to the terrain. However, we must not become too attached to our desires. We must learn how to find balance in all that we do, all that we believe, and all that we love. Allowing our egos to dissolve and seeking integration of mind, body and spirit is essential. Returning to precognizant memories of our true essence is our task. A Yoginī is a woman who challenges cultural norms. She is a force to be reckoned with. Betsy Prioleau in her book, *Seductress: Women Who Ravished the World and Their Lost Art of Love* describes such an archetype as the "paradigmatic liberated woman, empowered with men and empowered in life. She is a threshold model who can reinstate feminine sexual sovereignty and holistic happiness and remap the future."[51] Prioleau's, like Audre

Lorde's, definition of erotic, emphasizes the power of our Śakti, the creative force that is so necessary on this path. She notes how a woman carrying such empowered qualities "combines erotic supremacy with personal and vocational achievement."[52] While she refers to such a woman of the threshold as a seductress, I prefer the more autonomous word, Yoginī.

Yoginīs are threshold beings of the East. They rule the liminal realms where form has not yet swirled into manifest being. They occupy the boundary places, places where one can cross over into other realms of consciousness, of lived experience. They express fluidity, enchantment, bedazzlement, passion, and power. Men and women can both benefit from the alluring presence of such a woman. Prioleau notes, "(men) achieve their fondest dreams in the arms of a seductress, a goddess to venerate who keeps them interested and ignites their inner hero. She leads them to their best self and restores them to true masculinity, their predestined place in the cosmic scheme."[53]

Prioleau's book *Seductress* speaks to the current societal crisis of women who have lost access, even knowledge of their erotic power. She speaks of the college students that "flooded her office" and lamented over "elusive bad boys, soulless hookups, sapped confidence, wrecked pride, and total mystification about how to prevail in love."[54] The majority of men, on the other hand, "cling.to their historic prerogatives of the initiative, double standard, promiscuity, mate trade-ins, domination, and domestic copouts."[55] She notes that "the population of single women, especially middle-aged professionals and first wives, has swelled to one in four, with most wanting and failing to "get married." This desperate desire to find a mate and marry is a lot of the problem for women. Pining over men or a relationship causes a woman to lose her creative energies regardless of whether she wishes she were with a man or a woman. Such endless brooding and feelings of incompleteness without the "perfect" partner prevent a woman from knowing and being her authentic self. The same can be said for men who are endlessly trying to be in relationship; however, there are obvious differences as the power dynamics and ratio of women to men tend to be more in men's favor. I know few single men and a lot of independent women. While partnership can be a beautiful, albeit challenging, experience, women would do well to stop romanticizing about the "til death do us part" fantasy of marriage. We need to find new ways of being in relationship. Moreover, we need to develop a deeper relationship with ourselves and be okay with being alone. We need to learn how to keep the Śakti flowing, to envelop all we encounter in the mesmerizing life dance of passion, creation and destruction. Women who tap into these energies feel empowered, expanded, vibrant and alive. The glow a sexually assured woman emanates is magnetic, alluring, arresting. Sexual energies do not need to remain confined to stale worn-out models of relating. When set free these energies open doors within our psyches that lead to creation, manifestation, and liberation. Sexual energies set things in motion. They can also bring things to an end. The erotic is the dance, the līlā or play, the māya or illusion of Goddess. Its tantalizing energies cannot be bound. Raising such energies breaks through conventions—that is why the patriarchal establishments, particularly religious ones have attempted to hold it down. A woman's unbridled sexual and creative energies are a dangerous force for they "foil all systems of power."[56]

While we can look to the Yoginīs of past and present, we also need to create our own models of relating to our lovers and partners. In a speech on "Motherhood and Matriarchy" at Sonoma State University on International Women's Day in 2008, Vicki Noble suggested that heterosexual women "consider making a legal binding contract with one or two female friends to share a house while they are raising children, letting the boyfriends come and go—which is what they tend to do anyway! Why not admit that marriage is a failed institution and get on with the creative work of building new forms?" She goes on to say, "I suppose, alternatively, if the next generation of men decided as a group to give up male-dominance and privilege, and vowed to practice making the theory into daily reality, then marriage might be an institution where that hands-on practice (of matriarchal values where women and men live in harmony, without domestic abuse, rape, incest, and illegitimacy) could take place."[57]

Dharmanidhi Saraswati, Founder of the Kashmiri Shaivite Trika Institute and Tantric priest and Yogi has given numerous lectures on this very subject of partnership and relationship. He cites three different models of marriage for the yogin. The first path includes the more traditional monogamy but can eventually lead to a consciously chosen open relationship of multiple partners. Obviously open relationships are very challenging for most of us in this twenty-first century, unless we have willingly worked on layers and layers of conditioning and societal and traditional roles around female and male dynamics. Even with clear intent and dedication, open relationships can be very dangerous to the psyche. The second path Saraswati describes is called *Yoginī bhu*. This is a pioneering path of consciousness where practitioners redefine marriage and child bearing by choosing to have children as their sādhanā or practice. He describes how this path harkens back to the more matriarchal communal living of our ancient ancestors. The third form, sādhanā, is a yogic partnership that focuses on doing Tantric practices and sharing responsibility in our own and our greater community's evolution of consciousness. In each of these models, it is crucial to understand that the partner is essential to the practice and that human relationships provide a fertile ground for the yogin to develop their consciousness. Such contracts are not your standard patriarchal husband and wife model. There is a necessity for partners to divide responsibilities around labor and also to create time for individual as well as partnered practice.[58]

In this day and age we stand at a crossroad where we can choose between the outworn and limiting model of conventional marriage and Śākta Tantric expressions of relating that are not only empowering, but potentially liberating. "According to Amma, empowering women doesn't mean rebuffing men and settling old scores with them. On the contrary, Amma's is a vision of forgiveness, mutual understanding and love. Only action based on such an expansive vision can carry humankind to both spiritual and material heights."[59] As Amma notes, "Only love can bring about a permanent change in the mind-sets and, therefore, the realities of women and men."[60] Amma continues, "To prevent this extinction of love itself, human beings must return to respecting, worshiping and reposing their faith in a divine power. That power is not outside. But in order to discover it inside, we need to adjust our perspective."[61] Divine Love is about deep intimacy. It is a Love that must be cultivated from within. Contrary to what we have been conditioned to believe, the secret to our fulfillment is not to be found in a conventional marriage or relationship governed by dualistic notions of reality. On the path towards self-realization and self-liberation, what matters most is that we have *choices* around whom or what we choose to devote our love and passion. The great Indian philosopher Haridas Chaudhuri comments on the process of soul-searching as it relates to love:

> Such soul-searching leads different people to make different decisions. Some are very cautious in their choice of a life mate and then decide to marry. Some may say this is not right for them. But they may more or less successfully transfer their love for a person to some other love. For example, they may transfer their love to some great ideal or to the pursuit of knowledge or truth or art. Some may decide to transfer their love to God, the spiritual ideal of life. Then, after choosing something to which they can completely devote themselves, to which they can love with all their hearts, there will be a fulfillment of self-existence and an unfolding of one's own inner individual being.[62]

But what if this does not happen? What if we do not find an outlet for our love and passion, or what if we do not even know what or who it is we love? Then what happens? According to Chaudhuri:

> Spiritual death. This means one is not successful in bursting through the ego shell. [He] is incapable of transcending the fetters of [his] own narrow ego and therefore embraces so-called living death. . . when an individual chooses not to give [himself] to anything, not to society, not to a life partner, not to a great ideal of life, not to a great social institution—when this self-dedication is lacking in any form—[he] experiences the potent cause of neurotic disturbances and regression. In the name of self-existence and freedom rests the utmost imprisonment of the self—self-imprisonment within the ego."[63]

To some, this may not matter, for we may not even be aware of the limitations of the mind or of the ways that we are not living life fully. Patriarchy is about conditioning and domination—not choice and freedom.

But, ultimately, Unconditional Love is what frees us and benefits us all.

To be a Yoginī means being courageous, having high self-esteem and having a strong sense of self-worth. It requires feeling invincible, empowered and strong. A Yoginī does not need nor have to rely on another to take care of her emotional and physical needs. However, she knows when and how to ask for help and support. She cultivates relationships that are balanced, egalitarian and have complementary energies. She is discriminating and listens to her body when it comes to choosing to engage emotionally, sexually and/or romantically. She knows she contains the mysteries of the universe within her female body. She knows her yoni is the pīṭha, the sacred seat of all power. She understands that life is a dance between balance and chaos, darkness and light, suffering and joy, death and life. She is able to ride the cosmic tides that ebb and flow through our lives, sometimes bringing love, other times pain, but always lessons of who we truly are.

To really know the Yoginī and to experience the infinite choices She offers, a woman must become Her. If called, she will go through a series of rites and passages. She must confront and come to terms with her deepest fears. Death, illness, suffering, loneliness, chaos all must be approached with compassion and detachment. A woman who wishes to embark on such a path toward freedom will be tested, but her experiences can be transformed into creative energies. To become a fiercely independent woman, we must cut our way through the patriarchal constructs that continue to bind us and open to another way of being. Fearlessness is necessary. To go against the grain requires tremendous strength and self-confidence. Śakti. We all have it in us. We can live the lives we want to lead. Like the Matṛkās and Yoginīs, we can have our own epithets that reflect our unique choices and divine self-expression.

Notes

1. The use of the word yogi is a way some teachers refer to both women and men. The correct term for both sexes is yogin. Yogi is not an inclusive term of the female.
2. Sheba Chhachhi in Kathleen Erndl, "Is Shakti Empowering for Women?" in *Is the Goddess a Feminist: The Politics of South Asian Goddesses*, eds. Alf Hiltebeitel and Kathleen M. Erndl (New York: New York University Press, 2000), 99.
3. Elinor Gadon, "Probing the Mysteries of the Hirapur Yoginis," in *ReVision: A Journal of Consciousness and Transformation*, vol. 25, no. 1, (2002): 40.
4. Vidya Dehejia, *Yogini Cult and Temples* (New Delhi: National Museum, 1986), x.
5. Ibid., 17.

6. Ibid., 9-10.
7. See Mark Dyckowski, *The Doctrine of Vibration. An Analysis of the Doctrines and Practices of Kashmir Shaivism* (Delhi: Motilal Banarsidass, 1989).
8. Dehejia, *Yoginī Cult and Temples*, xii.
9. Ibid.,78.
10. Ibid., 85.
11. Angela Dietrich, *Tantric Healing in the Kathmandu Valley* (Delhi: Book Faith India, 1998), 168.
12. Ibid., 39
13. Ibid.
14. Dehejia, *Yogini Cult and Temples*, 35.
15. Ibid., 34
16. Michael Magee, *The Yoni Tantra* (Harrow, England: Worldwide Tantra Project, 1995), 6.
17. *Kaulajnananirnaya* of Matsyendranath (Prachya Orakashan, Benares, 1986, 24) quoted in Magee, *The Yoni Tantra* (Harrow, England: Worldwide Tantra Project, 1995), 6.
18. Ibid., 8 in Magee, *The Yoni Tantra*, 6-7.
19. Dehejia, *Yoginī Cult and Temples*, 63.
20. Ibid., 12.
21. David Gordon White, *Kiss of the Yoginī: "Tantric Sex" in Its South Asian Context* (University of Chicago Press, Chicago, 2003), 256.
22. Dehejia, *Yogini Cult and Temples*, 15.
23. Ibid.
24. Ibid.
25. Judy Grahn, *Blood, Bread, and Roses: How Menstruation Created the World* (Boston: Beacon Press, 1993), 113.
26. Stephen Harrod Buhner in Vicki Noble, *Double Goddess. Women Sharing Power* (Rochester, Vermont: Bear & Company, 2003), 98.
27. Grahn, *Blood, Bread, and Roses*, 113.
28. Vicki Noble, *Double Goddess*, 97.
29. Ibid.
30. Ibid., 99.
31. White, *Kiss of the Yoginī*, 6.
32. Amarananda Bhairavan, *Kali's Odiyya* (Maine: Nicolas Hays, 2000), 179.

33. Narendra Nath Bhattacharya, *History of the Śākta Religion*, 128.

34. Dehejia, *Yoginī Cult and Temples*, 53.

35. Ibid., 53-54.

36. Ibid., 54.

37. Ibid., 55.

38. Gadon, "Probing the Mysteries," 38.

39. Ibid., 40.

40. Ibid., 133-134.

41. White, *Kiss of the Yoginī* and Dehejia, *Yoginī Cult and Temples*.

42. White, *Kiss of the Yoginī*, 5.

43. Vicki Noble, *Motherpeace: A Way to the Goddess through Myth, Art, and Tarot* (San Francisco: HarperSanFrancisco, 1983).

44. Dehejia, *Yoginī Cult and Temples*, 50.

45. Ibid., ix.

46. Vasudha Narayan, "Brimming with *Bhakti*, Embodiments of *Shakti*: Devotees, Deities, Performs, Reformers, and Other Women of Power in the Hindu Tradition," in *Feminism and World Religions*, edited by Arvind Sharma and Katherine K. Young (Albany: State University of New York Press, 1999), 43.

47. Ibid., 36.

48. Ibid.

49. Tori Amos, Tori http://www.samesame.com.au/features/565/, July 17, 2009.

50. http://everythingtori.com/go/galleries/view/993/1/992/press, in "Harp," August 2007, July 17, 2009.

51. Betsy Prioleau, *Seductress: Women Who Ravished the World and Their Lost Art of Love* (New York: Penguin Books, 2003), x.

52. Ibid., xii.

53. Ibid., xv.

54. Ibid., xi.

55. Ibid., xi.

56. Ibid., xv.

57. Vicki Noble, "Motherhood and Matriarchy" (Paper presented on International Women's Day at Sonoma State University, Sonoma, California, March 8, 2008).

58. Dharmanidhi Saraswati, "Mahasiddhas and Relationship" (Paper presented at Yoga Maṇḍala, Berkeley, California April 28, 2008).

59. Sri Mata Amritanandamayi Devi or Amma,"The Infinite Potential of Women: An Address by Her Holiness Sri Mata Amritanandamayi Devi" (Jaipur, Rajasthan, India, March 7, 2008), 13.

60. Ibid., 34-35.

61. Ibid.

62. Haridas Chaudhuri, The Philosophy of Love, ed. Dionne Marx (New York & London: Routledge & Kegan Paul, 1987), 74.

63. Ibid., 74-75.

day seven
kali: goddess of transformation

Dakshin Kālī

We visit Dakshin Kālī, the ancient sacrificial temple site to Kālī. It is also devoted to Ajimā, the ancient Grandmother Goddess. The name of this sacred stomping ground to Kālī, Dakshin, *means south, a direction that is associated with the realm of the dead. Dakshin is also the same word for the right-hand Tantric path.*[1] *The dense forests surrounding the valley temple on the river give it the perfect ambiance for powerful Tantric rituals. In the* Devī Māhātmya *myth Kālī springs from the forehead of Durgā to lap up the blood and the felled demons with her lolling tongue. Kālī is also part of Durgā's collective group, the Mātṛkās, and it is common to find Her in temple and ritual iconography in the form of* Cāmuṇḍā, *an emaciated, terrifying woman with sharp teeth, a skull cup full of blood in Her hand and a necklace of skulls. Nepalese worshipers also refer to Her as Kālī, or Bhadrakālī, which means Gracious Kālī.*[2]

Saturday and Tuesday are Kālī's days of worship because they are related to the planets Saturn and Mars. Both planets share qualities that express Kālī's nature. For example, saturnian qualities of discipline, control, and time all fall within Kālī's domain. Mars' association with warrior[3] *and activating energies are equally part of Her essence. This Saturday is especially important because it is the first Saturday during Durgā Pūjā in 2000. Along with hundreds, perhaps even over a thousand other devotees, we arrive to pay our respect to Kālī. Just the day before we had had the honor of visiting Ratna Māyā Devī Mātā (Kusali Devī) and received Her blessing. She encouraged our group to pay homage to Kālī at Dakshin Kālī, and we promised we would go on Saturday.*

Lines and lines of people carrying animals that will be offered to Goddess—and according to the tradition, liberated from the endless cycle of birth and rebirth—snake down steep stairways, over bridges, across the courtyard and into the sacrificial pit, which houses the central mūrti. As we make our way, my feet stick to the bloody and monsoon muddy ground. It is here at this ancient Mother site that I get a full dose of the significance that death plays in this festival. Along one bank of the river, along which the temple and shrines of this forest compound are built, are burning ghats, or platforms where people burn the deceased. Yogis, Yoginīs and lower caste people comb through the ashes looking for gold fillings and any jewelry that has remained, and then the corpse's ashes are emptied into the river, returned to Mā Herself. As I continue walking through the open-air temple complex, smoke mixed with the scent of fresh blood fills the air. Despite my enthusiasm, I feel a bit queasy from the pungent smells. We arrive at the main temple that houses an open shrine, lined by the Matṛkās on the inner walls. Animal sacrifices to the Matṛkās take place throughout the day. The central shrine of every Hindu temple is called the Garbhagṛha, *which translates to "the womb of the Goddess." When we enter a temple, we enter the body of Goddess and the central rites of worship all take place in Her symbolic and mandalic womb.*

Several devotees push through the throngs of people. They carry platters of ghee-soaked cotton wicks, which are burned in terracotta cups before the various mūrti or divine images. Others carry trays of fruit, coconuts and flowers. I feel as if I have been transported into another realm. I am enveloped in a vortex of Śakti. I am mesmerized, captivated and feel totally alive. A rich array of sounds, sights, smells, and feelings pervade my senses. The whole experience takes on qualities of a dream. Suddenly Ranju points to a woman deep within the crowd of devotees at the central shrine. She is different in behavior from the others and the sea of bodies part as her Śakti palpably intensifies. "Watch her." Ranju firmly tells us. We watch, eagerly awaiting the unfolding of a great cosmic drama. While most Nepali women with long hair bind it in a ponytail or bun, this particular woman, has a long mane of wild black hair. She looks like Kālī. I cannot take my eyes off her. She is being held up from under her armpits by another woman who is behind her. She looks fierce and determined and all the while twists her legs into asanas and her hands into mudrās. Her eyes seem to grow larger by the second and her tongue extends out and laps at the air around her. She touches the foreheads or chests of devotees who come up to her. Sometimes she holds them; sometimes she whacks them on their heads or hearts. Before long I begin to feel a desperate longing for her touch.

Ranju explains that this woman is a devotee of Kālī who had come to the temple for the pūjā and spontaneously became a channel for the Goddess while she approached the central image. I have read about this type of trance possessions in Kathleen Erndl's book Victory to the Mother *and here a living example has manifested before me. It is clear that this beautiful Nepali woman is no longer expressing ordinary consciousness. As she slowly moves through the crowd, people rush up to Her to receive Her blessing. Some even move away from Her, perhaps out of respect and fear. I watch as She stops and fixes her eyes on someone, and then moves her hands into various mudrās while simultaneously sticking her tongue out as far as she can, then rolling it back into her mouth. Here, before my very eyes I am witnessing the iconographic gestures I have studied in books and seen on stone statues, live! Here is another living Goddess.*

I gravitate toward the woman in trance, who is so clearly manifesting Kālī. My prayers for a direct experience of the Mother have been answered once again. Ranju approaches her, and then stands behind her to support her. Ranju motions for me to come and stand before her to receive the Goddess' blessing. This Kālī-possessed woman looks deep into my eyes and locks her gaze with mine. She smiles, and then starts twisting hers lips almost as if she is sucking my aura. She starts blowing at me then reaches out to grab me and pull me closer to her. Her eyes roll back into her head, and She begins convulsing. She reaches out to me and places her trembling hands on my head, forcing me to slightly bow in front of Her. As soon as I feel her graceful, yet electrifying touch, I feel emptied and overcome with a sense of expansion and connection. In that moment I return to the void, the eternal womb of the Mother. This living Kālī guides me to stand up straight and then pulls and pulls at my heart as if she was removing some of my pain, rage, and suffering. Staring deep into my eyes, She touches my soul with Her penetrating stare. Instinctively, I start chanting KĀLĪ MĀ KĀLĪ MĀ KĀLĪ MĀ *over and over. Waves of gratitude and profound recognition wash over me. I feel a physical lightness and sweet coolness throughout my body. She pulls away and moves to bless the next pilgrim and I burst into tears (as does every one of us who was blessed by Her). As long as I am in Her presence, all I can feel is a deep burning desire to return to HER. And stay. It is very intense. I want to return to You, I need to return to You, I just want to be with You. I find myself telling Her from my heart. Oh Bhadrakālī, How can I serve you better? How can I do my Work more efficiently so that I can merge with You and soon?*

Kālī: Goddess of Death, Power and Transformation

The final three days of the Durgā festival are devoted to one of the fiercest aspects of Goddess—Kālī, Goddess of Death, Power, and Transformation. It was especially on these three days in 2000 that participation in the festival allowed my consciousness to shift into a greater understanding of the power and necessity of the more formidable aspects of existence. Among many things, Kālī teaches that death and decay are just as important to our overall existence as birth, growth and abundance. Kālī is a Goddess who defies convention. She is free from societal expectations and demands. Kālī is described as having a horrible, dreadful, and terrifying appearance. She dances wildly and ecstatically on the battlefield or in the cremation ground. She is uncontrollable. Because of Her untamable nature, She is associated with the periphery of Hindu society. Worshiped by tribal or low caste people in uncivilized or wild places, this is a Goddess who is also understood as the Supreme Mother of Existence in the Tantra tradition. David Kinsley writes in *Hindu Goddesses*:

> Kālī's shocking appearance and unconventional behavior confront one with an alternative to normal society. To meditate on the Dark Goddess, or to devote oneself to her, is to step out of the everyday world of predictable dharmic order and enter a world of reversals, opposites, and contrasts and in doing so to wake up to new possibilities and new frames of reference. In her differentness, strangeness, indeed, in her pervasiveness, Kālī is the kind of figure who is capable of shaking one's comforting and naïve assumptions about the world. In doing this she allows a clearer perception of how things really are.[4]

Kālī is a Goddess of the periphery. She carries a human skull cup that contains menstrual blood—the essence of Śakti power, of life force energy. The skull symbolizes the transient nature of existence. With this ritual accoutrement alone we find the essence of the Kaula, Śākta, Tantra tradition expressed in the blood (life force) and skull (death). We are reminded that life and death are one.

Kālī is black like the cosmos and dark like the earth. She is described as being garbed in space or sky clad. Sometimes she is described as being blue-black. When we immerse ourselves in the ocean or fly on a plane through the sky, the water and air no longer appear blue, because the element is actually transparent. Likewise, all colors, names and forms emerge from and disappear into Kālī. Her disheveled hair is sometimes referred to as a curtain of illusion. Her hair reminds us of the illusory reality of waking life. Worlds are contained in Her dark locks. Her loose and wild hair also indicates her sexually free nature. Her tongue hangs out indicating her sexual desires and their all-consuming ecstatic essence. She wears a garland of fifty heads representing the fifty letters of the Sanskrit alphabet. Each letter is a sonic universe, grounded in physics, and containing a repository of knowledge and wisdom. A girdle of arms drapes from her hips. These arms and hands remind us of our choices and actions in life. They constantly remind us that ultimate freedom in body and consciousness is to be attained as the fruit of karmic action. Kālī wears serpents as bracelets.[5] Serpents have been demonized in orthodox religion; however, in the ancient and Tantric world, they are closely associated with the sexual powers of women, and specifically their menstrual cycles. Much like a snake sheds its skin, so too does the uterine lining of menstruating women release from the yoni every 27 to 29 days.

Kālī's three eyes can see the past, present and future. And the three gunas are expressed by her white teeth (quality of purity-sattva), red lolling tongue (quality of desire and passion-rajas), and an inert Śiva at her feet symbolizing the earthly qualities of density and inaction (tamas).[6] Śiva, Kālī's beloved, is ontologically inseparable from Kālī. The union between Śiva and Kālī expresses the necessary and complementary tension between opposites. Kālī dances on Śiva's corpse-like body. From a philosophical perspective, Śiva is the Ground of Being and the

Foundation of Existence. A Tantric dictum states that *Śiva without Śakti is but a corpse*, implying that the dynamic essence of Goddess gives life to Śiva. However when we consider Kālī and Śiva as complementary qualities that go beyond human notions of sex and gender, we see how interdependent and symbiotic the relationship between the two deities actually is. In some respects, Kālī relies on Śiva's foundational nature. In some of the iconography we see Her standing on him. There are various interpretations for this. In some myths Śiva lies on the ground to stop the Goddess' wild dance of destruction after She becomes intoxicated from consuming copious amounts of demon blood. Other interpretations find this positioning suggestive of Kālī's dominant sexual nature. And still others describe the necessity of Śiva's foundational and quiescent essence that serves as a neutralizing ground for the Goddess' fiery Śakti. They speak to the līlā or dance between polarizing aspects of existence. Nevertheless within the Śākta Tantra tradition, Śiva never tames Kālī for She is ultimately untamable. Despite philosophical theories around the symbiotic nature of their union, it is Kālī who holds the supreme power of the Divine in the Śākta Tantra tradition. Without Her enlivening Śakti, Śiva would remain but a corpse.

Kālī is most often depicted with four arms; however, in Her Mahā or Great/Supreme forms She can have eight, twelve, or more. In Her left hand she carries a severed head symbolizing the ego. In Her right hand She holds a sword of discriminating wisdom. With Her other two hands She gives mudrās that dispel fear and give spiritual protection and strength. Kālī is the power of time. She teaches us about the indifference and neutrality of natural forces. She reminds us of the inevitability of death. Tantric practices and rituals all address our inescapable approach towards death, our return to Her great Yoni. Kālī governs death but She is not only death and a harbinger of this state, but also represents the triumph over death. In the Tantric worldview, death is both an ending and a new beginning. It is a passage into the next phase of our soul's evolution. Tantrikas spend their lifetimes doing practices that prepare them for death. The ultimate goal is to be conscious at the moment our soul leaves our bodies so that we will not be caught in *samskāra*, the endless wheel of karma and reincarnation. Although this world is considered Divine, when we are unconscious of the governing force behind all existence, we become trapped by this reality and a limited dualistic view.

For a Hindu, to be returned to the Mother's life-giving waters, for example, the great river Ganges and other rivers like the Bāgamātī in Nepal, is the ultimate sādhanā. Cremation practices are observed on the river banks, and, contrary to death rituals performed by women in the ancient past, today only the men prepare the body and funerary pyre. When I was in Varanasi, India in 2003 I went to the burning ghats to watch the practices with a Tantric practitioner I was studying with. I was the only woman in the crowd and asked him where all the women were.

He told me that today women are excluded from the rituals because they are "too emotional." He said that a woman's emotions, particularly her tears, prevent the astral body of the departing soul from crossing into other realms. Immediately I was triggered by this obvious patriarchal overlay. Indeed, on the Tantric path the goal is to learn to modify our emotions and to become more neutral to all so-called positive and negative experiences. But we inhabit human bodies. Inevitably emotions will arise; it is how we choose to respond, as opposed to react that matters. Nevertheless his comment demonstrated how authentic female expression has often been used against women in ways that exclude us from participation in various life experiences. However, this limited view has obviously not always been the perception concerning women and death. Vicki Noble's research over the past three decades has repeatedly demonstrated that in the ancient past, death was the domain of women (especially older women), of the Yoginīs and priestesses. Much like women have been healers, and midwives of the birth of a human baby, we have also served as midwives of death for members in our kula/community for millennia. Moreover, we can still find vestiges of female spiritual authority within rituals honoring death by the mere worship of Kālī as a Goddess of Death, Transformation and Birth by millions around the world. To Her Tantric devotees, Kālī's vulva serves as the gates of birth and death. Furthermore, considering the social role (or lack thereof) of human beings who are closest to Kālī's gates, namely babies and the deceased, gives deep insight into Kālī's nature and what she demands from us. Kinsley writes:

> Both the dead and infants have a liminal nature. Neither has a complete social identity. Neither fits neatly or at all into the niches and structures of normal society. To approach Kālī it is well to assume the identity of a corpse or an infant. Having no stake in the orderly structures of society, the devotee as a corpse or infant is free to step out of society into the liminal environment of the goddess. The corpse is mere food for her insatiable fires, the infant mere energy, as yet raw and unrefined. Reduced to either extreme, one who approaches Kālī in these roles is awakened to a perception of reality that is difficult to grasp within the confines of the order of dharma and a socialized ego.[7]

Kālī is at home outside the moral order and is not restrained by societal expectations and demands. Whether we are faced with the reality of our own deaths, or that of a loved one, Kālī strips away all the illusions we have held about our selves and our individual place in this world, forcing us to come to terms with the inevitability of death. These are obviously not pleasant lessons, and yet at the root of our suffering is a deep need for us to surrender—to Her. There is ultimately nothing we can do to stop death, sickness, aging, natural catastrophes, etc. Kālī reminds us we do not have control over such realms of experience. She asks us to let go of our ideas of how things "should" be, and through our acceptance we may experience the deep loving compassion of this Dark Goddess.

While the fiercer and more erotic qualities of Kālī's more socially benign manifestations, for example Lakṣmī and Saraswatī, have been eclipsed within orthodox circles, Kālī has retained her primal and wild nature. Although She is considered uncouth and threatening to the conventional social order, She is nevertheless tolerated. She will not go away. She is feared and therefore propitiated. While She is sometimes relegated to the periphery in certain cultural settings, she stands supremely in the center of the Kaula, Śākta and Tantra tradition. Kinsley writes:

> Many of the Tantras emphasize the fact that it is Śakti that pervades reality with Her power, might, and vitality and that it is she (Kālī and others) who is immediately present to the adept and whose presence and being underlie his [sic] own being. For the Tantric adept it is her vitality that is sought through various techniques aimed at spiritual transformation; thus it is she who is affirmed as the dominant and primary reality.[8]

This reality and consciousness still pervade the rituals, beliefs and practices of Her many devotees who refuse to submit to conventional order.

Kālī is not merely a Goddess of Death: She is a Goddess of Death, Birth and Transformation. She is Mā, the all-nurturing and blissful Mother. Dark like the earth and black like the night sky, Mā Kālī contains all the mysteries of existence in Her Universal Body. Her darkness contains the Great Mystery of the Unknown. We fear the Dark Goddess only because we cannot control the domains that She governs. When we resist, or hold on to certain attachments, She comes with her sword of discriminating wisdom and slices through our delusion. Her lessons may feel severe to our ego minds, but ultimately She comes to free us from all the limitations and conditioning that society and we, ourselves, have imposed on us. Perhaps Kālī has kept Her edge and Her uncontrollable wild spirit because She embodies a very real, inevitable and undeniable aspect of existence namely death, destruction and decay.

Kālī and the Devī Māhātmya

Kālī not only teaches us about physical death. In Kālī's chapter of the *Devī Māhātmya* myth, Durgā battles the demon Raktabīja. He is tenacious, stubborn, and every drop of his blood produces more demons. When two demons Caṇḍa and Muṇḍa approach Durgā she becomes enraged and manifests as Caṇḍīkā, She Who Tears Apart Thought. The Great Goddess turns within and calls forth Her Śakti, Her innate power, which emerges as the Matṛkās. Kālī is the first Goddess to burst from Durgā's forehead and take on the proliferating demons on the cosmic battlefield. As all the other Matṛkās appear, the skies are filled with a roar. The appearance of these paradoxical Goddesses whose very natures are so primal, stirs us because they summon a voice that is stronger than our own. They will not tolerate any form of injustice and do whatever is necessary to help liberate the oppressed. A powerful message to women (and men) about the Śakti we carry within, specifically in the Matṛkās who represent the various aspects of our self, is presented in this myth. Our own inner Matṛkās can assist us in fighting any demons in our lives.

Every time an arrow or sword pierces one of the demons, another demon springs up from the felled blood. When Kālī rushes onto the battlefield, She unrolls Her tongue and laps up the blood and demons. As She devours the forces that are creating injustice, She transmutes the poisons that are pervading the worlds thereby neutralizing the life-threatening aspects of existence.

Kālī devours the demons just as She hungrily consumes the negative thoughts that continuously arise in our minds. Kālī emerges from Durgā's mind and is especially helpful to those who wish to combat the ego. In this carita, we learn how Kālī receives the epithet, Cāmuṇḍā. Two of the demons She devours are Caṇḍa and Muṇḍa and so in a Tantric way the demons become Her and remember their Divinity. In this appearance She is ferocious, untouchable, and totally wrathful. She is the crone, the wise one, and the soothsayer. She cuts all that impedes us from expressing our truest nature. She severs ties with thoughts, people, beliefs and actions that limit and inhibit us. She slays all ego constructs that bind us whether they are internal or external. She forces us to confront death in all its forms. With Cāmuṇḍā we must be fierce, strong, and often go at it alone. And She gifts us with the wisdom of our experience.

Whether worshiped in Her emaciated yet empowered aspect as Cāmuṇḍā, or as the Dark Mother Goddess Kālī, this terrifying form of Goddess has become an empowered model of righteous rage for feminists in the West. While She teaches us the potential path of liberation inherent in our anger, She is not restricted to such horrifying forms. Kālī's devotees know firsthand that She is ultimately the Great Mother of Bliss and Love. To many She is conflated with Durgā and is the Divine embodiment of all existence. She is a force that cannot be held back. She is unbridled primal energy. She teaches us to find constructive ways of expressing our anger rather than turning our rage against ourselves and acting out in ways that are self-destructive.

Depression is Kālī's realm. She represents the will, and when our creativity feels blocked, Kālī is the inertia we experience. Depression shows what in us is not flowing in accordance with the Divine. However, in this state we may be too possessed by our emotions to see with any clarity or spiritual objectivity. Depression has its own cycles for those who are familiar with this terrain of consciousness. Depression has its own timing and wisdom. We can become mired in Kālī's tamas. Life can become heavy and stagnant and depression can feel all-consuming. Despite the risks and suffering that accompany this state, depression can also become a fertile breeding ground of inspiration and gestation. While depression can be conducive to force us to look within to find our inherently divine natures, there is danger in dwelling in this underworldly realm for too long and getting stuck. Kālī teaches about the natural cycles within our lives. She is the embodiment of constant motion and evolution. We cannot always be high-spirited and happy. We need to have periods of going within and experiencing pure stillness. We can find contentment in our deepest selves by just sitting in meditation and being, or by chanting *Krīm Krīm Krīm*, Kālī's bīja or seed mantra. The resonance of Her mantra shifts our consciousness and affects the emotional body. We can meet Kālī in this liminal realm of depression, and we can use Tantric tools to help us transform. Kālī helps us navigate the dark underworld terrain of the psyche. She guides us to the jewels of our essence that have been buried in our pain, our ignorance and unconsciousness. She helps us break free from emotional states that bog us down. Whether we surrender to Her or not, if Kālī has chosen us as Her initiate, She will take all of our physical and emotional attachments until we are stripped bare and only have our Self to turn to, we who are She.

Betty Deshong Meador describes the process of retrieving parts of our selves that have been oppressed, denied, and lost as a descent to the underworld. Across the globe we can find Goddesses of the Underworld who demand we remember our full female nature. But the cost of remembering is sometimes quite high. Often we are forced to let go of our "narrow spectrum of desires, (and) stunted vision of what life is and can be."[9] In *Uncursing the Dark: Treasures from the Underworld*, Meador looks to the ancient Sumerian myth of Goddess Inanna's descent into the Underworld as a guide for women who are undergoing such a process. Inanna, Queen of Heaven, must meet Her sister, Ereshkigal, who has been relegated to the underworld. As Inanna descends She is stripped of all Her most beloved possessions. All the adornment and clothing that defines Her in this world must be removed. She appears naked and vulnerable before the dark and furious Ereshkigal, who is actually a repressed and unexpressed part of Inanna's self. Inanna must enter the underworldly terrain of Her psyche to confront the wild aspect of Her nature. Meador notes, "No one who has endured a descent will ever treat lightly the suffering it demands. Any descent I know or have heard of is disorienting, emotionally battering, depressing, full of anguish, shame, envy and despair."[10] Of course, the severity of the experience varies from person to person. However, Inanna's journey is one that many women in the West are familiar with today. Ereshkigal and Inanna are a Sumerian Kālī. Regardless, this is not an easy path nor is it necessarily a chosen path. Some events just naturally or karmically occur. We can attempt to harness the energies through certain meditative, mantra and ritual practices. However, if the Dark Goddess has called us we cannot escape the lessons She has come to teach us. Crisis after crisis, trauma after trauma may continue until we fully surrender to Kālī. Kālī is a Goddess who awakens us to our inherent nature—often through excruciating means.

Reclaiming Kālī is about restoring the lost or repressed Divine Female to our natures. Kālī and Durgā are two sides of the same coin. There is much to learn from how both Goddesses participate in this mythic battle. Durgā is resilient, invincible and poised. Durgā is the calm center of a torrential storm, while Kālī is the howling wind and pelting rains. Sometimes we need to express the fierce yet composed qualities that Durgā exemplifies. At times showing our rage at injustice and "devouring" anything in our way is certainly needed. The Dark Mother is not only about anger, She also teaches us about the strengths that come from our sorrows. She is a formidable force of rectitude and justice. Her myth shows how the various qualities we carry within can be called on for us to more deeply engage in life. Whether we call the Divine Mother Kālī or Durgā, we witness how She engages in Her mythic battle not out of a lust for violence, but in order to restore harmony to the worlds. She will not tolerate any form of discrimination. She is compassion, She is unconditional love, and She is bliss. Those of us who walk the path of Kālī/Durgā are continuously confronted with opportunities that although challenging, ultimately enable us to practice responding from our center—that inner place of stillness and perfect alignment with the Divine.

Kālī and Sexuality

Kālī carries an explicit sexual autonomy. Her tongue is emblematic of Her yoni and has distinct sexual connotations. The sexual significance of the Goddess' outstretched tongue has been inverted in more conservative religious circles who claim that Kālī's tongue represents Her lajjā (shame). This is a very curious explanation for why images show Kālī with an outstretched tongue. Sticking out one's tongue in the West has more to do with warding off people or energies we find distasteful. Or in a less prominent way is used to make sexual advances or to lure our desired partner into our arms and bed. I have never witnessed *shame* being expressed by someone sticking out their tongue.[11] Disgust yes, but not shame. In general, Kālī is feared by those who in all likelihood suffer from a deeply ingrained fear of female sexual power. Female repression includes the many ways we are not allowed to speak our truth. The tongue is the instrument of the voice and therefore power. When women are not able to voice our feelings, concerns, expectations and experiences, the repressed energies can perhaps become internalized as shame. But I highly doubt any woman would protrude her tongue to express shame. Perhaps Kālī is sticking Her tongue out at all those who have disdained and tried to control Her.

Regardless of patriarchal interpretations of Kālī's iconography, Kālī has become a model of sexual independence to many in the West. Indeed, Her roots are ancient and shamanic. Her evolution has retained and continually expresses much of the

Goddess' original nature. As a sexually empowered Goddess, She is worshiped interchangeably with Bhagawatī and Kāmākhyā. Often She is offered garlands of hibiscus or marigolds. One of Kālī's favorite flowers is the hibiscus, a symbol of passion, and awakened and liberated sexuality. When distilled in spring water and used as a flower essence, the hibiscus is said to stimulate the libido and help one heal emotionally from sexual trauma. The brightly colored marigold holds cooling properties and is one of Durgā/Bhagwatī's flowers. It has many medicinal uses from treating irritated skin to reducing menstrual pain. Marigolds contain estrogenic properties that treat menstrual discomfort and slow heavy bleeding. These flowers can also be used to treat yeast infections.[12] The rose, yet another flower that has been compared to a woman's vulva and sexuality is one of Kālī's cherished offerings. Marigolds, roses, hibiscus and even Lakshmi's lotus are all flowers that express the power of female sexuality and are significant to the rituals. The end of any Hindu ritual generally includes the Puṣpāñjali Mantra. *Puṣpa* means flower and flowers are offered to the Divinity while this mantra is recited. The mantra does not necessarily extol the virtues of flowers, but it does honor the natural world in its description of the origin and evolution of the five elements and their effect on our consciousness.

Kālī Yantra

The Kālī yantra is another symbol that expresses both her elemental and sexual nature. Kālī's yantra is a series of five downward pointing triangles with a dot (bindu) in the center, representing the source of consciousness and womb of the world.[13] The five triangles represent the five elements and realms of consciousness. As a whole, Kālī's yantra expresses the Yoni—the great cosmic womb through which the entire universe is birthed. Her yantra is to be meditated upon and experienced as a manifestation of Her transcendent and immanent nature. Practices include interiorizing the form of the yantra through the recitation of mantras and specific visualization techniques. The lines each relate to a different Goddess or aspect of Kālī and Her respective quality. The mantra and meditative practice associated with each line stimulate certain energy centers and meridians in our bodies. Ultimately such practices can activate our kuṇḍalinī, which to Śāktas and Tantrikas is essential. Kuṇḍalinī is the Goddess. She is the sexual and creative energy that lies dormant at the base of our spine until it is awakened. In *Kuṇḍalinī Tantra*, Swami Satyananda Saraswati notes a very essential difference between Kālī and Durgā and the sexual and creative energy we call kuṇḍalinī. He writes, "When Kuṇḍalinī has just awakened and you are not able to handle it, it is called Kālī. When you can handle it and are able to use it for beneficial purposes and you become powerful on account of it, it is called Durgā."[14] Saraswati is referring to Kuṇḍalinī as Kālī in the sense that She is the unawakened force of the unconscious. When kuṇḍalinī has just awakened, that force is more or less out of control, scary and potentially dangerous, and this is Kālī. When you have mastered and harnessed the same energy it becomes an expression of Durgā as an evolved and refined essence of consciousness. However, one could argue these Goddesses are one and the same Divine Force. It is important to have guidance from a spiritual teacher when doing practices that stir kuṇḍalinī as this energy can be disruptive to the psyche if we do not know how to channel and harness it properly. From the perspective of the destructive power inherent in kuṇḍalinī, we can understand Kālī as the unbridled power of unconscious energy. The journey of kuṇḍalinī through the subtle channels (nāḍīs) and energy centers (cakras) stimulates these energy centers thereby moving stuck energies and clearing the energetic body for the energy to flow uninterrupted to the crown of the head, where it flowers as the Kula-kuṇḍalinī, and the Divine Union of Śakti and Śiva.[15] We can perform numerous practices and trainings to harness these energies. However, sometimes, as it did for me in 1999, Kuṇḍalinī opens spontaneously. My own awakening was, in part, stimulated by my introduction to Vajrayoginī, a Buddhist form of Kālī and Durgā.

Vajrayoginī

To speak of Kālī in Nepal, one must describe Her formidable Tibetan Buddhist form, Vajrayoginī. During the Durgā festival Vajrayoginī is sometimes worshiped interchangeably with Durgā. There are four Yoginīs who guard the outer maṇḍala of the Valley. Vajrayoginī is the "eldest of the four sisters of the Valley." The others are Guhyeśvarī, the Pharphing Yoginī and Vidyāśvarī.[16] In the Yoginī Tantras, Durgā is the Queen of the Yoginīs. To the Buddhists, Vajrayoginī is the Queen of the Dākinīs. Put very simply, Dākinīs are the Tibetan equivalent of Yoginīs (although arguably they do have both conflated and diverse functions and appearances). Durgā and Vajrayoginī with their cohorts of female beings or manifestations of Her great power are probably energetically the same Goddess with different names and slightly different attributes depending on religious tradition and locality.

Vajrayoginī's iconography is similar to Kālī's. She stands naked wearing a garland of skulls, holds a skull cup of menstrual blood, and carries a crescent shaped dakinī knife. She stands on two demons in a warrior posture within a ring of fire. In other appearances She stands in a classical dance posture common to Yoginīs. Her nature, like Kālī's and Durgā's, will liberate the devotee. "Vajrayoginī takes form so that women, seeing enlightenment in female form, will recognize their innate divinity and potential for enlightenment."[17]

Vicki Noble and Miranda Shaw are two feminist scholars and Tantric Buddhist practitioners whose research focuses on the Dākinī and the potency and Divinity of the female body. Noble cites Shaw in her essay, "Dakini-The Goddess who Takes Form as A Woman":

> Vajrayoginī repeatedly states that she reveals herself in and through women, "announcing in one of the Yogini-tantras, "Whenever in the world a female body is seen, that should be recognized as my holy body."For women, Shaw says, "the relationship with Vajrayoginī is one of identity. Women must discover the divine female essence within themselves. This should inspire self-respect, confidence, and the 'divine pride' that is necessary to traverse the Tantric path. . . . This pride is an antidote to self-doubt."[18]

Noble's teachings repeatedly emphasize how Vajrayoginī subdues the demons with splendor. She is a model for finding compassionate but nevertheless formidable ways to respond to any threatening situation rather than fighting fire with fire. Looking to wild Goddesses like Vajrayoginī, Kālī, and Durgā is undeniably cataclysmic in our understanding of our selves. Here are Goddesses whose very nature is transgressive, defying orthodox society's repressive mores regarding women. I have known and read about countless women who had no idea of the Dark Goddess and when first encountering Her through an image, ritual and/or chant, felt totally mesmerized. Their receiving Her darśan, often without even consciously knowing what was happening, instigated change within and around them. Often such changes have been dramatic and life-changing. Sometimes the Dark Goddess comes through illness or experiences of loss and death. However, She does not only appear through tragedy, but also in experiences kissed by grace. Her ultimate nature is Love and Bliss.

Encounter with the Goddess

I had an extremely potent visionary experience during the first workshop I attended with Vicki Noble in 1999. Although I had met the Kumārī in 1998, I was not yet familiar with the Dakinī or Yoginī. I felt very drawn to Nepal and India, but I hardly knew Kālī and was more familiar with Goddesses like the Sumerian Inanna or Greek Hecate. From the first time I read Vicki's work, I felt a deep resonance and longing to meet her. Her words spoke to my consciousness. She was a big part of the reason I moved to California. The first time I met her, I attended her Dākinī workshop. Noble led the class in a guided meditation to prepare us to create mandalic collages. The visualization was very shamanic in nature, inducing an altered state by the repetitive shaking of a rattle and a chant to Goddess. We set an intention for guidance from a spirit ally, power animal or aspect of the Divinity. As I felt my ordinary consciousness release its controlling grasp, I began to experience some of the elements within my vision. I heard a gentle breeze rustling through trees, ravens and other majestic birds calling out to one another. I felt the cool dusk air and I smelled smoke from a bonfire. I walked and observed the terrain shifting and becoming more mountainlike. Although I had begun this meditative journey intending to visit one of my favorite pristine beaches in Thailand, I realized I had returned to the foothills of the Himālayas. Vicki advised us to stop at a natural place in the landscape, which resonated like a personal power place. I found myself standing in a circle of large stones surrounded by dense forest at twilight. In my vision I sat down on a rock to wait for a sign from Goddess. Suddenly a dark-skinned female appeared. Her black hair was loose and cascaded around her like a lion's wild mane. She was stunningly beautiful and yet a bit frightening. She exuded a very raw and primal energy which commanded authenticity, courage and integrity. Her body was smeared with blood. Vicki's voice continued in the background of my consciousness, suggesting we ask whatever being appeared for a message or gift and to give a symbolic offering. I offered Her a raven's feather. . . and she placed Her hand between Her legs then offered me cupped handfuls of Her menstrual blood. She motioned for me to drink, so I did.When I came out of trance, Vicki asked the class to share some of their visions. I was unsure of what had just happened. It seemed totally crazy that I had just drunk menstrual blood offered from an Indian-looking Goddess. I was afraid of speaking out and being judged by the other students. My vision was so extreme and so personal: I questioned whether I should even describe what had happened. And yet, I was deeply curious, and I remembered the fearlessness that had so struck me about Her eyes. When I shared the details of my deeply felt vision, Vicki was stunned and asked if I knew of Yeshe Tsogyal. I did not. She told me to read about her right away as Yeshe described a very similar experience with a Dakinī in her autobiography. Noble explains:

> Yeshe Tsogyal's autobiography, which was discovered and revealed as a "treasure" (terma) a few hundred years ago, has now been translated into English three different times and is available for western students of Tibetan Buddhism to read. In it we find the following remarkable narrative, in which Tsogyal tells us that she had reached the brink of death in her advanced meditation retreat and she called out to "the Teacher": "Then I had a vision of a red woman, naked, lacking even the covering of bone ornaments, who thrust her bhaga against my mouth, and I drank deeply from the copious flow of blood. My entire being was filled with health and well-being, I felt as strong as a snow-lion, and I realized profound absorption to be inexpressible truth."[19] It would seem that the essential female bodily substance, menstrual blood, is shown here to be the nourishment par excellence. At the very least it is a striking metaphor for female-to-female direct transmission in a lineage of wisdom, in this case from the Goddess to a dakini in human form.[20]

My kuṇḍalinī was fully awakened after experiencing this vision. I had experienced the direct female-to-female transmission that Noble describes. About an hour later as Vicki was showing images of Dākinīs and shaman women across the globe, I became very lightheaded and started to shake uncontrollably. The darśan from the images penetrated me to my core activating a tingling and pulsating energy that began in my yoni and began uncontrollably spreading through the rest of my body. It scared me. I had no idea what was happening, and I was also mortified that my body was calling so much attention to itself. Vicki suggested I lie down but the shaking only intensified. Vicki had the other women come and put their hands on me to directly receive some of the healing energy that was charging through my body. She guided me through some prāṇayama breath work to stabilize the energy. After awhile she led all of us in chants. The combination of touch, mantra and prāṇayama grounded me. Kuṇḍalinī's serpentine movements responded to the tones and my breath. I began to relax and feel a deep sense of opening, especially in my heart.

Kuṇḍalinī experiences continued for months and during this time I experienced very supernatural and direct experiences of Kālī. The energy was so intense I lost my appetite and could hardly eat or sleep. I had intense visions that kept me up for days. I made an altar to Kālī and experienced three, fortunately small, fires in my apartment. The fires were evidence that I desperately needed to eat tamasic (heavy, dense, earthy) foods and ground myself. At times I felt I could lose consciousness walking down the street as waves of undulating energy overcame me. A flower, a butterfly, a bird would send me into ecstasy. I encountered snakes all around me and was fascinated by them. On the morning of the winter Solstice I found a dead baby snake on my city driveway in the Castro district of San Francisco. Books on snakes and volcanoes came to me as gifts. An Italian English as a Foreign Language student approached me for guidance on shamanism although I had never revealed my spiritual beliefs in my classes. One night I turned on the television to an image of writhing snakes covering the entire screen. Another day I turned on the radio and someone was talking about the medicinal properties in snake venom. Everywhere I turned I was confronted with serpents. It excited me. One of my favorite stories about my mother is of her being a child and loving snakes. My Mammy told me how one day my mother came in from the yard with about ten garden snakes wrapped around her arms. By my late twenties I was familiar with the Snake Priestesses of Ancient Crete, who were oracles for the community and who danced with snakes entwining their arms. Although my maternal line is not conscious of Goddess from earliest times, indeed Her energies and mysteries have been revealed through such fabulously unorthodox experiences. Thanks to the appreciation my mother and grandmother have had for serpents, I have always felt a sense of awe and reverence for them.

The months following the workshop with Vicki were a time of deep awakening and initiation that opened gateways of consciousness that I have been exploring ever since. Fortunately Vicki and another powerful Kālī woman in my life, my therapist Kyle, guided me in harnessing the energies and dealing with the fears and pain that inevitably arose with this awakened energy. I had to examine and reexamine all the unprocessed material from years of illness, abuse, and living as a woman in the dominant patriarchal culture. I had to find my voice and my power: no easy task. I had to stand at the gates of my psyche and look the Dark Goddess in the eye as She removed everything, yes, *everything* that I was attached to at that time (relationship, home, friendships, family, a beloved dog, even a pregnancy). From that point on, I have been aware that I have been fully immersed in Dark Goddess Consciousness, ever learning to navigate between pain and joy, suffering and ecstasy.

Kālī Power

The Dark Goddess has been maligned in conservative circles, but Her mysterious darkness contains much power that has the potential to shift our global consciousness. Chandra Alexandre, Priestess and Director of a feminist spiritual organization called *Sharanya* writes:

> Dark Goddesses continue to exist. . . despite the tremendous energy that has been and continues to be exerted against them. Yet because of the incredible ability Dark Goddess have—in part by virtue of their (symbolic) alignment with the forces of nature—to challenge patriarchal modes and meanings, they are motivators and leaders for transformative action, social justice and (r)evolution in the hearts of humanity. They have indeed become a symbolic voice of the peoples and planet suffering under all forms of tyranny. They are indeed today's liberators.[21]

More and more women and men are awakening to the consciousness of the Dark Mother and liberating our selves from old patterns and conditioning. Female-centered myths of the Śākta tradition and various Tantras help us to look to the Dark Goddess through our individual and collective suffering as role model and guide. She is very much a living reality. Kālī shows Herself in snakes, ravens, death and illness, but also in living women, some who have saint status, or more specifically are realized beings or Goddesses who are fully conscious of their Divinity. Numerous contemporary women such as Ammachi, the Hugging Saint and incarnation of Kālī from Kerala; Sri Maa from Kamakyha; Anandamayee Maa from Northern India; Amma Pratyangirae, a fierce emanation of a multi-headed lion Goddess of Singapore; and numerous other Living Mās,[22] as well as Buddhist practitioners, teachers and scholars such as Vicki Noble and Tsultrim Allione,[23] along with many other women provide explications of female power and Kālī-esque experiences in their narratives and teachings. We can read and listen to their teachings on their own trials and victories. We learn how they have been ostracized and/or honored, and through these tales, can often find insight into our own fears and strengths. They hold up a mirror to our own lives and show us at the root of all our fears lies a deep-seated fear of the unknown, and of death.

Notes

1. Right-hand Tantric path practitioners follow ascetic, dogmatic and more traditionally orthodox practices than those on the left-hand path of Tantra. For example, right-hand practitioners follow strict moral codes while left-hand practitioners embrace and utilize substances that orthodox cultures consider taboo. Right-hand practitioners do not share a non-dualistic view of everything in the physical realm, especially bodily substances, as ultimately Divine. One of the main differences between both paths is that left-hand practitioners seek to awaken our inherent Divinity and maintain that we not only become, but are Divine. Those on the right-hand path maintain a belief in the Divine and the possibility for direct relationship with Divinity; however, they do not share the belief of human Divinity.
2. John Stratton Hawley and Donna Marie Wulff, eds. *Devi: Goddesses of India* (Berkeley: University of California Press, 1996), 20.
3. Kālī expresses Mars warrior qualities in the sense of protection and liberation, not violence and oppression.
4. David Kinsley, *Hindu Goddesses: Visions of the Divine Feminine in the Hindu Religious Tradition* (Berkeley: University of California Press, 1986), 130.
5. Much of the interpretation of Kālī's attributes and tools come from Ajit Mookerjee, *Kali: The Feminine Force* (Rochester,Vermont: Destiny Books, 1988), 62.
6. Ibid.
7. Kinsley, *Hindu Goddesses*, 131.
8. Ibid., 122.
9. Betty DeShong Meador, *Uncursing the Dark: Treasures from the Underworld* (Wilmette, Illinois: Chiron Publishers, 1992), 44.
10. Ibid., 45.
11. In a personal conversation with Vicki Noble, she shared how Tibetans stick out their tongues as a gesture of honor, especially toward someone who is higher-ranking. Sticking out the tongue is accompanied by a specific hand gesture. June 28, 2009.
12. Monterey Bay Spice Company, http://www.herbco.com/p-622-marigold-calendula-petals.aspx
13. Madhu Khanna, *Yantra: The Tantric Symbol of Cosmic Unity* (London: Thames and Hudson, 1979), 55.
14. Swami Satyananda Saraswati, *Kuṇḍalinī Tantra* (Bihar: Bihar School of Yoga Publications Trust, Inc., 2000), 15.
15. Ajit Mookerjee, *Kuṇḍalinī: The Arousal of the Inner Energy* (London: Thames and Hudson, 1982), 12.
16. Mary Shepherd Slusser, *Nepal Mandala: A Cultural Study of the Kathmandu Valley*, Vol 1 of 2: Text (Princeton: Princeton University Press, 1982), 327.
17. Miranda Shaw, *Passionate Enlightenment: Women in Tantric Buddhism* (Princeton,

New Jersey: Princeton University Press, 1994), 41.

18. Vicki Noble quoting Miranda Shaw in "Dakini: The Goddess who Takes Form as A Woman," in *Goddesses in World Culture. Vol. 1: Africa, Asia, Australia and the Pacific*, ed. Patricia Monaghan, (Santa Barbara, California: Praeger (an imprint of Houghton-Mifflin), Spring 2010).

19. Keith Dowman, *Sky Dancer: The Secret Life and Songs of Yeshe Tsogyel* (Ithaca, New York: Snow Lion Press, 1996), 71.

20. Noble, "Dakini: The Goddess Who Takes Form as a Woman."

21. Chandra Alexandre, "Why She. . . and Why a Dark Goddess?" http://www.sharanya.org/shacan/darkgoddess.php4.

22. See Linda Johnsen, *Daughters of the Goddess: The Women Saints of India* (St. Paul, Minnesota: Yes International Publishers, 1994).

23. Tsultrim Allione, Buddhist teacher and emanation of Machig Lapdron, a reincarnation of Yeshe Tsogyal, has written a wonderful book of historiographies on strong female practitioners and teachers of Tibet and India within the Buddhist tradition called *Women of Wisdom*.

day eight
taleju: women's blood mysteries

Astami: Blood, Sacrifice and the Dark Goddess

Astami, the eighth day, is one of the most significant days of the Durgā festival. Millions of devotees from various religious and ethnic backgrounds come together to worship Goddess Durgā. In some parts of the Hindu world, for example in Bengal and Assam, only the final three days (seventh, eighth and ninth) of the nine-night festival are fervently celebrated with grandeur and glory. In Nepal these final three days are equally significant because according to the final carita of the myth, Durgā's great battle with the buffalo-headed demon and his minions intensifies until it reaches the climax. The community's anticipation of Goddess' triumph over the demons and hope for the restoration of harmony and equilibrium in all the worlds are symbolically reflected in the daily rituals.

The eighth night is especially important as the ritual sacrifices are said to symbolize the many demons Goddess Durgā annihilates. Sacrifices are made to a Tantric form of Goddess known as Taleju. Taleju has a central temple in the three main sister cities of the Valley, Kathmandu, Patan, and Bhaktapur. Each of these cities was a medieval Malla kingdom during the Middle Ages when Tantrism flourished. Taleju was central to the royal families of that era, and She still plays an important role to the Valley inhabitants. Taleju is considered to have a milder temperament than fierce Durgā or Kālī, yet She contains similar Tantric qualities and like Her more ferocious sisters has a close relationship to the vegetative world. Taleju is a manifestation of Durgā in Her role of chief protective deity. So powerful is Her tutelary presence throughout the Valley, She is considered to be not only a presiding deity, but an embodiment of Nepālmaṇḍala. Taleju is the Kathmandu Valley itself: She is the land, the buildings, and the people. She is everything that exists in seen and unseen realms. She became a symbol of power, protection and resistance just as Kālī "became connected with Bengali resistance during periods of political strife."[1] Clearly Taleju, Kālī and Durgā are powerful Divine models for our resistance efforts in the West.

Taleju is associated with royalty and Her temple, which is located at the heart of the kingdom, is open to visitors only once during the year at the Durgā Pūjā.

During the Middle Ages Taleju and Durgā became martial Goddesses and were worshiped to gain control of new territories. These Goddesses were invoked because their powers are real, all-pervading and effective. Tantric texts tell of kings who performed rituals to the various forms of Durgā in order to secure their authority and strengthen their power on all levels. Why Goddess would be complicit in war and violence is a complex moralistic and philosophical question. It is striking that the Divine in female form is understood by the dominant class to be a necessary and powerful force to be reckoned with. The Fierce Goddess is paid respect and called upon, while Her presence in living women continues to be marginalized and even feared and denied. We see the repression of female sexuality in the Kumārī, the Living Virgin Goddess, an incarnation of Durgā/Taleju, until she has her first menstrual period. It is said the Goddess chose this young form to be worshiped as so She would not be sexualized. Moreover, the loss of Divine Power that is associated with the Kumārī's menarche is a clear patriarchal and brahminic overlay when we consider the centrality and sacrality of menstrual blood in Śākta circles.

Unlike the orthodox Saraswatī or even Lakṣmī, Taleju has not lost Her erotic allure. She is also known as a sexually mature Mother Goddess. Taleju is strongly associated with the land and the harvest. She is unique to the Kathmandu Valley and is perhaps an evolution of an earlier regional Earth Goddess. Etymologically, Taleju's name comes from various sources. The root, *tala,* may derive from a Tantric designation for genitalia, and takes different suffixes: *ju, monde, esvari*[2] all endings that refer to the earth or physical realm. *Tala* may also be a root word for field or hamlet in ancient India and Nepal and could reference an earlier role as a Grāma Devatā or Village Goddess.[3] *Tāla* is also a name for Śiva in his lingam form. It is interesting to note how the word Taleju expresses a relationship between field, which can be a metaphor for the yoni, and lingam or penis. For millennia sexual rites have been performed in fields across the ancient world to bless the harvest and stimulate female fertility. Taleju is a Goddess who rules over such rites.

In Her esoteric Tantric form, Taleju has thirty-two heads, among them cat, jackal, coyote, tiger, lion, donkey, and boar.[4] Taleju, like Kālī and Vajrayoginī, also carries a human skull cup full of blood in Her hand. Interestingly, aside from a multi-headed icon above the magnificent golden temple door in Bhaktapur, there are no other images or statues of Taleju. When I first encountered Taleju in 2000, one of our guides explained that there is no true image of Taleju because She is so powerful and fierce that if we laid eyes on Her, we would fall into a state of trance and shock! Therefore, to alleviate the power of this magnificent and horrific Goddess, She is propitiated with animal sacrifices on Astami and Navamī, which are the final two days of the festival and the mythological peak of Durgā's bloody cosmic battle with the demons. Taleju, Durgā, and Kālī are considered "Dark" Goddesses for each represents the mysterious embodiment of Earth and Cosmic energies.

To some, their "darkness" is something to fear, a point we will return to shortly. Throughout the year people make vows to the Dark and Fierce Goddess in Her various manifestations. They promise to have animals sacrificed during the festival in exchange for the Dark Goddess' protection of their families, or Her alleviation of an illness or infertility, and any or all the other countless reasons why humans pray to the Mother Goddess. Even Newar Buddhists participate in the sacrificial rituals; however, in keeping with Buddhist tenets of nonviolence, they offer coconuts, eggs and bananas instead of an animal's life.

When I asked our guide Ranju about the reason behind sacrifice, she explained that in Hinduism there are four roads to liberation or mokṣa, which is the ultimate goal in Hinduism. Artha (wealth), dharma (right action), and karma (devotion to family) are three paths that bind us to the physical world, but the fourth path mokṣa (liberation) is approached through ritual practices such as sacrifice. She explained that it is not just a matter of randomly choosing and ruthlessly slaughtering any animal that comes along. There is a definite system to each choice. There are specific guidelines as to which animals can be sacrificed. For example, if an animal moves its head in a certain way or gives some other action that has come to represent the Goddess' refusal, its life will be spared. There are sheep in the Kathmandu Valley that are covered in long dreadlocks or jata. They have been left to wander freely as chosen children of Kālī after having been rejected from the sacrificial pit. Jata are understood as a sign that the human or animal wearing them is a beloved of Kālī. Each of the sacrificial animals represents a human quality or emotional "demon" that needs to be destroyed in order for virtue to prevail. The buffalo represents anger and ignorance; the goat, injustice; sheep, stupidity; chicken, timidity; and duck, apathy. The animals become the embodiments of people's deficiencies and are offered to the Dark Goddess for transformation. Furthermore, since Hindus view everything in the cosmos as a manifestation of the Divine Mother, only male animals can be sacrificed. Supposedly Durgā prefers uncastrated water buffaloes as they symbolize the buffalo-headed demon She defeats in Her myth.[5] Aside from water buffaloes, only black animals may be sacrificed because they are said to symbolize the Dark Mother and the earth. Since the female is the life-giving force, female animals are never sacrificed. Hindus believe that by sacrificing the lives of these animals, these beings will be reincarnated into human form in the next life, thus enabling them to eventually achieve mokṣa (liberation).

Despite such justifications, I cannot help but question who created this system and who gets to decide which animals are slaughtered. The "fact" that they must be black carries racist undertones, especially when we consider how the lighter skinned Brahmins carry out the rituals. Many of the darker skinned people in South Asia come from the Dravidian culture, one of the earliest cultures in South Asia we know of today. Dark carries many negative and derogatory connotations throughout the contemporary world. Darkness is too often equated with all that is negative, violent, and unpleasant. Demonizing darkness has been one of many inhuman ploys of racist agendas, perpetuating beliefs of inferiority and servitude towards those who do not look like the ruling class. The white patriarchal dominant culture has other-ed and marginalized dark-skinned and nonwhite peoples out of fear and a desire to control, exploit and possess. In the United States we finally have an African American president, but we still have far to go in fighting racism in all its hideous forms. The Dark Goddess offers us solutions for accountably addressing and healing the devastating effect slavery has had on human consciousness here in the West and throughout the world.

Fortunately, the Dark Goddess continues to appear in both manifest and subtle forms as a warrior of social justice and rectification to many outside of Tantric South Asia. She is a potent social, cultural and spiritual model for healing both external and internal divides and wounding. It is interesting that Dark Goddesses like Kālī, Yoginīs, and the Mātṛkās have a similar marginalized status within orthodox culture, and yet they remind us that the Greatest Mysteries of our Existence all come from the cosmic and eternal darkness. The presence of Dark Goddesses in our psyche and in our communities provokes us to reexamine what we hold as dark, and how we feel about and define that "darkness." Tantra and other mystery traditions teach *without the dark, there is no light*. Central to many of these teachings is the idea that we all come from the dark primordial womb of the Mother Goddess.

To sacrifice means to make sacred. During the Durgā festival animals are offered as sacrifice; however, can such an act truly be considered making them sacred? The intentional act of *taking a life* still brings up questions as to the integrity of this practice. The interpretations behind the need for sacrifice seem as paradoxical as the practice of sacrifice itself. To most of us in the West, animal sacrifices are difficult to understand. We come from a culture that negates the destructive aspects of *natural* cycles and keeps strict taboos around the discussion of physical death. The only socially "acceptable" observation of death has to do with Hollywood action and horror films depicting grotesque and heinous images of killing that on one level serve to perpetuate violence and machismo ideals, and on another desensitize the majority to the reality and even sacrality of natural death. Hindu Goddess Scholar David Kinsley offers an interesting perspective on why sacrifices take place in South Asian communities. He suggests that the festival's close association with the harvest gives the sacrifices another meaning aside from their mythological association of battle. He writes:

> My suggestion is that underlying blood sacrifices to Durgā is the perception, perhaps only unconscious, that this great goddess who nourishes the crops and is identified with the power underlying all life needs to be reinvigorated from time to time. Despite

her great powers she is capable of being exhausted through continuous birth and the giving of nourishment. To replenish her powers, to reinvigorate her she is given back life in the form of animal sacrifices. The blood in effect resupplies her so that she may continue to give life in return.[6]

Patriarchal culture takes and takes from Mother Earth with little regard to the Earth's limited natural resources. Most people are taught not to even *feel* the need to give back to the Earth. A respect for the fragile interconnection between all life forms goes ignored, even unnoticed. However, in Nepal, sacrifice is viewed as crucial in maintaining natural cycles and the Great Goddess' favor and protection. Moreover, in the fall in preparing for the coming barren season of winter, a natural and necessary culling of the herd takes place regarding male animals that are not needed for breeding. In agricultural societies, male animals are killed for food and feasting in the fall; therefore, sacrifice was probably, at least partly, initiated as a form of gratitude or sacralization in this necessary process. All parts of the animal's body are used after the sacrifice. In fact, the head of the buffalo is said to be the most honorable part. The buffalo's importance is connected to the myth of Durgā's victory over the buffalo demon. After 108 buffaloes are sacrificed on Astami, their heads are taken home and divided among family members according to seniority. The eyes, ears, nostrils, tongue, all have significant meaning. No part of the animal goes to waste.[7]

Another possibility for the reasons behind sacrifice in the contemporary Hindu world is as a ritualistic means for people to face and participate in death. There is an inherent recognition in the Hindu and Tantric worldview that without death, there is no birth. Death is an inevitable component of every new life. However, the practice of animal sacrifice that today is so central to rites around Durgā, Kālī, the Matṛkās, and Yoginīs seems to be a degenerate practice of a much earlier woundless sacrifice. The irreverent nature of this practice is especially evident when we consider how the relevance of the female body and the inclusion of women in most of the orthodox rituals, especially those around natural death, are overlooked. Considering how the powers of menstrual blood are highly lauded by Kaula, Śākta and Tantric practitioners, it is curious that the natural, nonviolent offering of menstrual blood, the kula, that holds direct liberating potential for practitioners is offered only in esoteric circles. This has not always been the case.

Vicki Noble writes in *Shakti Woman,* quoting Irish scholar Lawrence Durdin-Robertson, "the first blood at the altar was menstrual blood, the free flow of the priestess giving back to the Earth Mother."[8] The work of scholars such as Vicki Noble, Chris Knight, Penelope Shuttle and Peter Redgrove demonstrate that the practice of human sacrifice has roots in menstrual ceremonies. The only blood that is shed without pain or harm to another being is menstrual blood: yet this source of female power has been maligned and shamed since the beginning of patriarchy. On the Indian subcontinent, human and animal sacrifice came to replace the original menstrual offerings. The fullness of all cycles from birth to fruition to death reminds all who live in accordance with the natural cycles of earth and sky that equilibrium is only achieved through balance. Blood sacrifice can be considered a form of placating the spirit realm, of propitiating the Great Goddess of Life and Death who gives us our existence. Goddess has been offered blood by indigenous and earth-honoring peoples of past and present to prevent the natural catastrophic disasters: disease, floods, hurricanes, earthquakes, and tornadoes. However, animal sacrifice replaced the original woundless offering of menstrual blood, thereby stripping women of their inherent power that was in natural alignment with natural forces. Outside of Tantric and Kaula circles, menstrual blood is no longer the holy sacrament. Instead hundreds if not thousands of animal sacrifices take place to appease the Goddess on Astami. In some instances the Dark Goddesses' life-giving function has been disregarded and forgotten as local people, out of fear of Her wrath, primarily propitiate her.

In her article, *An Archaeomythological Investigation of the Gorgon*, Joan Marler attributes the demonization of Goddess to the rise of heroic consciousness that sought to conquer death (and) could not tolerate reminders of natural mortality and ties to the earth, that. . . took horrific female forms"[9] As societal values shifted towards violence, warfare, material possession and domination, death became the expression of patriarchal power. Male creation deities usurped the life-giving powers of the Great Mother Goddess and death and warfare became central around 5000 years ago. "The blood ritual imitations of women's functions were turned into taboos against women's function."[10] Women were no longer allowed to participate fully, or especially lead death rituals, as they had done for thousands of years. Biological female functions were turned against women to prevent them from participating in any rites. Vicki Noble notes:

> On planet earth, it is women who most directly experience the reality of natural cycles, through the continuous ebb and flow of our ovulation and menstruation, in sync with the moon, for most of our adult lives. And research shows that it has been women who facilitated the rituals of dying, death, and rebirth around the world—until very recently in most places.[11]

Woman's power to give and nurture life as well as the collective understanding that it was this same Goddess whose womb we all return to were replaced by violent acts of patriarchal men taking life.

Bloody Impressions
Astami – Eighth Day, October 5, 2000

As I walk through the blood-stained streets amidst the heightened fervor of thousands of Goddess devotees, I begin to understand that the blood and skull imagery used in Śākta Tantric rituals are not necessarily bad or negative. Gradually I am able to understand the deeper meaning of these symbols especially in their relation to Goddess Kālī. In a quintessentially Tantric way, I can witness the rituals without my mind going into judgment—and yet my stomach still churns at the sight of the blood. What is the wisdom of my body telling me? My heart has a hard time staying open in these rituals. It goes out to the animal that is being sacrificed and I find myself praying for its soul, but I am not sure how effective my prayers are. Regardless of how quick and supposedly "humane" the practices are I do notice fear in the eyes of each sacrificial victim. It is confusing to be from the West and to try to understand the meaning and history, and also not to impose my limited Western dualistic judgments on what I am witnessing. By nature my experience of sacrifice is paradoxical. I understand that a blood offering is important to the ritual, and yet the act of taking another life, even in a ritual context, does not feel like something Goddess would demand. Perhaps a Tantric practitioner would argue: If Goddess is Everything, then She is the sacrificer and the sacrificed, and the act of sacrifice would be a natural expression of Her power and will. While I can tolerate the practice while I am at the sacred sites, I intuitively sense that killing another being has not always been part of the rituals.

What most impresses me is the visibility of and acceptance of death. There are sacrifices taking place all around me. The iron pungent smell of blood is everywhere. On these final days, traces of blood and animal carcasses seem to be wherever I look. There is a constant stream of symbols of life and death no matter where I turn. Blood is smeared on rickshaws and motorbikes that also are decorated with garlands of orange and yellow marigolds. The juxtaposition of the delicate balance between life and death is fascinating. Each offering to these inanimate objects asks for blessings of protection from the Fierce Goddess. Flowers hang from license plates and rearview mirrors and garlands are strung across the trunks and hoods of cars while blood is splattered over the windshield and wiped across the rest of the vehicle. I remind myself that this is symbolically the blood of the lustful demons that Durgā slays in Her battle for justice. Everywhere I walk, I feel the sticky grip of wet blood on my shoes, rooting me to the earth. Red all around me—the blood, the saris, red combs, reddish pink-dyed chapatis, huge daubs of vermilion red tikas of curd and rice placed between the eyebrows, ribbons on offering plates symbolizing the umbilical cord and our connection to Mother. Seeing so much blood and many hues of red adorning every object, place and person makes me think of life more than death. Death is present and the Goddess of Death is certainly honored, and yet Śakti, the animating life-giving force pervades the sites. I feel embraced by the worldly and cosmic dance of death and life and understand that one does not exist without the other. This sheds new perspective on the emotional and spiritual cycles in my own life. It especially makes me think of my menstrual blood and how, despite all the suffering I have endured from endometriosis, I still cherish the time this natural monthly ritual affords me. We have been taught to feel shame about our monthly blood, a sacrifice that does not inflict harm or pain on another. We have been conditioned to hide it and anything that is associated with it. We learn at an early age that our blood is dirty and is unmentionable.

And yet, as I wander through these city streets I marvel at how phenomenal it is that every month life and death is expressed through the rhythmic nature of a woman's menstrual cycle. Our bodies are the microcosmic expression of the powers of the Universe, of Goddess Herself. All this red is the color of women's POWER. Our power to give life. Our power of creativity. Our blood is the sacred elixir of our Śakti power.

Blood Roots

Durgā is a Dark Goddess. She is dark like the soil of the earth and the night sky. The essence of Śakti is expressed through the color red, while the male essence, Śiva, is expressed by the color white. To a Kaula, white is the semen, red is the menstrual blood and the mingling of the two produces an elixir par excellence that has the power to transform and expand consciousness. A woman's kula or blood connects her directly to the Supreme Consciousness that is Goddess Durgā. D. White's research on the Kaula emphasizes this connection: "The cosmic force that activates and energizes every facet of tantric practice—that originates from the womb of the Goddess and passes through every link in the chain of transmission. . . is ultimately nothing other than a stream (*ogha*) or flow (*scrotas*) of sexual fluid." He goes on to say that even contemporary Tantrikas in Assam "identify their "lineage nectar" (*kulamrta*) with the Goddess' menstrual fluid or the commingled sexual fluids of Śiva and the Goddess."[12]

From a less esoteric and more socially accepted perspective, red Śakti is the life force energy—it is the cosmic blood of existence that gives us all life. Durgā, Śakti, menstrual or birthing blood, all contain the same Divine essence. Tantric teacher Nandu Menon grew up in a matriarchal village in Southern India. His village's creation myth describes the origin of the universe as coming out of Mother Kālī's menstrual blood. Her black body is the entire cosmos and when She decides She wants to create, She bleeds. In Her blood are cosmic eggs, each associated with one of the Mahāvidyās, Tantra Goddesses of Liberation. Each Goddess represents a different level or reality of consciousness, and ultimately all life comes from this cosmic flow of menstrual blood.

As we have seen, the most powerful rituals in Tantra celebrate the natural cycles of the cosmos, earth and female body. Both rituals and iconography honor the conspicuous relationship between women's menstrual cycle and the lunar cycle. Many feminist scholars[13] have written extensively about the metaphoric relationship between our menstrual cycle and the lunar cycle. The opalescent full moon mirrors the ovum we release when we ovulate with the full moon every month. When our female bodies are not exposed to artificial light and chemical substances, the dark invisible moon triggers the flow of our blood. Kaula and Śākta Tantric ideologies view polarity and the tension between opposites as central to the tradition. Tantric ideology is played out in the "bipolar nature" of our monthly menstrual cycles.[14] Noble notes, "the innate back-and-forth mystery of ovulation and menstruation, unique to our species and magically (magnetically) synchronized with the cycles of the Great Goddess Herself in Her dual planetary aspects as Earth and Moon, and the mythic forces of life and death."[15] Eric Neumann, one of the earliest contemporary Western writers on Goddess describes the bipolar nature of women's emotions and hormones. He describes the two extremes of women's menstrual experience as "fiery productivity and meditation and dreaming."[16] The qualities that both authors describe are reflective of the qualities of the Śakti/Śiva active/receptive polarity that later became central to the Tantric tradition.

In her fascinating book, *Blood, Bread and Roses: How Menstruation Created the World*, Judy Grahn describes how the ancients' conception of the dark period of the moon was most likely inseparable from their understanding of darkness as the source of menstruation.[17] According to Grahn, Noble, Alexander Marshack, and others, our ancient ancestors experienced a connection between women's reproductive cycles and the lunar cycle and this perception influenced the evolution of consciousness. Archaeological discoveries in burials and caves include 25,000 plus year-old female figures with full breasts, bellies, and hips. Etchings of 28 or 29 lines, the number of days in the lunar as well as a woman's menstrual cycle, have been found on crescent-shaped horns.[18] The influence of menstruation on consciousness is greater than we have ever considered. Grahn contends that women's menstrual cycles induced the female creation of arithmetic, erroneously believed to be a male-originated science. She writes: "It is possible that the ideas of measurement and ratio in human society originated not solely from the moon in the sky, but also in the emerging rhythm of the woman's cycle as civilization grew, and the effects of woman's cycle on the people among whom she lived, which includes men and children as well as herself."[19] Furthermore, it is logical to ascertain that early women's invention of agriculture came, in part, from an understanding of menstrual blood as a potent fertilizer. Noble contends that "the healthy vibrations from the blood, and the yogic sexual practices that accompanied the bleeding time, were useful in growing food for the community."[20] For millennia many farmers and gardeners have understood the gravitational and cyclical influence the moon has on the growth and vitality of plants. Farmer's Almanacs, containing advice still followed by farmers today, have been created in many parts of the world to chart the phases of the moon and to suggest the most conducive times for planting, growing and harvesting.

In addition to prehistoric archaeological evidence of the significance of the moon, linguistics also provides insight into how the moon has always been a central focus in culture, ritual and myth around the world. Etymologically, words for moon and menstruation are related in many languages. *Mens, mensis* are Latin words meaning 'month', and also 'moon'.[21] In English "our words for 'mind' and 'civilization' came from moon experience(d).[22] The German word *Regel* means rule as in govern and measurement. In Spanish *las reglas*, and French, *regle* "mean 'measure' or 'rule' as well as 'menstruation' and are cognate with the terms regulate, regal, regalia, and rex (king). In Latin, *regula* means 'rule.' These terms thus connect menstruation to orderliness, ceremony, law, leadership, royalty, and measurement."[23] The Sanskrit word for menstruation, *ritu,* is related to ritual, suggesting the sacred nature of menstruation as well as the repetitive nature of ritual; and *mātr* refers to both measurement and mother and is a cognate of the word, *Mātṛkā*. *Men* (Moon) and *mensis* (month) belong to the root *ma* and the Sanskrit *mas.*[24] These words all express the wider influence of woman's monthly menstrual moon-related ritual on human consciousness and society.

Rituals associated with Durgā today also point to a history of honoring the female blood mysteries of menstruation, death and birth. Durgā's festival begins on the dark moon, the day when thousands of women, whose bodies have synced with the natural lunar cycle, bleed. Moreover, Khanna points out that in Tantric mythology the God of Love, Kāmā, travels over a woman's body through an entire moon cycle. She goes on to state "Consequently, each phase of the moon is equated with certain energy zones of the woman's body in its waxing and waning aspects. The energy points marked zones for contemplation during the sex-yogic ritual."[25] Bleeding can be a time of deepened intuition and profound states of conscious awakening for women who are in tune with the rhythms of their bodies. For a Tantric practitioner menstruation is the most suitable time for performing sexual rituals because at this time "menstrual blood consists of ova—energy-containing properties with large amounts of estrogen substance. It has been scientifically validated that 'in its idle state in the body, it is the purest form of blood.'"[26] Menstruation is a potent female experience that patriarchal man has tried to control through religious, cultural and social laws, perhaps because at its essence menstrual blood offers the possibility of reaching a more integrated level of consciousness through the female.

Menstrual Taboos and Seclusion

For centuries under patriarchy there has been an overwhelming sense of fear and disgust toward our menstrual blood. Every woman with a healthy womb bleeds until she goes through menopause; and yet menstruation has euphemistically been called a "curse", the "rag", or even the more benign, "Aunt Flo." These words all serve to hide what is completely natural and relevant to women's existence. There are cultural taboos around a woman bleeding just as there are strict rules or taboos around sacrifice. However, the root of the word *taboo*, is *tapua*, a Polynesian word for *sacred* or *menstruation*.[27] The female body naturally detoxifies by shedding the uterine lining every month. However, this blood is not necessarily toxic. Why it is understood as polluting stems from the patriarchal disdain for women's bodies and fluids. In primal cultures, menstrual blood has been understood as carrying potent energies, but they are not polluting in the way the Brahmin caste has deemed them. In fact, in Śākta-centered cultures menstrual blood is "a special kind of blood. It didn't come from sickness or injury. It was related to a woman's ability to give birth, and that ability was and still is a power that only women have."[28] Anthropologist Frederique Apffel Marglin's research on menstrual rites in a village in Orissa have parallels in other Śākta and Kaula villages and communities within India (particularly Assam) and some parts of the Kathmandu Valley. There are earth and agriculturally based rituals where the Earth Herself menstruates in such places. During these times, although these are typically considered festivals of women, men also observe the traditions. Foremost for all participants is an opportunity to rest. All work ceases. Humans and the earth are given a break. On the final days of the Durgā Pūjā we find this in many of the rituals on the bloodiest days of the festival that mirror menstrual seclusion rites. No one works, all accoutrements associated with any form of learning and labor are put to the side.

Similarly, a menstruating woman is secluded with other menstruating women so she can rest. To a Kaula, Śākta or Tantric practitioner, it is understood that the Goddess is bleeding though Her. Marglin interviewed many women and men about the meaning of a festival called *Raja*, honoring the menstruating Goddess in Orissa. One of her male informants explains:

> Women are prakriti srusi sakti (the creative energy) and we (men) are purusa (the male principle) and we come here to worship the adisakti (greater energy), ma (the mother). We come here now because She is at her period which is good for each and everyone. This means that She is ready, that She will give forth. She will give us good crops and cause many things in nature to grow. Women are reflections of the Mother and of the pruthibi (earth). The Mother, the earth, and women are the same thing in different forms. During the four days of Raja, the earth, the Mother is bleeding.[29]

When Apfell-Marglin asked if menstrual blood was dirty, she received the response. "No, it is not dirty! Dirty blood is something that comes when the body is sick. . . . The blood of menses is given by Satidusi" (a name of the local goddess).[30] Menstrual seclusion rites developed partly from the recognition of women's powers during her bleeding time and the need for her to be secluded from everyday tasks. Such rites characteristically consist of three taboos: the menstruant not seeing light and thus spending her bleeding time in a hut or dark cavelike shelter; her feet must not touch the solid ground for fear of the power of her blood contaminating the earth; and she must not touch water as she will contaminate it.[31] However, practices which may first appear to be degrading to women, actually may speak to her natural affinity with both the life giving and destroying aspects of Divinity. In her menstrual state, a woman contains qualities of the undomesticated earth and cosmic Goddess, who both gives and takes life. She expresses energies that cannot be contained by patriarchal man.

In Kaula, Śākta and Tantric culture, a menstruating woman is understood to be Goddess in Her highest power. She is not supposed to bathe, comb her hair, or cut and touch any plants because in this state she contains extraordinary powers that can upset the ordered balance of the community. As Noble points out menstruation is "explicitly non-ordinary and requires we be set apart from the ordinary tasks at hand."[32] She continues, "During our menstruation we have a wide range of paranormal abilities and experiences available to us."[33] The need for seclusion was originally not meant to ostracize a woman from the community, but rather it gave the menstruant the time and space to rest, nurture her body and get in touch with her creativity and intuition. Gradually the taboos around menstruation lost their original meaning of sacred in the communal consciousness and began to take on negative connotations. Such negative perceptions were based *not on fact but on fear* coupled with a loss of trust in the natural cycles of Goddess. The patriarchal and scientific dismissal of bodily wisdom and intuition in favor of overidealization of logic and the rational mind has produced a modern consciousness in which women's lives are especially degraded, fragmented, and impoverished. With this shift in consciousness, menstrual blood becomes polluting in orthodox tradition and the reasons behind seclusion rites become inverted. Although blood has been demonized and misconstrued, the underlying acknowledgement of its *potency* albeit solely in a destructive capacity, remains.

Every Woman Bleeds: The Liminal Realms of Female Consciousness

Each month women around the globe experience Kālī/Durgā in Her death aspect as they release their blood, the fleshy uterine lining that had the potential to nourish a human life, and yet was naturally released. Not all women wish to conceive a human child, nor does every menstrual cycle end in conception, so it is important to consider menstruation as a cycle of generation and regeneration, rather than seeing it strictly as a reproductive cycle.

Anthropologist Frederique Apffel-Marglin has written numerous essays and books that emphasize an understanding of the powers of menstruation that go beyond the dominant and disempowering scientific view. She argues how "scientific knowledge concerning menstruation has profoundly affected the manner in which menstruation is lived, understood, and spoken about by many women."[34] Apfell-Marglin speaks to the split between culture and nature and private and public spheres that are dominant in the dualistic patriarchal worldview. She notes how anything associated with female bodily processes are deemed "an intensely private matter."[35] She describes how advertisements for menstrual products euphemistically refer to them as *feminine hygiene* and notes how

> they all promise to eliminate or disguise any outward signs that you are menstruating. They are all designed to reassure one that the product will enable one to act as if one were not menstruating. In the public realm there is an insistent need to deny the existence of menstruation. Most women would be acutely embarrassed by physical signs of menstrual blood in public.[36]

Indeed, this threat of embarrassment and the repudiation of female fluids within science have gone so far as to offer a menstrual suppression pill so that women do not have to be bothered with the "inconvenience" and "messiness" of this monthly female occurrence. Apfell-Marglin goes on to state how menses *happens* in healthy women. It is a natural cycle that cannot be induced or controlled unless science intervenes. This need to hide and suppress female blood is one of many ways patriarchy desires "to erase as much as possible the experience of menstruation, an event experienced as a curtailment of freedom of action."[37] We live in a world that overemphasizes doing and acting and does not honor the natural need for periods of rest and just being. Most of us have great difficulty in stopping all our actions. Moreover, Western culture does little to support our need for downtime as more and more distraction—for example, Facebook, Twitter, email, iphones and Blackberries—to name a few; keep us from truly living in the moment. Arguably the dynamic essence of Śakti is constantly in a state of becoming, but this process includes down periods, times of reflection, gestation, and rest. Periods for regeneration and generation.

Every woman within childbearing years bleeds naturally each month unless she has some illness that is preventing this natural monthly purge. Every woman on the planet menstruates and has done so across millennia. Every woman regardless of race, ethnicity, sexual orientation, and class from her preteen years until midlife bleeds, and she has the capacity to share a cycle that flows in accordance with the moon. The exclusively female potential of lunar entrainment, and the way our cycles sync with women in our communities by mere proximity of our female bodies are fascinating and mysterious phenomena. Women's menstrual cycles distinguish the human race from other animals on the planet. Our menses is directly related to various levels of consciousness. The cyclical nature of our hormonal cycle allows us to instinctively tune into the natural world. When women eat fresh organic fruits, vegetables, and grains and are not exposed to chemicals and artificial light, we bleed with either the full or new moon. Women's bodies naturally emulate and participate in the cosmic rhythms of existence.

Experiences of and around menstruation must not be defined and controlled by the patriarchal culture. When forced to repress and deny the reality of our bodies, the reality of our authentic female experience, the emotional pain and estrangement we feel from the dominant patriarchal culture translates onto our bodies, taking its toll as illness and pain. Reproductive illnesses: PMS, endometriosis, fibroids, pelvic pain, and ovarian cysts are all too common.

The majority of women on this planet are not aware of the rich lineage of female healers, shamans, Yoginīs and priestesses who have had knowledge of yogic practices, breath work, body work and medicinal herbs to treat any disease and to bring us into natural balance. These women all respect and honor the natural powers of a woman's menstrual cycle and blood. Rituals are performed with the intent to alter consciousness and bring about some empowering or healing effect individually, communally, and globally. Barbara Tedlock's book, *The Woman in the Shaman's Body* presents numerous examples of women in cultures around the world from past to present who have been in touch with their quintessentially female power, but questions how this knowledge has been lost to so many of us. She writes:

> How is it that we've lost sight of this ancient woman shaman and what she represents? For despite the proof of language and artifacts, despite pictorial representations, ethnographic narratives and eyewitness accounts, the importance—no, the primacy—of women in shamanic traditions has been obscured and denied. That women's bodies and minds are particularly suited to tap into the power of the transcendental has been ignored. The roles that women have played in healing and prophesy throughout human history have been denigrated.[38]

True female empowerment requires not only knowledge of the female mysteries, but also acceptance and respectful expression of the female mysteries of menstruation, birth, and death. Woman's experience is far from linear, stagnant, and strictly logical. Women's blood flows in a cyclical dance of releasing and becoming. Our female bodies hold the power of the kula, the female lineage, and produce the blood and sexual fluids around which the Śākta Tantric cultures are structured.

Menstruation is an expression of female consciousness that is instrumental in inducing healing and an internalized sense of empowerment. Tantra, Śākta and Kaula ideologies and practices help us to reconnect with the repressed creative and sexual power that our yonis demand we express.

Notes

1. Gérard Toffin, "A Wild Goddess Cult in Nepal. The Navadurgā of Theco Village (Kathmandu Valley)," in Wild Goddesses in India and Nepal: Proceedings of an International Symposium Berne and Zurich, November, 1994, eds. Axel Michaels, Cornelia Vogelsanger, Annette Wilke (Bern: Peter Lang, 1996), 248.
2. Mary Shepherd Slusser, Nepal Mandala: A Cultural Study of the Kathmandu Valley, vol 1 of 2: Text (Princeton: Princeton University Press, 1982), 317.
3. Ibid., 317
4. A cultural guide and University of Tribhuvan professor of Hindu iconography, art, architecture, and religion, Mukunda Aryal explained the nature and iconography of Taleju during a tour of Durbar Square in Patan. The various animal heads on this Goddess suggest Her ancient shamanic lineage.
5. Mary M. Anderson, The Festivals of Nepal (New Delhi: Rupa & Co., 1988), 149.
6. David Kinsley, Hindu Goddesses: Visions of the Divine Feminine in the Hindu Religious Tradition (Berkeley: University of California Press, 1986), 112-113.
7. Anderson, The Festivals of Nepal, 150.
8. Vicki Noble, Shakti Woman: Feeling our Fire, Healing our World, The New Female Shamanism (San Francisco: HarperSanFrancisco, 1993), 14.
9. Joan Marler, "An Archaeomythology of the Gorgon," in Revision: A Journal of Consciousness and Transformation, (Vol. 25, Number 1, (2002)): 16.
10. Monica Sjöö and Barbara Mor, The Ancient Religion of the Great Cosmic Mother of All (Trondheim, Norway: Rainbow Press, 1981) in Noble, Shakti Woman, 25.
11. Noble, "Dakini: The Goddess who Takes Form as A Woman," in Goddesses in World Culture. Vol. 1: Africa, Asia, Australia and the Pacific, ed. Patricia Monaghan, (Santa Barbara, California: Praeger (an imprint of Houghton-Mifflin), Spring 2010).
12. David Gordon White, The Alchemical Body: Siddha Traditions in Medieval India (Chicago: University of Chicago Press, 1996), 138.
13. Noble, *Shakti Woman*, Judy Grahn, *Blood, Bread, and Roses: How Menstruation Created the World.* (Boston: Beacon Press, 1993), Chris Knight. *Blood Relations: Menstruation and the Origins of Culture* (New Haven and London: Yale University Press, 1991), Penelope Shuttle and Peter Redgrove, *The Wise Wound: The Myths, Realities, and Meanings of Menstruation* (New York: Grove Press, 1986).
14. Vicki Noble, *Double Goddess. Women Sharing Power* (Rochester, Vermont: Bear & Company, 2003).

15. Ibid., 3.
16. Eric Neumann in Shuttle and Redgrove, The Wise Wound, 131.
17. Judy Grahn, *Blood, Bread and Roses*, 14.
18. Alexander Marshack, *The Roots of Civilization* (Mount Kisco, New York: Moyer Bell Limited, 1991).
19. Grahn, Blood, Bread and Roses, 128.
20. Noble, Shakti Woman, 15.
21. Shuttle and Redgrove, The Wise Wound, 127.
22. Ibid., 134.
23. Grahn, Blood, Bread and Roses, 5.
24. Shuttlegrove and Redgrove, The Wise Wound, 130-131.
25. Madhu Khanna, "The Goddess-Women Equation in Śākta Tantras," in *Faces of the Feminine in Ancient, Medieval, and Modern India*, ed. Mandakranta Bose (Oxford: Oxford University Press, 2000), 117.
26. Dudley in Khanna, "The Goddess-Women Equation," 118.
27. Grahn, Blood, Bread and Roses, 5.
28. Frederique Apffel-Marglin, "The Sacred Groves. Menstrual Rituals in Rural Orissa" in Manushi Journal (Number 82), 25.
29. Ibid., 28.
30. Ibid., 27.
31. Grahn, Blood, Bread and Roses, 11.
32. Noble, Shakti Woman, 14.
33. Ibid., 56.
34. Apffel-Marglin, "The Sacred Groves," 22.
35. Ibid.
36. Ibid., 22-23.
37. Ibid., 23-24.
38. Barbara Tedlock, The Woman in the Shaman's Body: Reclaiming the Feminine in Religion and Medicine (New York: Bantam, 2005), 4-5.

day nine
nine durgas: goddesses of liminality

Navamī

Hundreds of women line up outside the Taleju temple that is only opened on Navamī, the ninth day, during the festival each year. Brightly orange, purple, red, blue and green-colored saris lined with gold threads and intricate floral and vegetative patterns weave through the throngs of people gathered in the main square of Kathmandu. Military truck after military truck pushes through the crowded streets, parting the crowds like water, and then after each has passed, the people fill in the space like an oceanic flow, only to ebb as the next entourage advances. Festivalgoers parade through the streets banging on pots, pans, and playing various instruments in a cacophony of passionate revelry. Vendors parked out on the ground since before dawn sell flower garlands, candles, incense, and pūjā baskets of fruit, eggs, and other ritual items. It is loud, bustling, and slightly overwhelming. Truck fumes, fresh blood and thick wafts of incense all compete for my olfactory attention. Every object is worshiped, every person is adorned, and each of the five senses is given ample consideration. Pujaris sit on triangular seats, a white scarf laid out before them, with pages of mantras held down by stones, awaiting recitation. Entranced Ajimās give blessings. Children, wild dogs and cats race through the crowds. Bulls, cows and ravens add their own mythological aura to the great gathering.

Today is the final day of ritual festivities honoring Durgā in all Her forms. While Navamī is the final of the three days to Kālī, Goddess' maiden form is also honored and celebrated. On this day girls between the ages of one and sixteen are dressed and adorned in full Goddess regalia and worshiped as Kumārīs in homes. Premenarchal girls are honored as embodiments of Goddess Durgā either alone or with other girls in elaborate rituals. Above all it is a day that marks the completion of the cosmic cycle and the final night of Durgā's battle for justice over the demons. Throughout the day while householders attend rituals at the Taleju temple, secret rituals at shrines to Durgā's collective form, the Aṣṭa Mātṛkās, also known as the Navadurgā, are conducted to invoke these Goddesses' energies into the bodies of men from the Gardener class. The completion of tonight's dance rituals will catapult the energies of the Navadurgā out into the Valley over the next nine months where a cosmic dance of creation, fruition and destruction will be reenacted by the ritual dancers in the hope of maintaining balance in all realms of existence, and especially in the physical world. While the Navadurgā perpetuate the dance of the seasonal life cycles as they move through the Himālayan Valley over the next nine months, the Aṣṭa Mātṛkās maintain their peripheral ancient stone abodes around the cities and villages as holy places of worship and protection.

Navadurgā

In Nepal the collective manifestations of Goddess Durgā, the Aṣṭa Mātṛkās and Navadurgā, a number of other Goddesses, and certain other deities are known in Nepalmaṇḍala as *pīṭha devatās* (Gods having a place/altar embedded in the landscape). All of these deities are ancient and have a powerful presence which is intricately tied to the land and the seasons. The Navadurgā carry similar functions to the Aṣṭa or eight Mātṛkās and in some places they are worshiped interchangeably. Like the Mātṛkās, the Navadurgā serve as Divinities demarcating the boundaries between order and chaos, internal and external realms, and seen and unseen forces. However, while the Mātṛkās are more strongly tied to a particular place; for example, a specific stone, shrine or tree, the Navadurgā are a governing force in the sense of time and movement.

On an esoteric level, the collective form of the Navadurgā narrates the temporal process of a human life. Each of the Navadurgā relates to some sphere of the birth, life, death cycle. Their natures speak to different life phases from conception Brahmāyaṇī, to youth Kaumārī, to maturity Vaiṣṇavī, and Vārāhī to motherhood, Mahākālī or Cāmuṇḍā to death, and Mahālakṣmī or Tripura Sundarī to spiritual blossoming and union. They also directly influence the spiritual development of their devotees. They are not mothers of biological children, nor do they have deity offspring in any of the myths or legends. As with the Mātṛkās, any association with children refers to these Goddesses' protective role in the early years of a child—or the *practitioner* as child of the Divine Mother. These Goddesses take the spiritual initiate through a process of awakening during the ritual activities. Through Tantric practices the practitioner is able to activate certain spiritual and evolutionary qualities that aid them in living a more consciously integrated and spiritual life. Often these energies are a direct expression of the wide and diverse spectrum of influence of the Navagraha or nine planets.

The advanced science of Jyotish or Vedic Astrology and the influence of the nine major planets[1] have played an important part in understanding the soul's evolution in South Asia for hundreds of years. Jyotish is a complex system that expresses the relationship between the micro and macrocosm. It is beyond the scope of this book to fully explicate the philosophy and science behind this tradition, but it is important to consider the nature of the relationship between the Navagraha and the Navadurgā as it emphasizes their cosmic and temporal function. The Navadurgā are not only guides, but mediators between worlds. The concept of bridging earth and the human body (microcosm) with Divinity and Universe (macrocosm) is expressed in each of the Navadurgā's association with both a planet and a plant. Let's first look at their relationship to the Navagraha.

Graha also means *seizer* and speaks to the governing influence of the nine planets on our lives: Sun, Moon, Earth, Mercury, Mars, Venus, Jupiter, and Rahu and Ketu the ascending and descending nodes of the moon. It is interesting to note how many of the Navagraha have a malevolent presence that must be propitiated. These are forces that are inseparable from all that we are and experience in worldly life, and yet they have a strong and very real presence that must be honored—and in some cases harnessed so that they will not wreak havoc on the civil or personal and internal order. The Navadurgā and Navagraha have a similar reputation of being a pervasive and powerful presence that cannot be ignored. Both the Navadurgā and Navagraha express elemental and cosmic energies which not only influence but possess individuals. Slusser explains how the planets are called "seizers" because of their possessive nature.[2] The transits and influences of the natal placement of these planets in one's astrological chart (a map of the soul) give profound insight into the mysteries of the universe and the reflective cycles in our own natures. For thousands of years people all over the world have turned to the sky for illumination of the human psyche and its relationship to the cosmos. There are specific practices that can be done to enhance and alleviate the planets' influences. Being under the influence of certain planetary cycles is its own form of possession albeit not as direct and visible as the spirit possession of the Navadurgā and other fierce female deities.

Possession—Shamanic and Female

Possession is a spiritual experience one finds the world over. It is an opportunity for direct communication with the deity without having to go through a mediator such as a priest, rabbi or some form of hierophant. Possession and trancelike experiences are still common throughout South Asia and have typically been woman's domain. Kathleen Erndl notes: "The most dramatic way in which the Goddess manifests herself to her devotees is through possession of human, usually female, vehicles."[3] People can also be possessed by malevolent spirits that cause disease and other worldly disruptions. Possession by Goddess "is seen as a gift, a sign of grace, a positive, albeit troublesome experience."[4] She defines possession as "troublesome" because of the intensity of the energies and the responsibilities the human must accept in being a vehicle for such powers and truths. It can be challenging for women, in particular, due to cultural and social denial of any sort of public female authority. On a physical level, this trancelike state can cause discomfort as blocked energies are moved by awakened kuṇḍalinī. But ultimately, the recipient of these intense energies may also experience profound personal healing. When a possession occurs repeatedly in one woman, her role as soothsayer and healer inevitably has both positive and potentially negative repercussions in her family and community. Lhamo, the Tibetan healer I encountered during my first visit to Nepal in 1998, was initially ostracized by her community. The possession symptoms she experienced were considered bizarre and threatening to the status quo. For years she was considered crazy. Eventually His Holiness the Dalai Lama learned of her behavior and powers and wrote a letter endorsing her as a channel for Goddess.[5] It is interesting to note how sometimes female healers and oracles are held with the same mixture of awe and fear as their fierce Goddess counterparts.

Throughout the world, communities that exhibit more shamanic and earth-based qualities tend to view possession as an experience of receiving the *grace* of the deity. My own experiences of humans embodying Fierce Goddesses (Kumārī, Ajimās, Ratna Māyā Devī Mātā, Lhamo, the Navadurgā dancers, and Ammachi) have affirmed that such otherworldly interactions and expressions have not always been considered as something threatening or to be feared. In fact, possession is also understood as a benefit to the entire community. These women and girls are living oracles who predict calamity and blessings, advise on the timing of certain events, and serve as spiritual advisors in a variety of capacities. They become mediators between the worlds. Moreover, women who become or have become possessed often have more authority and agency in their communities.

Invoking the Navadurgā belongs to a category of controlled and planned possessions. In such cases the Goddesses are intentionally called into the body of the worshiper. A possession is "any complete but temporary domination of a person's body, and the blotting out of that person's consciousness, by a distinct alien power of known or unknown origin."[6] However, any single definition is inadequate because possession is a "complex set of related phenomena."[7] In some cases, the possession can occur spontaneously. The woman who was manifesting Kālī at the Dakshin Kālī temple is an example of this. Such experiences tend to be shamanic at their core. Extreme bodily shaking, a change in voice, "miraculous" healing and oracular powers are some of the various expressions of a deity's presence in the devotee or practitioner. It is interesting to note that fierce female deities are the most common to appear in possession experiences. As one scholar points out, we rarely hear of women or even men possessing the male spirits of a deity.[8] Instead it is Kālī, Durgā, and any of the numerous collective and individual forms of the Fierce Goddess that come through. I wonder if the Fierce Goddess has always been the one to come through a medium? And if She is coming so frequently and has such a demanding presence, what is She trying to tell us?

While most of the Mātṛkās and Navadurgā have names derived from the male gods, it is interesting to consider certain Kaula and Śākta Tantric ritual qualities that are evident in their expression and rituals. The first of the Navadurgā in the Kathmandu Valley is often Brahmāyaṇī[9], the Goddess of Generation and Creation. She initiates the yearly agricultural cycle from the harvest (September) until the monsoons (May/June). Her shrine is the first to receive offerings. Brahmāyaṇī is associated with the moon. Aside from festival days Her general day of worship is Monday. The generative implications we explored around a woman's menstrual cycle are evident in many of the components of Brahmāyaṇī's worship; for example, Her association with the moon and preferred offering of menstrual and birthing blood. In fact, most taboo substances are common for all the individual and collective forms of Fierce Goddesses. Brahmāyaṇī's plant form *Kadalī* (plantain) is suggestive of the phallus or lingam and could signify the relationship between Śīva/Śakti. Brahmāyaṇī's female-related planet form and male-reminiscent plant form speak to the unification of male/female energies. Although She is an independent Goddess, Brahmāyaṇī contains all the tensions Her eight sisters and culminating form as Durgā possess.

Within the physical world, the Navadurgā manifest as the Navapatrikā or nine plant forms of the Goddess. Further study of the qualities of the nine plants used in the rituals would most likely illuminate the nature of these Goddesses. At the most primal level they express the fecundity of nature and are manifestations of the Yakṣī or tree spirits. While the list of sacred plants may vary from region to region, Hillary Rodrigues presents the following variation of plants worshiped in Bengal:

> Kadalī (plantain), Māna (a broad leaf plant related to Camunda), Kacvī (a black-stalked plant), Haridrā (tumeric), Jayantī (a kind of creeper or barley), Śrīphala (bilva branch containing two fruits resembling breasts), Dāḍimahamī (pomegranate), Aśoka (large shady tree with small red flowers), and Dhānya (rice paddy plant).[10]

Each of these plants relates to some aspect of Goddess' nature, whether it be Her dark complexion (black-stalked plant) or golden one (turmeric), or the sexual and fecund symbolism of the other plants. One of the Navadurgā in Bhaktapur, Siphadyaha,[11] is related to the red oleander plant. The red oleander plant carries qualities that express sexuality as well as death. In addition to the menstrual red leaves and flowers, the plant has a milky white sap reminiscent of semen. The oleander plant is extremely toxic and its crushed seeds have been used in many suicide cases in South Asia. The plant embodies the fierce and alluring energies of the Goddess Siphadyaha. Goddess possesses the oleander plant's essence and its nature subtly expresses the sexual and destructive elements of reality that are inseparable from existence.

A different Navadurgā is associated with each of the nine days of the Durgā Pūjā or Navarātri (nine nights). As embodiments of these Goddesses' energies, one of the Navapatrikā (nine plants) is worshiped each day with one of nine kinds of water.[12] Nine is a number of completion and culmination. It contains all the numbers leading up to it. Many traditions numerologically describe it as the Universal Teacher.[13] Nine days and nine nights of Durgā Pūjā, the nine planets, nine Durgās and the nine months they dance through Nepālmaṇḍala, the nine plants and nine waters, each corresponds to some necessary expression of the cosmic and worldly web of existence. We find ideas about the natural cycles repeated in the various manifestations of Goddess. While the Navadurgā are independent Goddesses, they do not necessarily exist outside the fold of their collective form and are understood as ultimately part of the Great Goddess Durgā. These Goddesses are parts of the greater whole. And the whole, Herself, Goddess Durgā is described as the pillar or axis of the three worlds and is said to contain all the gods.[14]

The order and names of these Goddesses seems to vary from region to region[15] and in Nepal the list is also inconsistent. In his essay, "A Wild Goddess Cult in Nepal," which describes their presence in the Valley town of Theco, Gerard Toffin lists seven of the nine as: Brahmāyaṇī, Kumārī, Viṣṇudevī, Vārāhī, Kālikā, Mahālakṣmī, and Indrāyaṇī. Their names vary slightly in Bhaktapur but the syncretism between the Navadurgā and Aṣṭa Mātṛkās remains evident: Brahmāyaṇī, Maheśvarī, Kaumārī, Vaiṣṇavī, Vārāhī, Indrāyaṇī, and Mahākālī. Mahālakṣmī is worshiped as the red-leaved oleander goddess, Siphadyaha.[16] The Nepalese Navadurgā includes "favorite deities such as Vatsaladevī, Jayavāgīśvarī, and Guhyeśvarī[17], with the remainder of the complement filled out with obscure divinities according to personal preference."[18] When the Navadurgā and the Aṣṭa Mātṛkās are danced, they are publicly worshiped as a group of thirteen deities. In addition to the nine Goddesses, four other protective deities are included in the mix: Simā, Dumā (who are a lion and tiger Goddess), Gaṇeśa and Śvetabhairava (white Bhairava). Thirteen is a lunar number and in parts of South Asia is considered magical.[19] Durgā Pūjā begins on the dark of the moon.

The Navadurgā and Navāratri

Durgā Pūjā heralds the awakening of the Navadurgā after a long absence. After dancing through the Valley villages in a mandalic pattern over a period of nine months, the dancers put the Navadurgā masks away before the monsoons begin. To some the summer monsoon months mark a time when the Navadurgā are asleep in the fields and will rise at the harvest festival to Durgā. With the planting of the barley seed on the first day of the ritual, they awaken. While some describe their three-to-four-month hiatus as a long sleep, others refer to their "disappearance" as a death and their reappearance on the first day of a festival as a rebirth. Many of the Durgā Pūjā rituals welcome and celebrate these Goddesses' return.

The nine-day invocation summons the creative and destructive energies of evolutionary cycles of existence. This cosmic dance is expressed on myriad levels. Each night the Navadurgā are invoked through Tantric dance performances. Beginning early in the morning the male ritual dancers go to each of these Goddesses' shrines on the periphery and then to god-houses within the city or village. They perform rituals to empower the jewels and costumes with the spirit of the deities. They put on masks that are decorated with esoteric Tantric symbols that will stimulate the uninitiated and activate the energies of the initiated who witness them. The masks carry special features characteristic to the particular Goddess whose energy they embody. Pronounced jaw lines, protruding chins, tusks, fangs, and starkly contrasted colors all express certain tensions that dominate daily life: female and male, menstrual blood and semen, minimum and maximum power are a few of the truths that are presented.[20] Yak tail manes are fixed to the masks giving the appearance of the wild hair of Durgā/Kālī.[21] In many respects, the masks are treated as living deities, even when they are not being worn. In Theco, a village in the Kathmandu Valley that plays an active role in the rituals of the Navadurgā throughout the Valley, the masks are stored during the summer months in a special temple-like god-house. On the seventh day of the Durgā Pūjā (Kālī's day) the masks are taken out, the symbols are repainted. Every twelve years the old masks are burned at the end of the festival and the following year new masks for the next twelve year cycle are made.[22] However, in Bhaktapur the masks are destroyed in special cremation rites after the festival each year. The ashes of the masks are returned to the river just as the mūrti of Durgā is returned to the river on the final day of the festival. When the new masks are made the following autumn, some ashes from the old masks are mixed in with black soil from a river bank. Death and Life are honored in every gesture and every creative act. When these men put on the masks, they become the Navadurgā and dance their energies in a shamanistic ritual that allows them to participate as co-creators in the cycle of time as well as life, death, and birth. They dance to align cosmic energies that will protect the moral order of city and village life. As we see in these dances, the untamed and fiercest forms of Goddess are most venerated, perhaps because of their undeniable power to bestow life and/or death.

In the chapter on day five and the Aṣṭa Mātṛkās, we looked at the androgynous implications behind the dancers and how the idea of a third gender is common in many shamanistic communities. It is interesting to consider the community these dancers come from, as not just any male can participate in the ritual. The gardener class, the Guthi is now responsible for performing the Navadurgā rituals and for reenacting the dances in the Valley city of Theco in Lalitpur and in Bhaktapur. Originally these rites were said to be maintained by the Jyāpu agricultural caste. Some of the values of the Guthi are reflective of matriarchal elements: "egalitarism, territorial bonds, village unity. . . emphasis is put on "horizontal solidarity," cooperation within a single localized caste rather than the vertical and hierarchical caste structure usually enforced."[23] In Bhaktapur, the gardener class (Gāthā or Mali in Nepali) "grow flowers and sell them in the early morning to specified customers or on the occasion of festivals."[24] While a Tantric priest or ācāju "presides over the secret calendar of the dances, the 'mistress' or nakhi of the god-house is a woman."[25] Despite the presence of matriarchal elements within the Guthi class women are excluded from the Guthi association, which functions like a secret society. Women do not participate in the public rituals, except as observers. They are also not invited to the various feasts that take place as part of the rituals. They are forbidden from entering places where such rites are held. Their role, outside of the wife of the Tantric priest who watches over but also cleans the god-house is restricted to observer or servant. Although women are not allowed to directly participate, the largest groups of observers of Navadurgā rites are the women of the Guthi and Jyāpu castes.

It is interesting to note these two classes' association with the natural world and the significance that agriculture and the vegetative world have played in rituals for millennia. The Navadurgā are fringe deities in most parts of South Asia. They most likely originated from earlier agricultural and Village Goddesses or are a collective that evolved from the Aṣṭa Mātṛkās. Bloodthirsty chthonic Goddesses like the Navadurgā are the focus of devotion "from Hindu and Buddhist high castes to the middle and low castes. Pacified, domesticated goddesses hold a secondary place."[26] Their formidable natures as well as their legend, attributes and preferred offerings indicate their undeniable presence in the world. The Navadurgā are powerful Goddesses that one scholar describes as a brutal force "problematic to the orderly social world."[27] It seems that such rituals are performed, in part, to assuage the fears in the minds of men and to give these aspects of existence a place in the order of the cities and villages. White describes these Goddesses as "beings that, because they are closer to the human world than are the high gods, are generally viewed as having a more immediate impact on human life."[28] We can regard the Navadurgā as intermediaries for Durgā. Sometimes Durgā is difficult to directly access, as Her name "The Inaccessible One" suggests, but Her planetary and vegetative manifestations give direct opportunity for experiencing and tapping into Her permeating presence.

The Navadurgā and the Military

The Navadurgā also had a distinct military and royal role during the Middle Ages. While it is beyond the scope of this book to examine the reasons and use of the Fierce Goddess in a patriarchal and militaristic agenda, it is necessary to mention as it is a part of their history. "Down to the nineteenth century, the kings of Nepal worshiped the Nine Durgās at the end of the autumnal festival of the Nine Nights

(Navarātrī) precisely because this was the beginning of the season of military campaigns, which lasted until the onset of the rainy season."[29] Military strategies from this period contain descriptions of astrological diagrams (with references to the Navagraha and Navadurgā) for determining when and where to attack.[30]

Masked dance performances, similar to the trance-inducing Navadurgā or Aṣṭa Mātṛkās dances we see in the central square during the festival today, were performed in royal courts.[31] Only recently did the Kathmandu Valley shift from being the last Hindu Kingdom in the world to a democracy.[32] White contends that the ontological identification of Goddess with king in mythology and royal ideology must have been a conscious one.[33] Throughout the ancient and medieval world from Egypt to Sumer to China to Cambodia we find an association of Goddess with royalty. In the case of South Asia, the militaristic use of these Goddesses played an undeniable role in the history and mythology. I do wonder if the Fierce Goddesses' powers were usurped by the male military agenda, one that was directed at conquering people, possessing land and exploiting natural resources. I also question if man-made violence is a realm of Goddess if the military is invoking Her for their battles? According to Roger Friedland's essay "Religious Terror and the Erotics of Exceptional Violence": "Violence, including violence towards women, expresses a masculinity at risk."[34] This is the masculinity of the patriarchal male, one of dominance, abuse of power, control, and hierarchy. He contends: "Controlling and defending female boundaries is at the core of masculinity."[35]

Patriarchal masculine power must conquer, own and possess in order for it to thrive. Female boundaries, whether body-based, psychological, spiritual or territorial need to be forcefully kept in check to preserve the dominant masculine agenda. Organized violence, especially war, in the name of religion, becomes the means for exerting the rapacious desire of the patriarchal male. However, any defeat is menacing to the male ego. "For both secular and religious nationalism, unwanted penetration by other nations—their guns, their money, their culture, their people—is experienced as a feminization, a humiliating unmanning."[36]

When we consider Durgā's myth, we are presented with the indomitability of the female spirit and fiercely protective female power that will not tolerate injustice. The buffalo-demon can only be destroyed by a woman. Only She has the Śakti, the power, to resolve the situation. Her act is not violent, but liberating. Hers is not a battle fought to oppress and conquer. I contend that Durgā's battle is not literally a violent one. She intervenes to stop the endless bloodshed and man-made violence. Durgā engages in battle because She has come to liberate us from a system of oppression, hierarchy and dominant values. Perhaps She has come to remind us of the passionate, sensual, erotic and egalitarian values of Śākta Tantric tradition.

War is not endemic to the human spirit. War does not exist outside of patriarchy.[37] War is not inclusive of values of compassion, fierce protection, integrity and love.

In patriarchy sex becomes used as a weapon, and the female body, the battlefield. Friedland observes how "Politicized religions—and the religious warriors in particular—are obsessed with sex, with the displays of female flesh, with the regulation of sexual organs, with veils and sexual fidelity. Feminine flesh in particular attracts their ire."[38] Sexuality becomes "a medium for the exercise of power, or a metaphor through which domination, particularly male domination, is imagined and enacted." He posits that without reverence for the human and creative erotic (Śakti), war and violence is eroticized in this patriarchal world and anything related to sensuality is targeted and deemed threatening. The use of violence as a means of defense is often "directed at women, particularly the women of groups threatening the boundedness and purity of the territorial nation-state." He asserts, "manhood as defined by the patriarchy is at stake in this struggle."[39] This is a familiar theme in Durgā's battle with the demon. Here we also witness the struggle between patriarchal values of domination and exploitation and the fierce, valiant and liberating justice of indigenous and tribal peoples who are part of the Goddess tradition. The use of force is employed to perpetuate the patriarchal agenda. In the myth, the demon king tells his generals to bring the Goddess to him, even if they have to drag Her by Her hair. Goddess declares that she will only marry the man who defeats Her in battle—and of course, no man can. When Mahiṣāsuramardinī asks for a boon from Brahmā, he does not even think to ask that he cannot be defeated by a woman. He mistakenly only asks for victory over all men. In his omission, we glean how patriarchal consciousness is ignorant and exclusive. It does not even consider the power of the female, and when it does, it does everything it can to restrict, repress, exploit and annihilate Her presence. Or, it utilizes Her generous, nonjudgmental energies to do its own bidding.

On the ninth day of the festival, the military conducts rituals to Durgā within the main square of Kathmandu where their weapons and vehicles are blessed with a tika or mark of the Goddess made of curd, rice and red vermilion powder. They invoke Her protection and victorious strength for the coming year of defense and battles. The military presence in the midst of the rituals is unsettling and paradoxical. It presents an obvious clash between the ancient and matrifocal ritual practices of this festival with more dualistic and patriarchal approaches to life and death. Durgā's role as a warrior Goddess and patron of the military is an interesting tactic employed by the dominant powers.

The legend around Her tutelary form, Taleju, and the Kumārī affirm Friedland's theories around female sexual power and violence. Remember, this is a legend where the Goddess Taleju chooses to appear in the body of a prepubescent girl so that the King will not make any sexual advances at Her. While there is no guarantee that worship of a Kumārī will prohibit sexual advances, we can understand the power the mature female body has over men. The King was distracted from his work because he always wanted to have sex with Her. Taleju's desire not to be sexually objectified by the King and the transference of Her power into a pre-sexual female body reminds me of the way women split off parts of our psyche when we are being molested, harassed or abused. Women cannot be fully embodied, fully sensual, passionate, erotic and free in patriarchy. So often we repress our erotic nature for it is not understood and the target of too much male control and abuse. Perhaps the Navadurgā collective reminds us of the power of strength in numbers. Bonding with like-minded women and men who respect and honor the erotic is empowering, and one form of defense that is called for in any kind of battle.

The Legend of the Navadurgā in Bhaktapur, Nepal

The legend of the Navadurgā in Bhaktapur is particularly revealing of the wild and powerful natures of these Goddesses. However, in its retelling it has become more of an admonition about the dangers of the uncontrollable primal and naturally chaotic aspects of existence. The distinction between legends and myths is important because legends often reveal events that are related to a specific place on the earth rather than a cosmic and all-pervading nature. Legends recount encounters between deities and humans in the mundane world. They portray events of great importance not for the cosmos, as in myths, but for the city or town with which they are associated.[40] The legend of the Navadurgā is not a universal South Asian story; however, it does carry some common orthodox themes around possession, control, pollution and civil order.

According to this medieval legend, the Navadurgā live in the dark forest outside the city boundary of Bhaktapur. It is believed these Goddesses will capture and devour anyone who enters their terrain to feed their insatiable thirst.[41] One day an adept Tantric practitioner comes upon them as they are dancing their secret dance of creation. They notice his intrusion and capture him. He begs them to let him go and promises to worship them if they do. The Navadurgā set him free. Instead of fulfilling his promise of worshiping them, he binds them with powerful mantras, draws on his ritually acquired siddhis (supernatural powers) and shrinks their size. He then takes them into his home and locks them in a room for his sole enjoyment. He continues to "worship" these Goddesses in captivity and commands them to dance for him. Because they are under his spell, they are forced to oblige. But they warn him that the spell will be broken if anyone else sees them.

One day when the Tantrika is out, his wife cannot resist opening the door to the secret room. Her husband spends so much of his time there, she is curious to know what is inside. She steals her husband's key and opens the door. The Goddesses rush out in a fury threatening to leave the city forever, knowing full well that their absence will leave the inhabitants in dire circumstances. Without their fiercely protective presence, unmoral order would overcome the city. As the Navadurgā flee the Tantrika's house, they capture, sacrifice and eat a pig.[42] The Tantric practitioner is of the Brahmin caste and to a Brahmin, pigs are polluted. Because they have touched and eaten a polluted substance, he cannot take them in his house again. He can merely perform ritual practices to transmute the energies, thereby accessing the sacrality inherent in all things. (It is curious that he does not touch them because they have eaten a food considered polluted by the orthodox tradition—a Tantrika has no opposition to anything considered impure to the conventional order).

It is not clear how the Tantrika finds the Navadurgā again, but the legend states how he begs them to stay since their leaving will bring disaster to the city. The Goddesses agree on condition that every year the people will perform a special dance and that dancers will embody their fierce spirit. A Goddess-house is built for each of them and their respective masks are kept in this small shrine until they are worn for the Navadurgā dance during Durgā Pūjā.

The legend of the Nine Durgās has many layers of interpretation that are helpful in understanding some of the rites that take place during the Durgā Pūjā festival in the Kathmandu Valley as well as the shift from female-centered traditions to the brahminic/sanskritized and patriarchal order. First, the narrative makes the distinction between the concept of outside and inside that is played out today through festival rites and ideologies around such collective forms of Goddesses. These fierce Goddesses were taken from the wild forest and locked inside a man's home. Goddesses have long been associated with forests and other such places within the natural world. The forest could be considered as a symbol for tribal India/Nepal, when aboriginal Goddesses and their elemental natures were respected and understood as integral aspects of cyclical existence. The forest also represents the wild, dark, dangerous and unknown. Some of the beings that exist in a forest are considered uncontrollable and feared. For example, tigers, poisonous snakes and spiders, and other creatures that have been connected to fierce Goddesses in mythology and practice the world over are part of the repertoire of untameable and life-threatening beings. There are other categories of disembodied beings such as ghosts and a host of benevolent and malevolent beings (Yakṣas,Yakṣīs, Yoginīs and Yogis, Navadurgā, Aṣṭa Mātṛkās and others) that are considered powerful and in some cases dangerous. In contrast to the wild and formidable nature of the forest, the house represents structure and order. It is a domain that is controlled by men. Chaotic "female" energies are not allowed expression within this sphere. As we have seen, second century C.E. Laws of Manu enforced strict codes of conduct for female domestic roles as wife and mother. Within city walls, and within the home, femaleness is only allowed very restrictive and limiting modes of expression.

Through the Navadurgā legend we learn that these Goddesses do not come willingly into the male-ordered city and domestic sphere. They seem content with a life outside man-made boundaries where they are free to express their primal and elemental natures. It is likely they speak to the lives of women in tribal or forest societies from earliest times. Moreover, their powers, which are so integral to human experience, although repressed, remain enticing and alluring. The priest wants what they have, perhaps, because it is an aspect of himself and of existence that has been denied in the orthodox order. The priest becomes a symbol of those who are intrigued by this power and must, on some level, desire its presence within the ordered world. But he cannot simply invite them in; he must coerce them into coming into his sphere of control and order. In order to separate these Goddesses from their natural environment, i.e., their primal, autonomous natures, they must be captured, abducted, and then kept under lock and key. It is interesting that patriarchy has done this to women in various ways for the past 5000 years. However, in the old matrifocal traditions women were not controlled by or inferior to men. In fact, marriage as an institution has not always existed.

According to Vicki Noble in her essay, "From Priestess to Bride: Marriage as a Colonizing Process in Patriarchal Conquest," the institution of marriage marks part of the transition from female-centered societies to male-dominant ones.[43] Women were exchanged for livestock, or money, and became part of an economic contract. Marriage was a business arrangement; it was a means to acquire allegiances and territory. With conventional marriage we see a shift in the status of women. Women lose agency, authority, as well as egalitarian and complementary relationship between females and males that are prominent within matriarchal, even matrifocal societies. In considering the roles and rites of Hindu women, Sanjukta Gombrich Gupta points out:

> Marriage is her only major life cycle rite. A widow has no position in this society. Daughters are treated as beloved temporary members of their natal family but are most unwelcome as permanent members. . . a wife is held responsible for her husband's death by failing to secure his long life. Her sexuality becomes once again a source of danger.[44]

She goes on to state how Hindu women, by employing the means they find in unorthodox religious systems such as the Śākta Tantra tradition, are able to transcend the restricted position in the family hierarchy and the passive role in Hindu religions that have been accorded them by the law books of Hindu dharma—for example, the *Manusmṛti*.[45] Women have always found a haven in spirituality and Tantra and the devotional Bhakti movement offer just that. Ecstatic dancing has always been a devotional way women commune with the divine. Gupta observes:

> (women's) natural affinity for the values of the religion of bhakti has helped them to follow their own ways with confidence. The ecstatic bhakti religion does not condemn

passion—even sexual passion. In that religion, women have found religious freedom and dignity. Historically, with the help of that religion, they rose above their debilitating "innate nature" and became spiritual equals to the best of the religious personalities in the ancient and modern history of the Hindu religions. Instead of being a source of danger and degradation to her family, a woman is looked on as the repository of family welfare and spirituality.[46]

But women dancing freely and ecstatically for and by themselves, as we see in the Navadurgā legend, outside of the moral order of the city or home, are conceived as dangerous. Women who live outside patriarchal conventions and tradition, "in the dark forest on the edge of the dominant society" (a metaphor for our psyches, perhaps?) cannot be governed in the traditional sense. In some respects the Navadurgā legend is the familiar patriarchal tale of the woman/wife whose curiosity could not be contained. She must see what is inside the locked room and in turn her disobedience threatens the male-established order. Because this woman let the Navadurgā free, these Goddesses upset the stable order of the city. Wife is excluded and their powers are held in secrecy by the male. They must be contained in a locked room and kept against their will. Although they are female, the wife is not permitted to engage with the primal female energies they impart. They may dance, for the cosmic dance is their very nature, but only their male possessor is allowed to observe them. He wants their powers all to himself.

In the legend, the Navadurgā are portrayed as hungry demonesses who will devour anyone who passes them by. But upon their release, instead of wreaking havoc on the civilized order of the city by causing some natural disaster, they eat a pig as a direct act of rebellion. The pig is associated with fecundity and matriarchy in many parts of the ancient world. Many orthodox religions consider it polluted and filthy. But the sow, boar or pig has been conceived as Great Goddess or one of Her familiars in cultures around the world for millennia. By aligning with matrifocal elements and eating food brahmanic order considers contaminated, the Navadurgā regain their autonomy, thereby preventing the male order from getting close to them again.

Kumārī Worship on Navamī

On Navamī another female-centered ritual is central to the festivities: the worship of the Kumārī or young girls. On the morning of this day prepubescent girls in various communities throughout the Valley are worshiped as the embodiment of Durgā or Taleju. Each Kumārī is given a bath early in the morning and then is given a new red sari to wear. She is adorned with jewelry, flowers and a kumkum tika on the forehead. The Kumārī receives and later in the ritual assumes the power to give the tika blessing that adorns devotees' foreheads. However, she does not wear red sindoor powder in her parted hair (the mark of a married woman). Flowers that have been offered to Durgā are placed in each Kumārī's hand. Flowers, different leaves of the Navapatrikā plants, incense sticks, lamps and special food offerings are placed before her. Chants are recited and the sound of drums fills the air. Perhaps the drums are used to induce trance as they have done in shamanic rituals for millennia. Clothes, red bangles and gold and silver are some of the offerings given to each Kumārī as a gift. Another common gift for females during the pūjā is a red comb.

The comb is an accoutrement associated with female sexuality. Fairy tale and mythological depictions of mermaids combing their hair are a common image throughout the ages. In many mythic stories descriptions of women combing their hair carries an indirect reference to a ritual for changing the weather. We can consider the comb as a divine tool, one which has a personal use and also serves an esoteric community purpose. It not only empowers us by making us beautiful and coutured, but also has been used to shift weather patterns in order to produce a desired result in the physical surroundings. The etymological significance of this in the Greek language provides further insight into layers of meaning that point to female beauty and power. In Greek the word for comb *(kteis)* is the same word for vulva.[47] The comb is a universal tool and expression of female adornment for women, regardless of culture. We see it as part of the offerings to Goddess and Her living forms in South Asia; we also find it in the ancient burial sites around the globe. Even though African and other women who wear jata (dreadlocks), twists or braids need not use it to tame their hair as other women do, it is used to style the hair in various designs. Moreover, women from myriad cultures have been depicted with a comb stuck into their hair like a crown. Wearing combs sometimes gives the impression of regality, authority and power. In South Asia there are many ritual uses around hair from the shaven head of the brahmin ascetic to the dreadlocks of the devotee of wild Goddesses and Gods. Hair is a social and religious expression of power. In South Asia, women's loose hair is threatening and considered polluting for it is symbolically associated with menstruation and other socially deemed impure states such as widowhood.

The connection between hair, death and menstruation is interesting. In some menstrual seclusion rites, women are not allowed to comb their hair, but must wear it loose and wild. Menstrual rituals in certain cultures dictate that restricting or routing the natural flow of energies during such a potent period by combing the hair is not advisable. It is important that the energies can run unbound. We see how the innate powers of the Kumārī are kept in place for even in her virgin status she does not wear her hair open in public. When a Kumārī appears to give darśan at her palace window or while being paraded through the streets during the Durgā Festival or other festivals, Her hair is bound and she wears a crown. In public her energies are contained. The rajasic power that naturally comes with menstruation and which indicates to the dominant class that the power of Goddess is leaving, is, in part, expressed through a symbolic naga (serpent) necklace. And this special necklace carries powers that induce a possession experience for the royal Kumārī and strengthen her role as oracle during certain rites of the festival. While the ninth-day celebration of Kumārī honors the virginal as in the sense of pure and untainted female nature (since she has not yet menstruated), coded symbols pointing to the hidden (and dangerous) power of female sexuality are everywhere.

Worship of the Kumārī is yet another paradoxical ritual, especially since girls in the general society do not grow up with an understanding of their Divine status. Even the Kumārīs who hold office within the royal palace of the three medieval cities are marginalized once they menstruate. They lose their Divine status once they have their menarche. The girl is removed from her royal office and returned to the village of her parents where she leads an often very difficult life. Although she is no longer a Living Goddess, many are afraid to be near her and incite the wrath of the Goddess she once was. Her dismissal from office when she has her menarche reinforces the message that menstruation is polluting. It also idealizes the pre-pubescent state of femaleness—a time when females are not threatening to the male order and are more easily subdued and controlled. These girls do not have menstrual blood, so there is no risk of pollution from that, nor are they sexually mature enough to entice any "innocent" males. The Kumārī is said to be bereft of desires, making it easier for her to be controlled. In this state she is not a threat to the societal order. And yet the gifts she receives indirectly speak to a matriarchal, female-empowered past. She is gifted a comb, a symbol of the vulva, and bangles, accoutrements of female beauty rites and adornment. Even when her full power is deemed too threatening to the social order to emerge unbounded, aspects of these wild and inherent aspects of female existence are embedded in the ritual practices—both in the private and public spheres.

Goddesses of the Liminal—the Navadurgā, Mātṛkās and the Kumārī

To Luce Irigaray the place where sexuality and spirituality merge can be considered an "interval of between."[48] The Mātṛkās and Navadurgā, and all collective forms of Durgā are navigators of the *between* in their association with birth, sex, death and all boundary places: biological, physical, psychological, and divine. They are mediators between realities. These Goddesses govern liminal realms; the betwixt and between places of consciousness and experience. The Kumārī marks the transition from girlhood to womanhood and the threshold of menarche; the Mātṛkās and Navadurgā oversee time, physical space, and other rite-of-passage stages of the female life cycle. The collective forms function as transgressors of anything unnaturally ordered, restrictive, prohibitive, or forbidden. They do not submit to the patriarchal male-dominated expression of consciousness.

From the Tantric and Irigarayan perspective, the link between male and female and sexuality and spirituality must be both/and. It must create an alliance between the Divine and the mortal, between the micro and macrocosm—precisely what the Mātṛkās and Navadurgā and other collective forms of the Goddess are known to do. There is power in the communal natures of these Goddesses. They can teach us something about women working together as parts of the greater whole. Individual women coming together each with her unique gift (tool, attribute, vehicle) can make an impact on the world. Irigaray contends,

> it is very important for women to be able to join together, and to join together "among themselves." In order to be able to escape from the spaces, roles, and gestures they have been assigned, and taught by the society of men. In order to love each other, even though men have organized a de facto rivalry among women. In order to discover a form of "social existence" other than the one that has always been imposed upon them.[49]

We have all internalized the patriarchy. Often some of the deepest wounding comes between women who were allies and then turn against each other—often due to patriarchal power structures that at their root keep females apart so that we will not know and act from our individual and collective power.

Royal powers have turned to the Navadurgā and Kumārī for their militaristic and political agendas. Laypeople and spiritual leaders have propitiated and worshiped them to invoke harmony and protection within their communities. While the outcomes for which these Goddesses' powers have been called on in the last five-hundred years have not always been in alignment with matriarchal/Śākta Tantric values, the Śakti offered by these elemental female forces is undeniable. We need to take it back so it is not abused and exploited for violent means. These Goddesses are a living presence both within our selves and in our world. We may not recognize their appearance in the West as easily as we can in the East, but they are an integral part of the human and universal Spirit. It is important we look to Śākta Tantra myths, rituals and practices for models of our own creative and spiritual potential. We must also deconstruct legends and practices that place females on the margins or demean women and girls in any way. We can find qualities of the Navadurgā in women in our local communities and abroad. For millennia women have gathered to find solutions to violence, poverty and the various forms of suffering that infects our communities.

One contemporary example of a collective model of shared female leadership and matriarchal wisdom is the Council of Thirteen Indigenous Grandmothers. These are sagacious women who come together from different parts of the world to find conciliatory solutions to the environmental, spiritual, social, cultural and economic crises facing our world and communities today. Matriarchal models of reciprocity (for example, the gift economy),[50] conflict resolution and decision-making through consensus are part of their communal practices. Prayer, visions, dreams, ancestral worship, indigenous and shamanic healing practices are key elements of their collective. "The Grandmothers believe we must return to our inner spirit and the spirit of all things, which we have abandoned while looking elsewhere for happiness."[51] Their shared belief that stones not only have spirit, but hold ancient memories and are the oldest beings on the planet is reminiscent of the groupings of stones found throughout the Kathmandu Valley from which the councils of the Mātṛkās and Navadurgā most likely evolved. The Thirteen Grandmothers are living embodiments of the fierce female spirit we find in Durgā's collective form who are addressing ways we can bring about unity, sustainability and peace for all of humanity.

Of course, we need men to work with us. The inclusion of the male deities Ganeśa and Bhairava in the grouping of the Navadurgā, to me speaks to the conscious men who respect, honor and revere the sacred powers of Goddess and women. These are men who embrace Śākta Tantric values and understand the importance of honoring our sexuate differences. These are men who work with women in nonhierarchical and nondominant ways, encouraging women to lead in finding harmonious methods to celebrate the complementary energies between the sexes as well as find the unity behind our diversity. The Navadurgā teach us about power in numbers and the interconnectedness of the human spirit. Similar to the way the Navadurgā are ultimately aspects of Durgā, we are all part of the greater cosmos. And we each contain Goddess in Her singular and multiple forms within ourselves.

Notes

1. Two of the "planets" are actually not planets but the ascending and descending nodes of the moon.
2. Mary Shepherd Slusser, Nepal Mandala: A Cultural Study of the Kathmandu Valley, in vol 1 of 2, text, (Princeton: Princeton University Press, 1982), 344-45.
3. Kathleen Erndl, Victory to the Mother: The Hindu Goddess of Northwest India in Myth, Ritual, and Symbol (New York, Oxford: Oxford University Press, 1993), 105.
4. Ibid., 106.
5. Larry G. Peters, "The Tibetan Rituals of Dorje Yűdronma: A Fierce Manifestation of Feminine Cosmic Force," in Shaman's Drum (Number 45, 1997).
6. Erndl, Victory to the Mother, 106.
7. Ibid., 107.
8. Elizabeth Chalier-Visuvalingam, "Bhairava and the Goddess," in Wild Goddesses in India and Nepal: Proceedings of an International Symposium Berne and Zurich, November, 1994. eds. Axel Michaels, Cornelia Vogelsanger, Annette Wilke (Bern: Peter Lang, 1996), 295.
9. The first of the Aṣṭa Mātṛkās is Brāhmaṇī. Many of the names between the two groups

are very similar.

10. Hillary Peter Rodrigues, Ritual Worship of the Great Goddess: The Liturgy of the Durgā Pūjā With Interpretations (Albany: State University of New York Press, 2003), 129-130.

11. Niels Gutschow, "The Aṣṭa Mātṛkās and Navadurgā of Bhaktapur" in Wild Goddesses in India and Nepal: Proceedings of an International Symposium Berne and Zurich, November, 1994. eds. Axel Michaels, Cornelia Vogelsanger, Annette Wilke (Bern: Peter Lang, 1996), 197.

12. Rodrigues, Ritual Worship of the Great Goddess, 145-146. The nine kinds of water are: water from the Gangā, rain water, water from the Saraswatī River (collected from the Prayāga), water from the sea, water mixed with pollen from the lotus flower, water from a waterfall, water from different holy spots, water scented with sandalwood paste.

13. See Vicki Noble, Motherpeace: A Way to the Goddess through Myth, Art, and Tarot (San Francisco: HarperSanFrancisco, 1983).

14. Gérard Toffin, "A Wild Goddess Cult in Nepal. The Navadurgā of Theco Village (Kathmandu Valley)." in Wild Goddesses in India and Nepal: Proceedings of an International Symposium Berne and Zurich, November, 1994. ed. Axel Michaels, Cornelia Vogelsanger, Annette Wilke (Bern: Peter Lang, 1996), 247.

15. In India a popular list is: Śailaputrī, Brahmacāriṇī, Candraghaṇṭā, Kuṣmāṇḍā, Skandamātā, Kātāyanī, Kālarātrī, Mahāgaurī and Siddhidātrī, Jagadishvarananda, Svami (trans.) (1992) Shri Shri Candi (in Bengali) (Kolkata: Udbodhan, Shri Ramkrishna Math), 27.

16. Gutschow, "The Aṣṭa Mātṛkās and Navadurgā of Bhaktapur," 197.

17. Guhyeśvarī is a very important Goddess in Kathmandu. Her temple in Paśupathinātha is one of the Śakti Pīṭhas. Some say Her vulva fell here, others say Her anus. She is worshiped as a form of Durgā and has a very devoted and strong following of Her own.

18. Slusser, Nepal Mandala, 322.

19. Samjukta Gombrich Gupta, "The Goddess, Women and Their Rituals in Hinduism." in Faces of the Feminine in Ancient, Medieval, and Modern India, edited by Mandakranta Bose (Oxford: Oxford University Press, 2000), 98.

20. Robert I. Levy, Mesocosm: Hinduism and the Organization of a Traditional Newar City in Nepal (Delhi: Motilal Bandarsidass Publishers, 1990), 507-510.

21. Toffin, "A Wild Goddess Cult in Nepal," 235.

22. Twelve could correspond to the astrological solar cycle; however, Jyotish is a science that considers the lunar cycle as central so more research needs to be done into the significance of twelve for this village.

23. Gutschow, "The Aṣṭa Mātṛkās and Navadurgā of Bhaktapur,"194.

24. Ibid.

25. Ibid.

26. Toffin, "A Wild Goddess Cult in Nepal,"248.

27. Ibid., 248.

28. David Gordon White. Kiss of the Yoginī: "Tantric Sex" in Its South Asian Context (Chicago: University of Chicago Press, 2003), 133.

29. White, Kiss of the Yoginī, 129.

30. Ibid., 132-133.

31. Ibid., 142-143.

32. Nepal became a democracy in 1990. The 1990 constitution declared that Nepal is a multi-ethnic, multilingual, democratic, independent, sovereign Hindu Kingdom having a constitutional monarchy. In 2006 Nepal was declared a secular state. Whereas various ethnic groups and religions have coexisted amicably for centuries, if not millennia, today the gap between orthodox religious groups, nonorthodox practitioners, and groups who consider themselves nonreligious is widening. Modernity vs. Tradition influenced Nepal's internal conflict. In the past decade Nepal has experienced a civil war. There has been much violence and political unrest as part of a "democratic" movement by a group of revolutionaries that call themselves "Maoist." In some cases, the Maoists can be considered leftist revolutionaries rising up against the oppressive policies and practices of the Monarchy. For further discussion of this struggle see: Baburam Bhattarai, Monarchy vs. Democracy: The Epic Fight in Nepal, (New Delhi: India, Samkaleen Teesarai Duniya, 2005), and Understanding the Maoist Movement of Nepal, ed. Deepak Thapa, (Kathmandu: Chautari Center for Social Research and Development, 2003).

33. Ibid., 131-132.

34. Roger Friedland, "Religious Terror and the Erotics of Exceptional Violence" in Anthropological Journal on European Cultures, (Departments of Religious studies and Sociology, University of California, Santa Barbara, July 16, 2004), 20.

35. Ibid.

36. Friedland, "Religious Terror," 21.

37. Archaeologist and linguist Marija Gimbutas' work presents indisputable evidence of peaceful, egalitarian, gender-balanced and nonviolent cultures existing for thousands of years throughout Old Europe. Fortification or weapons, endemic to patriarchal civilizations, have not been uncovered at any of these archaeological sites.

38. Friedland, "Religious Terror," 2.

39. Ibid., 2.

40. Levy, Mesocosm, 612.

41. Ibid., 503.

42. Ibid., 503-505.

43. Vicki Noble, "From Priestess to Bride: Marriage as a Colonizing Process in Patriarchal Conquest," in The Rule of Mars: Readings on the Origins, History and Impact of

Patriarchy. ed. Cristina Biaggi (Manchester, Connecticut: Knowledge, Ideas & Trends, 2005), 188.

44. Sanjukta Gombrich Gupta, "The Goddess, Women and Their Rituals in Hinduism." in Faces of the Feminine in Ancient, Medieval, and Modern India, ed. Mandakranta Bose (Oxford: Oxford University Press, 2000), 92.

45. Ibid., 88.

46. Ibid., 103.

47. Barbara G. Walker, The Woman's Dictionary of Symbols and Sacred Objects, (San Francisco: Harper Collins, 1988) 129.

48. Luce Irigaray. An Ethics of Sexual Difference, trans. Carolyn Burke and Gillian C. Gill (London: the Athone Press, 1993), 48-51.

49. Luce Irigaray, This Sex Which Is Not One, trans. Catherine Porter (New York: Cornell University, 1985), 164.

50. Genevieve Vaughn, Women and The Gift Economy: A Radically Different Worldview is Possible, (Toronto: Inanna Publications and Education Inc., 2007).

51. Carol Schaefer, Grandmothers Counsel the World: Women Elders Offer Their Vision for Our Planet (Boston: Trumpeter, 2006), 7.

day ten
durga's victory

Vijaya Dashami, Victory Day

The tenth and final day of the Durgā Pūjā, Vijaya Dashami, is celebrated as the Goddess' victory day. It is the climax of the festival, and shouts of *Vijaya Dashami!* can be heard everywhere. The festival gets its name from this day: the great tenth day of victory.[1] The seeds that had been planted ten days earlier have now sprouted, and the yellow-green shoots are clipped and worn behind the ear after one receives a tika. In Kathmandu, people line up for hours around the royal palace gates waiting for the opportunity to receive a tika from the King and Queen, who are viewed as embodiments of Divinity. Giving and receiving the tika is an act of darśan—to see and be seen by the deity. Receiving a tika from an elder or higher ranked individual such as the Royal Kumārī, an Ajimā, or the King and Queen, and generally the patriarch of the common household, is a central act on the tenth day of the festival. Family members travel from far and near to the closest household hosting the eldest living family member. Anderson explains that the purpose behind this day is "to receive the tika blessing, a dot of red paste placed upon the visitor's forehead by [his] elder's hand."[2] Instead of worshiping a mūrti, humans receive the tika. The tika is placed on a living form imbuing her/him with sacred power. This red curd paste is a remnant of the original menstrual marking on the third eye—the seat of the pituitary gland that rules the endocrine system. This divine power aligns our energies with Durgā's and carries us through the next yearly and cosmic cycle until the next harvest when Durgā will come to bless us again.

Rice wine is drunk, music is played, songs are sung, chants are recited; each household carries a festive and yet nostalgic air, for everyone knows Goddess will soon be returning to Her cosmic mountain abode until the next harvest. After the communities spend the day in great feasting and celebration, a tearful farewell is offered to Goddess. Most of the community pūjās postpone the farewell as long as possible and arrange a grand send off for sometime after dusk. The mūrti that had been created and worshiped over the past ten days is carried in procession around the locality and finally is immersed in a nearby river or lake. Goddess has temporarily returned to the womblike waters from which we all come. The atmosphere is sad and melancholic. We are reminded of the ultimate goal in Śākta Tantra—to merge our consciousness completely with Hers so we can experience the Divine Union that She offers. But this is not always so easy. Even after the Pūjā period we often find we are still caught up in the mayā of our lives, the many details, relationships and responsibilities to which we must tend. For many, each Pūjā cycle brings a new level of understanding about our selves, our local environment, and even cosmic influences that pervade the worlds. Throughout the coming seasons, we can sometimes more easily recognize the Sacred, even Her enduring presence, when we become more conscious in our everyday acts. We may miss Her intensified presence that envelops and pervades us during the autumn festival; however, the festival rituals can make a lasting imprint on our consciousness. When we have been touched by Her grace and Śakti, it is difficult to live without hope and compassion. Even in the moments when we feel most alone, Goddess is right there with us. In the myth, as Durgā bids farewell, She assures Her devotees of Her return at the next harvest. She promises, *If you are ever in need, call on Me. I will hear you. I will come*. And She always does.

Tika Day 2000

Ram, a jewelry maker, who I had met the first time I was in Nepal in 1998, invites me to witness and participate in his family's celebration of Tika Day. I spend the evening engaging with family members of all ages who come to Ram's house to receive the tika from his mother and to celebrate Durgā.

Traditionally it is the father who performs the tika duties, but Ram's father is no longer alive, so, he explains, the role goes to the next eldest of the family, his mother. I find this to be surprising considering that several scholarly resources have said women are forbidden from the room where the barley seeds are sown. My experience defies that. I find it to be wonderfully auspicious to be receiving my tika from a woman, and in considering my own research can't help but feel certain that the lineage did go back to women.

Once again there is an offering of red vermilion paste mixed with rice, but instead of placing it on a statue or picture, today it will be placed on our foreheads. Today the Divine will be worshiped in human form. Within minutes of entering the room Ammā, Ram's mother and also a name for mother and affectionate name for the Goddess, motions for me to come and sit before her. She taps my shoulders while reciting prayers from the Śri Śri Chandī, *and then she puts several blades of the nine-day-old jamara plant in my hair behind my ear. Now that the barley seeds have grown into bladelike shoots, they represent the swords of Durgā. Putting the jamara blades behind our ear could symbolize the passing of Durgā's power, held in this symbolic vegetative life form, into the devotee. I find it interesting that instead of an actual sword, a freshly grown blade of green is a sign of Durgā's victory over the demons.*

Ram has two very dear teenage daughters, Babita and Sabita, who dote on me for hours. Both are around the age of sixteen and I can't help but look at them and think of Tripurāsundarī, a Mahāvidyā who has close associations with Durgā.[3] *I am fed and fed: lentils, curries, rice, chapati and greens. I sip a glass of incredibly strong rice wine. Everyone insists I eat and eat until I can't possibly eat any more. I am taken upstairs to be dressed in a red silk wedding sari. It is the most beautiful sari I have ever seen. His two daughters, about ten other female children, and several married women surround me. I know the women are married because they wear red sindoor paste in the part of their hair. Each takes a turn brushing my hair, making up my face, painting my finger and toe nails bright red and adorning my arms with colorful glass bangles.*[4] *Each of them wants to contribute in some way, even if it means touching up on what the last woman has done. They take my camera and photograph me both alone and with the collective of women in the house. We giggle and hug and play with each other's hair weaving more of the jamara plant into our braids. I feel like I am marrying Goddess. We play music and dance. For hours we honor each other as Durgā on the most favorable day of the festival.*

Hours later I return to my hotel and meet some women from our group in the lobby. They are astounded by my appearance. I am no longer wearing the red silk sari, but I am dressed from head to toe in red and black. My dark long hair has green barley blades woven through various strands and marigold petals sprinkled throughout. A humungous red tika of curd and rice takes up a good portion of my forehead. They describe me as having a glow and a certain radiance. A powerful energy, Śakti, has been unleashed in me and I look at each woman and see Durgā in each of them. And they see Durgā in me.

Tika Day 2006

Six years later I attend the Vijaya Dashami celebrations at Ratna Māyā Devī Mātā's home. Ajima, my beloved friend, is with me. Ratna Māyā Devī Mātā sits on her naga throne and instructs us in reciting mantras as we prepare for receiving our tikas. Today we will receive tikas from a Living Goddess whose Divinity is fully awakened. She wants to give my friend a spiritual name. She tells her that her spiritual name is Puntu Māiju. She is the "daughter of Ajimā." My friend has felt a connection to the Ajimā spirit at various shrines throughout the Valley. She tells Ratna Māyā Devī Mātā how connected to Ajimā she feels. She wants to be called Ajima after her spirit mother. A spiritual name honors our soul essence. When given by a guru, in a dream or through self-realization, the resonance of this name is like a mantra for our evolution. Ajima receives her tika from Ratna Māyā Devī Mātā while we chant to her Goddess essence. We each receive a tika. I am also honored and called by a spiritual name, Ambikā, one of my teachers, Nandu

Menon gave me. I tell Ratna Māyā Devī Mātā how I want to write a book about Durgā and with her permission and blessing I would like to share my experiences with her. "Ambikā Ki Jai!" She shouts and motions for the rest of us to join her. "Victory to Ambikā!" We all shout, and I feel my heart and soul shimmering with excitement. We are blessing the birth of this book.

Divinity Within

Years later I reflect on how everyone's inner Divinity is recognized and celebrated on Tika Day. However, for a Westerner, it is a difficult concept to fully embody at first. For years I found it easier to see other's divinity and not really believe or allow myself to experience my own. Chanting and doing sādhanā where I can tangibly feel the way the Śakti rises in me has helped me to find Goddess in myself as have numerous mystical and synchronistic experiences. A unified consciousness is not yet permanent within my own psyche, but I experience moments of sacred embodiment and divine knowing that are undeniably Goddess-like. And I know I am not alone in these realizations. It has been a great blessing to have shared this Tika Day experience with my soul friend, Ajima, and to also witness how so many other women and men in my life have been affected by this expansion of consciousness that embraces human and all beings as Divine.

For years I have contemplated this question: Are we divine? And if we are, what does that mean? In the orthodox religious traditions of the West Divinity is transcendent; humans, animals, and plants are not understood as Divine. But the Durgā Pūjā is a festival and ritual that honors the interconnection between vegetative, animal, human and cosmic realms—and where they intersect is a shared Divinity. When we live the themes of these myths and legends, when we see our struggles, our fears, and our hopes in them, what does this mean? Are we able to see them not only as guides, but also as reflections of, even extensions of ourselves? These myths and rituals help to illuminate our lives and what is often a very challenging existence. Tapping into these sacred rhythms through ritual, intention, and detached observation, opens our consciousness to a mystical and unifying reality permeated with bliss. Relating to these forces and believing in them gives meaning to our lives. Our experiences affirm our need for Durgā and remind us of the power that we ultimately carry within ourselves. A disciple of the Hindu spiritual teacher Swami Sivananda, Sri Swami Krishnananda contends "when we learn to see the significance of the presence of divinity or the universality of God even in our private actions, we are taken care of by universal forces."[5]

While I may turn to the Divine as Durgā, the Universal Divine Force is both formless and in form. Moreover, the idea of multiplicity and singularity coexisting is an important teaching in Śākta Tantra philosophy. Durgā's devotees know firsthand that She does indeed come to aid Her devotees though Her guises can be paradoxical. Her assistance and appearances are as diverse and multifaceted as Her infinite forms. Durgā and Her entourages of various manifestations offer alternative models of femaleness and female consciousness. There is a tolerance and acceptance of Her dual paradoxical nature within the Śākta Tantra tradition. She is a Divine model who expresses the complexity of the female psyche. Durgā and Her collective forms, the Mātrkās, the Navadurgā, and the Yoginīs are Divine *and* worldly, ecstatic *and* fierce, sensual *and* maternal, powerful *and* sensitive. In Śākta Tantra the Goddess isn't restricted to one role or expression, nor is She dichotomized and compartmentalized. Instead, here is a Goddess that embraces a full spectrum of power and emotions. Her collective and myriad manifestations exemplify fierce and powerful Goddesses whose peripheral and "uncivilized" status is highly respected in Śākta Tantric religious experience. The central text of this tradition, the *Devī Māhātmya,* expresses the nature of Her Reality. Embedded in the rituals and traditions that are enacted on the tenth and final day of the Durgā Pūjā, Vijaya Dashami, is a mythological and philosophical guide into experiencing our own Divinity and place in the universal scheme of existence.

Philosophical Significance

On the tenth day, the battles with the demons are over and all come together to celebrate the Goddess' great victory. Although She has many names and forms: Ambikā, Caṇḍīkā, Saraswatī, Lakṣmī, Kālī, Bhagawatī, She is ultimately one and the same Goddess. Regardless of emanation, each Goddess embodies the full cyclical nature of all existence. Goddess, in all Her forms, makes possible the functioning and sustenance of the Universe.

In the great myth, after She has conquered the demon king, Ambikā declares that She will take the name of Durgā, the demon She has defeated, to show that She too is the demon. However, there is an important distinction between the two figures: Goddess is infinite consciousness and the unity behind all diversity. The demon is "finite awareness whose subsequent manifestations symbolize human weaknesses and failings, the further fragmentation of something that is already partial and imperfect."[6] In other words, the demon represents the ego and our attachments and limitations. The demon speaks to the ways our individual egos are influenced by the dominant paradigm and controls the way we think, dress, and act.[7] When our attachment to being or looking a certain way is threatened, then our egos will perform any trick they have to try to manipulate the situation to suit their desired outcome. "Through the drops of blood that propagate more and more demons in the final battle, we metaphorically are shown how the ego is 'extremely elusive.' A common theme of rage fueled by desire run amok runs through the caritas. The ego retaliates by striking at anything 'other' in an attempt to gain dominance over Goddess and her minions."[8]

D. Kālī explains, "In total, the battle scenes teach that sādhanā involves every dimension of who we are, from our gross (physical) and subtle (mental) components, involving actions and attitudes, to the causal ignorance that masks our true nature."[9] He points out how for the first time, the weapons in the final carita are described as *divya,* which means wondrous and magic. He sees this as an indication of "a spiritual struggle well beyond the realm of day-to-day existence."[10] The final victory in the *Devī Māhātmya* expresses the calm, clear, serene potential of existence. It shows how when we let go of the ego, we open our understanding to a greater consciousness. "The 'death of ego' marks the passage from ever-changing becoming into pure being."[11] It expresses the soul's release into the inexpressible infinitude: Durgā. The ten-day festival provides participants with numerous ways to participate in this cosmic and worldly struggle. It helps us to see our place in the cyclical nature of existence. Regardless of where we are on our spiritual paths, however awake, or not quite so awake, the myths and rituals give us opportunities to explore universal themes of our existence. For the Tantrika and the sincerely devoted practitioner, the outcome is Union, which is the ultimate fruit of our dedication, austerities and devotion. D. Kālī notes:

> Mystical experience—the immediate, unmediated knowledge of the Divine—cannot be described, but that has not discouraged people of all times and places from attempting to describe the ineffable with the cultural metaphors available to them. Hindus call it saccididānanda ("Being-consciousness-bliss") or pūrṇa (full) referring to its absolute wholeness.[12]

To experience this wholeness, we must call on Durgā if we need help confronting both internal and external "demons." By interpreting the demons of the Durgā myth as ego constructs, societal conventions, and human failings, we are able to understand this myth on a personal and political level. When we see it as a roadmap of the heart and soul, we can turn to it for spiritual liberation. China Galland writes:

> Durgā had killed the Demon Mahisasura many times in earlier battles in this story, and though she cut off his head, he would come back to life in another form. He was not decisively defeated until his heart was pierced. This is the crucial element in what the story tells us. These human failings, these "demons" that threaten us can be defeated only when we go beyond reason, when we pierce the heart.[13]

This myth can help us to see how the heart will always lead us through. We must approach Durgā with an open heart. We must be brave and look to the heart of every issue and every matter. We must lay bare our fears and vulnerabilities. We need approach Her with humility. Durgā is inaccessible and inapproachable, as two of the meanings of Her name suggest, but only when we do not offer our egos. If the Goddess demands sacrifice, as so many scholars, priests and texts state, what would be a fitting sacrifice for the twenty-first century? Perhaps we need to sacrifice intolerance, prejudice, discrimination and all the *isms* that maintain the dominant and hierarchical status quo. Swami Sivananda says "the central purpose of existence is to recognize our eternal identity with the Supreme Spirit. It is to grow in the image of the Divine."[14] To do this we must confront the ego in its many guises.

There are countless images of Divinity in the Śākta Tantra tradition. Each of these manifestations carries infinite potential, and yet no name can reveal the fullness of Her true nature. We can turn to Lakṣmī's love, generosity and resourcefulness; the autonomy and wisdom of Saraswatī; the mystical sensuality of the Yoginīs; and the protective and healing powers of the Matṛkās. We can remember Bhagawatī, She of the Resplendent Yoni, whose blood mysteries open us to ecstatic and liberating realms. We can call on Kālī to confront our fears and dissolve our attachments. There is a Divinity for the infinite expressions of femaleness and of life. The Māīs, Ajimās, Navadurgā, Kumarīs, Vajrayoginī and Yakṣīs each express integral aspects of the earthly and cosmic cycles—and the kula. They speak to the mysteries around the sacred female as the essence of the universal clan. Matriarchal values of peace, gender and racial equality, and justice are eminent. In an address given for a Global Peace Initiative of Women Religious and Spiritual Leaders at the United Nations in Geneva, Sri Mata Amritanandamayi Devi, or Amma, spoke to the importance of the universal qualities of Motherhood; however, She does not refer to motherhood solely in the procreative sense. She contends we must all cultivate the qualities of "universal motherhood," qualities of fierce compassion, protection, courage and unconditional love. Anyone—woman or man—who has the courage to overcome the limitations of the mind can attain the state of universal motherhood. The qualities of motherhood are a woman's birthright. The love of awakened motherhood is a love and compassion felt not only towards one's own children, but towards all people, animals and plants, rocks and rivers—a love extended to all of nature, to all beings. Indeed, to a woman in whom the state of true motherhood has awakened, all creatures are her children. This love, this motherhood, is Divine Love—and that is God.[15]

To embody Durgā or any of the deities is to embody LOVE. She is both the ever-changing forms of existence and the formlessness of pure being. Durgā in any of Her forms offer teachings on a basic and foundational truth—the Love of the Universe. For Irigaray,

> The gods and goddess do not need to remain disembodied and merely objects of meditation; they prefigure the possibility of differentiated and loving relationships between men and women. . . these figures of divine and differentiated love provide the basis of

a renewal of sexual relationships, so that not only can the couple be transformed, but both the earth and the cosmos can be redeemed, signaling the birth of a new era. [16]

This new era offers a world that acknowledges the Divinity in all of us and expresses matriarchal values of peace, social justice and egalitarianism. Durgā has many liberating and transformative qualities to offer. We can turn to Durgā (and women and men who embody Her liberating qualities) for leadership. For example, we learn that there is no separation between "us and them"; that there is no pitting one way of being against the next; that there is tremendous beauty and unity behind all of life's diversity. She offers empowering paths for all who choose to live outside patriarchal expectations. Durgā displays "values of the independence movement: the struggle against oppression and slavery of any kind, including the fight for women's liberation from the domination by men. However, the final message is not violence, but love."[17]

To embark on a pilgrimage we must surrender. We must set aside immediate desires and any attachments and allow the momentum of mystical forces to propel us into uncharted territory. Over the years I have traveled to India and Nepal for the Durgā Festival, to visit Yoginī sites, and above all to pay homage to Goddess. I have gone as devotee and pilgrim, hungry for Śakti, for Her electrifying jolts of recognition and affirmation that have imbued my pilgrim experiences on so many of my world travels. I have had incredibly profound spiritual experiences: a state of reverence that is constant; veils between worlds disintegrating; the sacred merging with the mundane, no sense of separation or difference between one side or the other—in fact no sense of "other"; spirit and manifest realms integrated as one. And despite the patriarchal pervasion of culture and religion, I have found places both at home and abroad that were infused with a distinctly *female* consciousness.

Being in Nepal and India and participating in Śākta Tantra rituals has illuminated my own internal sense of power and helped me recognize aspects of myself that I needed to integrate. As I've learned to consciously embody the Goddess, as I have devoted myself to sādhanā—chanting, yoga asanas, prāṇayama, nyāsa and ritual—many of my psychological, mental and emotional wounds have slowly transformed into little pīthas, sacred places where the Goddess resides. Pilgrimage to India, Nepal and even experiencing the art of pilgrimage at home in California has been an awe-inspiring initiation into the integration of experiencing myself and the world from a *both/and* perspective rather than continuing to identify myself with the victimized end of the emotional spectrum. One of the deepest teachings has been that we always have choices about how we respond. Pain, illness and suffering are some of the most profound teachings of Goddess. It is healing and empowering to have a sense of the mysterious and awesome Source, Durgā, and to feel the Divine Unity between all the internal and external contradictions.

Durgā may not solve all the world's crises in the present moment. However, She will operate through us when we open to Her. She is a guide ever reminding us that we do not have all the information. Our dualistic judgments of what is right or wrong are limiting. They prevent us from seeing the magic. Durgā is here, and we have so much work to do. We must keep the long view. We have to have hope despite the horrors. It is important to remember the Earth has regenerative qualities. We must focus on examining our own negative habits and tendencies. We can do spiritual practices. We must cultivate inner peace, which, as so many great teachers have taught, will inevitably radiate outward. Understanding the various ways She manifests is empowering and transforming. In this day and age, the Kali Yuga, a time of destruction, great suffering, and disillusionment, we need to surrender to what Durgā has to teach us. Above all, we have to have hope. And when even that becomes unimaginable because our own or another's suffering seems unconscionable and unbearable, we can turn to dance. We must move our bodies, get our Śakti flowing, release pent up energies and bond through this timeless ecstatic ritual of bhakti, deep devotion. At the end of Durgā's battle, what do She and the Matṛkās do? *They dance*, ecstatically and with abandon—and surely shouting *Jai Mā!* Victory and Reverence to the Mother Goddess! Celebrating the Śakti, the Durgā, and the Divinity in each of us.

Notes

1. Mary M. Anderson, The Festivals of Nepal (New Delhi: Rupa & Co., 1988), 152.

2. Ibid., 150.

3. Tripurāsundarī is one of ten wisdom goddesses in the Tantric tradition. She is the creator, sustainer, and destroyer of the universe. She is also a warrior and royal Goddess. Tripurāsundarī and Durgā seem closely related through their myths and characters. Another name for this Goddess is Sodaśī, which literally means "she who is sixteen." According to Kinsley, "it is common for deities to be described as eternally sixteen years old, which is considered the most beautiful and vigorous human age." For further reference see David Kinsley, *Tantric Visions of the Divine Feminine: The Ten Mahāvidyās* (Berkeley: University of California Press, 1997), 112-129. Also, in Bhaktapur Tripurāsundarī is considered the central Navadurgā, representing the Goddess in Her full power.

4. In Nepal, jewelry is not simply a form of adornment; it especially has spiritual significance. While some sets of jewelry are worn only on certain occasions, it is generally believed that any piece of jewelry has auspicious qualities. In her pioneering work, *The Jewelry of Nepal*, Hannelore Gabriel gives the following explanation for why wearing jewelry is such a strong aspect of the culture: "Nepalese women say that jewelry is ramro, meaning beautiful, good. By wearing jewelry, one promotes goodness, attracting goodness to oneself and bestowing it on others. When a woman wears her finest jewelry on a ceremonial occasion she honors the divine in the universe and the divine in specific persons." (London: Thames and Hudson, 1999), 12. The Tantric concept of macro/microcosm is certainly played out here.

5. Sri Swami Krishnananda, "The Esoteric Significance of the Devi Mahatmya," from India: The Divine Life Society. http://www.dlshq.org/ (accessed March 13, 2002), 5.

6. Devadatta Kālī, trans. In Praise of the Goddess. The Devī Māhātmya and Its Meaning. A New Translation, with Commentary, of the Sacred Hindu Scripture and Its Angas, (Berwick, Maine: Nicolas Hayes, Inc., 2003), 149.

7. Ibid., 150-151.

8. Ibid.

9. Ibid., 150.

10. Ibid., 151.

11. Ibid., 150.

12. Ibid., 150-151.

13. China Galland, *The Bond Between Women: A Journey to Fierce Compassion* (New York: Riverhead Books, 1998), xxii.

14. Sri Swami Sivananda, "Durga Puja or Navaratri," in *Hindu Fasts and Festivals*, India: The Divine Life Society. http://www.dlshq.org/ (accessed March 13, 2002), 5.

15. Sri Mata Amritanandamayi Devi, "The Universal Motherhood" (Speech given at A Global Peace Initiative of Women Religious and Spiritual Leaders, Palais des Nations, United Nations, Geneva), October 7, 2002.

16. Luce Irigaray, "Practical Teachings: Love—Between Passion and Civility" in *French Feminists on Religion, A Reader*, eds. Morna Joy, Kathleen O'Grady and Judith Poxon (London and New York: Routledge) 2002, 77.

17. Axel Michaels, Cornelia Vogelsanger, Annette Wilke, eds. *Wild Goddesses in India and Nepal: Proceedings of an International Symposium Berne and Zurich, November, 1994* (Bern: Peter Lang, 1996), 33.

Glossary of Sanskrit Terms

Ajimā: The name of the Grandmother Spirit in Nepal.

Ambikā: A name of Goddess, means "Little Mother of the Universe."

apsaras: Celestial Goddesses, often described as nymphs.

artha: Material gain, worldly advantage, success.

āsana: Physical postures performed in yoga.

aṣṭa: Eight.

Astami: Eighth day of Durgā Pūjā.

asuras: Demons or demonic forces.

bhaga: Power, yoni, and dazzling light. Also means "go with the divine light."

Bhagawatī: A Goddess whose epithet means "She of the Resplendent Yoni." Similar qualities to Durgā/Kālī.

Bhairava: A fierce from of Śiva.

bhajans: Devotional songs to the deity.

bhakti: Devotion.

bhakti yoga: The path of devotion.

Bhavānī: A name for Durgā, means "Giver of Life."

Bhū Devī: Earth Mother.

bhukti: Spiritual power.

bījam: Root of word for seed (bīja). Refers to the seed mantra of the Tantric Goddesses.

bīja: Seed mantra of the Tantric Goddesses.

bindu: A philosophical concept that refers to the center of the universe.

Brahmā: Male Creator God.

brahman or brahmin: A member of the highest of the four major castes of traditional Indian society, responsible for officiating at religious rites and studying and teaching the Vedas. Brahmins are the more privileged and dominant group of society. One has to be born into this caste. Typically, Brahmins are an elite caste of scholars, priests and pundits.

Brāhmaṇī: Common, more generalized name of the first of the eight Matṛkās. Goddess of Regeneration. Her vehicle is a swan. Related to the male god Brahmā.

Brahmanic: Pertaining to the dominant, elite and exclusive caste of Brahmins.

Brahmārī: Bee Goddess.

Brahmāyaṇī: Common, more generalized name of the first of the nine Durgās.

cakras: Energy centers: there are seven, sometimes eight main chakras along the spinal column that begin at the perineum and end above the top of the head.

Cāmuṇḍā: Fierce emanation of Kālī.

Caṇḍa: Name of one of the demons in the *Devī Māhātmya* myth.

Caṇḍī: Name for Durgā/Kālī in the *Devī Māhātmya* myth.

Caṇḍīkā: Name of the Goddess, means the "Angry One."

caritas: Chapters.

Chanchalla: A name for Lakṣmī, means the "Restless One."

chapatis: A type of fried bread.

Dākinī: Tibetan incarnation of Goddess. Name means "Sky-walker." She can also be a living woman and practitioner.

Dakṣa: Father of Sātī or Dakṣayani. See Chapter Three for a description of the Sātī myth.

Dakshin Kālī: Ancient temple site in the Kathmandu Valley.

darśan: (Sanskrit *darśana*) The act of seeing and being seen by the deity.

Dashain: Nepalese name for the Durgā Pūjā.

Devī: Goddess.

Devī Māhātmya: Authoritative text about Goddess Durgā from around the fifth or sixth century C.E.

dhāms: Divine abodes.

dharma: Work, duty, virtue.

dhoka: Hole or gateway. Refers to millennia-old stones perceived as Goddesses in certain places of the Kathmandu Valley.

dikṣā: Initiation.

Durgāma: Name of the buffalo-headed demon that Durgā slays in the *Devī Māhātmya*.

duṣṭā: Vile woman, wicked woman, wretch of a woman, shrew and whore.

gandharvas: Demi-gods.

Gaṇeśa: Elephant-headed God. Remover of Obstacles. Lord of Wisdom.

Gaṇgā: Name of the River Goddess and the great river Ganges.

ganja: Marijuana.

garbhagṛha: Inner sanctum. Literally means "womb."

Garuḍa: A mythological creature that is part bird, part human. Most often associated with Viṣṇu and the Matṛkā Vaiṣṇavī.

Gaurī: Name of one of the benevolent and more peaceful incarnations of Goddess.

Ghata-sthāpana: The name for the first day of the festival in Nepal known as the "installation of the sacred vessel."

ghāṭs: River steps sometimes used to burn corpses.

grāhas: Planets.

Grāma Devī: Village Goddess.

gunas: Philosophical concept that refers to qualities or attributes of phenomenal existence. There are three presiding qualities: sattva or purity, rajas or activity, tamas or inertia.

Hanumān: Monkey god who is in service to Goddess.

Harītī: Buddhist Goddess of Small Pox. Protector of Children.

iḍā: Moon channel in the subtle body.

Indra: God of Rain and Thunder. Popular during the Vedic period.

Indrāṇī: Names for the sixth Matṛkā. Association with elephants and rain.

Indrāyaṇī: Name of the sixth of the Nine Durgās. Name and some qualities are related to God Indra. Association with elephants and rain.

Jai Mā: Greeting and expression of reverence and devotion. Means "Victory and Reverence to the Mother Goddess."

Jamunā: A river Goddess.

Jaya Mātā: Another way of saying Jai Mā, Victory and Reverence to the Mother Goddess.

jñāna yoga: The path of knowledge.

kalaśa: Sacred vessel, also refers to the womb.

Kālī: See Day Seven. Goddess of Transformation, Power and Death.

kāma: Love, pleasure, desire.

Kāmākhyā: Goddess of Desire. Name of Goddess at the site in Assam where Goddess' yoni fell in the Myth about Sātī.

karma yoga: The path of action.

Kaula: See Chapter Two.

Kaumārī: The third Matṛkā, sometimes related to the Kumārī.

kirtan: Group devotional expression through song and dance.

Kṛṣṇa: God of Love, Beauty, Music.

Kubera: King of the Yakṣas or tree spirits.

Kubjikā: An esoteric Goddess in Nepal of the Śākta Kaula lineage. She is sometimes conflated with Kālī or Tripurāsundarī.

kula: From Kaula. Means clan, female lineage, menstrual blood, and female sexual fluids.

Kumārī: A young girl who is an incarnation of the Goddess. See Day Two.

Kumārī Che: House of the Kumārī.

Kumārī Chowk: Temple of the Kumārī.

kuṇḍalinī: The sexual and creative energy that lies coiled like a serpent at the base of our spines. When awakened it travels up our spinal column through 7 energy centers, or cakras. See Ajit Mookerjee for a comprehensive and philosophical explanation.

Lajjā Gaurī: Early Goddess of Vegetation, first to fourth centuries C.E. Often depicted with Her legs open, vulva exposed and a plant instead of a head.

lajjā: Shame.

Lakṣmī: Goddess of Abundance, Harmony, and Beauty. See Day Four.

Lalitā: Goddess of Delight.

līlā: Divine play of the goddesses and gods.

Mahā: Great.

Mahākālī: The Great Goddess Kālī as the ultimate manifestation and expression of the Divine. In Her Mahā aspect, She is the Supreme Power behind all existence.

Mahālakṣmī: The Great Goddess Lakṣmī as the ultimate manifestation and expression of the Divine. In Her Mahā aspect, She is the Supreme Power behind all existence.

Mahāsaraswatī: The Great Goddess Saraswatī as the ultimate manifestation and expression of the Divine. In Her Mahā aspect, She is the Supreme Power behind all existence.

Mahāvidyās: Ten Tantric Goddesses of Wisdom and Liberation.

Maheśvarī: Second of the Matṛkās. Associated with Śiva. Rides a bull.

Mahiṣa: Short for Mahiṣāsuramardinī.

Mahiṣāsuramardinī: The shape-shifting buffalo-headed demon who Durgā slays in the second carita.

Māī: Mother, a name for the ancient Mother Spirit in the Kathmandu Valley.

māīthan: Place of the mother.

mala: Prayer beads upon which chants are recited.

Malla: The Mallas were a ruling dynasty of Nepal from the twelfth century to the eighteenth century.

maṇḍala: A sacred geometric diagram that is expressive of the cosmic whole. It is a symbolic form of paintings, cities, the Kathmandu Valley and temples.

maṇḍapa: Temple pavilion.

Manusmṛti: The laws of Manu. Sexist and classist laws that were codified around the second century.

Mātaṅgī: A Mahāvidyā. Goddess of Pollutants and Impurities.

Mātr: Mother.

Matṛkās: Seven or eight Mother Goddesses, see Day Five.

mayā: Illusion.

mokṣa: Liberation. Release from the cycle of rebirth.

mudrā: Gestures evocative of the deity.

mukti: Liberation.

Muṇḍa: Demon in the *Devī Māhātmya* myth.

muṇḍana: Placing the ashes of the dead in holy waters or a tīrtha.

mūrtis: Sacred images of the Divine in statue, painting or other iconographic art form.

nāda: Sound.

nāḍīs: Energy channels that run between the cakras and other energy points in the energetic body.

Nārāyaṇa: A form of the God Viṣṇu.

nava: Nine.

Navami: Ninth night.

Navarātri: Nine Tantric nights of worship of Durgā Pūjā.

Nayars: A matrilineal Hindu caste in Kerala and parts of Northeast India.

Nepālmaṇḍala: Name for the Kathmandu Valley.

Newar, Newari: A Tibeto-Burman speaking people. Perhaps the original inhabitants of the Kathmandu Valley.

Nīlakaṇṭha: Blue throat, a name for Śiva.

Niśumbha: One of the main demons in the *Devī Māhātmya* myth. Brother of Śumbha.

nyāsa: Worshipping the body as a Deity.

padma: Lotus.

pañca: Five.

pandal: Temporary shrine constructed for a ritual and/or festival.

Pārvatī: An epithet for the Great Goddess. Means "She of the Mountain." Wife of Shiva, Mother of Ganesha.

piṅgalā: Sun channel on the right side of the subtle body.

pīṭha: Means "seat." Sacred place of worship in the landscape that is associated with Goddess.

pranam: Blessing by joining the palms together and making a slight bow.

prāṇayama: Means "control of the breath." Practices to control the breath.

prasād: Food offering for a deity.

Prayāga: Confluence of three sacred rivers: Jamunā, Gaṇgā and now invisible Saraswatī.

pūjā: Ritual.

Purāṇas: In the fourth and fifth centuries C.E., the Purāṇas emerged as a new class of literature. The word purāṇa means "ancient." The texts present a highly mythologized history of the universe and present successive cosmic cycles of birth and destruction. They marked an ongoing process of assimilation of indigenous, non-Aryan cultures within the nomadic Aryan pastoral takeover.

puruṣa: A philosophical concept of the Sankhya school that refers to the self or universal human.

rajas: One of the three gunas. Qualities of movement, dynamism, passion, activity.

raja yoga: The path of passion.

Rig Veda: The earliest of the four Vedas central to the Brahmanical tradition, 1500 to 1000 B.C.E. Hymns of praise to divinities of the Vedic pantheon. Written by rishis.

Rishi: Sage or seer.

ritu: Rite.

sādhaka: Practitioner.

Sādhanā: Spiritual endeavor.

Sa'ham: I am She.

Śakhambarī: Goddess of Vegetation.

Śākta: A practitioner of the female-centered Śākta path; a spiritual path and religious belief system that honors and worships the supreme Divinity as female.

Śāktācāra: Rules of conduct followed by the Śākta practitioner.

Śakti: Creative, dynamic, activating power of the Universe that is female.

Śākya: A Buddhist caste—the highest caste of Newar Buddhists. The Royal Kumārīs must come from this caste.

Śākyamuni Buddha: Sage of the Śākya caste. Founder of Buddhism. He is also known as Siddhartha and Gautama.

Śaivite: Devotee of Lord Shiva and the Śaivite tradition.

samskāra: A personality characteristic.

sapta: Seven.

Saraswatī: Goddess of Creativity, Music, Learning, the Arts. See Day 1.

Sātī: The first wife of Śiva. Immolated Herself in the sacred ritual fire when Her father refused Her Yogi husband's presence at his celebration. Where various parts of Her body fell created the fifty-four Śakti pīṭhas.

sattva: Purity.

siddhis: Supernatural powers.

Sītā: A Goddess who is the wife of Ram.

Śītalā: Goddess of Small Pox.

Śiva: Lord of Destruction and Transformation, Beloved of Kālī/Durgā

śmāsanā: Cremation ground.

Śrī: Auspicious, benevolent. A title of respect.

Śri Śri Caṇḍī: Sacred text narrating the Durgā myth.

sthalā: A sacred, often ancient place.

sukhnā: Vows.

Śumbha: One of the names of the demon king.

Ṣushumṇā: Central channel of the subtle body.

Taleju: Royal Tantric Goddess of the Kathmandu Valley. Popular in Bhaktapur.

tamas: One of the three gunas. Refers to qualities of inertia, darkness, heaviness.

tamasic: Heavy, dense, earthy.

Tantra: See Chapter Two.

Tantrika: Tantric practitioner.

tejas: Heat.

thangka: Sacred meditational painting.

tikā: A blessing/offering made of rice, curd, and red powder and placed between the eyes.

tīrtha: Ford/crossing.

tīrtha-yātrā: Undertaking a journey to river fords.

Tripurāsundarī: She of the Three Worlds. One of the Mahāvidyās.

twā: Word for district in Bhaktapur. Also refers to a branch on a tree.

ugra: Fierce.

Umā: Epithet for Devī/Goddess in Her benevolent aspect.

Vāc: Goddess of Speech. Also means word.

Vaiṣṇavī: One of the Matṛkās. Related to the God Viṣṇu.

Vajrayoginī: Tibetan Goddess similar to Kālī. See Day Seven.

Vārāhī: Boar-headed Goddess. One of the Matṛkās.

Vastu Shastra: A traditional Hindu system of design based on directional alignments and subtle energies. It is primarily applied in Hindu architecture, especially for Hindu temples.

vidyā: Knowledge. Also refers to mantras to female deities.

Vindhyachal Mountains: Located outside of Varanasi in Uttar Pradesh. The mythological abode of Durgā.

Vindhyavasinī: An epithet for Durgā who resides in the Vindhyachal Mountains.

Viṣṇu: God of Preservation, Maintenance. Beloved of Lakṣmi.

Viṣṇupriya: Beloved of Viṣṇu.

vrata: Vows. Connotes a religious practice to carry out certain obligations and promises in exchange for a desired outcome or effect.

Yakṣa: Male tree spirit and elemental deity.

Yakṣī: Female tree spirit and elemental deity.

yantras: Geometrical drawings of the Divine.

Yogi: Male practitioner of yoga.

Yogin: Gender-neutral name for female or male practitioners of yoga.

Yoginī: Female practitioner of yoga. See Day Six.

Bibliography

Alexandre, Chandra. "Why She. . . and Why a Dark Goddess?" *Sharanya Newsletter: May Puja, Mudra & More!* May 28, 2009, http://www.sharanya.org/shacan/darkgoddess.php4.

Allen, Michael. *The Cult of the Kumari: Virgin Worship in Nepal*. Kathmandu: Mandala Book Point, 1996.

Allione,Tsultrim. *Women of Wisdom*. London: Arkana, 1984.

Amatya, Gehendra Man. *Religious Life in Nepal (Part Three)*. Kathmandu: Amatya Publishers, 1998.

Amatya, Saphalya. *Art and Culture of Nepal: An Attempt Towards Preservation*. Jaipur: Niral Publications, 1991.

Amos, Tori. http://everythingtori.com/go/galleries/view/993/1/992/press, in "Harp," August 2007, (accessed July 17, 2009).

—."Ophelia." Video Visualette produced and performed by Tori Amos *Abnormally Attracted to Sin*. New York: Universal Republic Records, 2009.

—."Meet Tori's Posse." *Feature* by Christian Taylor, March 28, 2008, http://www.samesame.com.au/features/565/ (accessed July 17, 2009).

Anderson, Mary M. *The Festivals of Nepal*. New Delhi: Rupa & Co., 1988.

Apffel-Marglin, Frederique. "The Sacred Groves. Menstrual Rituals in Rural Orissa." *Manushi Journal* Number 82, 22-32.

Auer, Gerhard and Niels Gutschow. *Bhaktapur: Gestalt, Funktionen und Religiőse Symbolik Einer Nepalische Stadt Im Vorindustriellen Entwicklungsstadium*. Darmstadt: Technische Hochscule, 1974.

Bhairavan, Amarananda. *Kali's Odiyya*. Maine: Nicolas Hays, 2000.

Bharati, Agehananda. *The Tantric Tradition*. London, 1965.

Bhardwaj, Surinder Mohan. *Hindu Places of Pilgrimage in India: A Study in Cultural Geography*. Berkeley, Los Angeles: University of California Press, 1973.

Bhattacharyya, Narendra Nath. *History of the Śākta Religion*. New Delhi: Munshiram Manoharial Publishers, 1996.

—.*The Indian Mother Goddess*. Delhi: Manohar, 1977.

—.*The World of Tantra*. New Delhi: Munshiram Manoharial Publishers, 1988.

Bhattarai, Baburam. *Monarchy vs. Democracy: The Epic Fight in Nepal*. New Delhi: India, Samkaleen Teesarai Duniya, 2005.

Biaggi, Cristina. *The Rule of Mars: Readings on the Origins, History and Impact of Patriarchy*. Manchester, Connecticut: Knowledge, Ideas & Trends, 2005.

Birnbaum, Lucia Chiavola. *dark mother: african origins and godmothers*. Lincoln, Nebraska: iUniverse, 2001.

Bista, Dor Bahadur. *People of Nepal*. Kathmandu: Department of Publicity, Ministry of Information and Broadcasting, His Majesty's Government of Nepal. 1967.

Bolon, Carolyn Radcliffe. *Forms of the Goddess Lajjā Gaurī in Indian Art*. Delhi: Motilal Banarsidass Publishers, 1997.

Brownmiller, Susan: *Femininity*. New York: Fawcett Columbine, 1984.

Buhner, Stephen Harrod. *Sacred and Herbal Healing Beers: The Secrets of Ancient Fermentation*. Boulder, Colorado: Brewers Publications, 1998.

Chalier-Visuvalingam, Elizabeth. "Bhairava and the Goddess." In *Wild Goddesses in India and Nepal: Proceedings of an International Symposium Berne and Zurich, November, 1994*, edited by Axel Michaels, Cornelia Vogelsanger, Annette Wilke, 253-300. Bern: Peter Lang, 1996.

Chamberlain (former married name of Laura Amazzone), Laura Kristine, "Durga and the Dashain Harvest Festival: From the Indus to Kathmandu Valleys." *Revision: A Journal of Consciousness and Transformation* vol. 25, no. 1, (2002): 24-32.

Chaudhuri, Haridas. *The Philosophy of Love*, edited by Dionne Marx. New York & London: Routledge & Kegan Paul, 1987.

Cixous, Hélène. "The Laugh of the Medusa." In "Feminine Writing and Women's Difference; Hélène Cixous." In *French Feminism Reader*, edited by Kelly Oliver, 257-275. Lanham, Maryland: Rowman & Littlefield Publishers, 2000.

—."The Laugh of the Medusa." *Signs* 1, no. 4: summer, (1976).

Coburn, Thomas B. *Devī Māhātmya: The Crystallization of the Goddess Tradition*. Delhi: Motilal Banarsidass Publishers, 1984.

—.*Encountering the Goddess: A Translation of the Devī Māhātmyā and a Study of Its Interpretation*. Albany: State University of New York Press, 1991.

Daly, Mary. *Pure Lust: Elemental Feminist Philosophy*. Boston: Beacon Press, 1984.

"Dashain: The Fortnight of the Mother Goddess." In *Nepal Traveller*. Fall 2000.

Dehejia, Vidya. *Yogini Cult and Temples*. New Delhi: National Museum, 1986.

Dempsey, Corinne. "Double Take: Through the Eyes of Yakṣīs, Yakṣas and Yoginīs."*Journal of the American Academy of Religion*, Vol. 73, No. 1, (March 2005): 3-7.

Deslauriers, Daniel. "Maturity as Paradox: The Fugitive Intentions of East-West Psychology." *Journal of East-West Psychology* Vol.1, Number 1, Winter, (1995): 65-69.

Dietrich, Angela. *Tantric Healing in the Kathmandu Valley*. Delhi: Book Faith India, 1988.

Dowman, Keith. *Power Places of Kathmandu: Hindu and Buddhist Holy Sites in the Sacred Valley of Nepal*. Rochester, Vermont: Inner Traditions International, 1995.

—.*Sky Dancer: The Secret Life and Songs of Yeshe Tsogyel*. Ithaca, New York: Snow Lion Press, 1996.

Durdis-Robertson, Lawrence. *The Cult of the Goddess*. Enniscothy, Eire: Cesara Publications, 1974.

Dyckowski, Mark. *The Doctrine of Vibration. An Analysis of the Doctrines and Practices of Kashmir Shaivism*. Delhi: Motilal Banarsidass, 1989.

Eck, Diana, L. *Darśan: Seeing the Divine Image in India*. Chambersburg, Pennsylvania: Anima Books, 1981.

Eliade, Mircea. *The Sacred & the Profane: The Nature of Religion*. Translated by Willard R. Trask. San Diego, New York, London: Harcourt Brace Jovanich Publishers, 1959.

Erndl, Kathleen, "Is Shakti Empowering for Women." In *Is the Goddess a Feminist? The Politics of South Asian Goddesses*, edited by Alf Hiltebeitel and Kathleen M. Erndl, 91-103. New York: New York University Press, 2000.

—. *Victory to the Mother: The Hindu Goddess of Northwest India In Myth, Ritual, and Symbol*. Oxford: Oxford University Press, 1993.

Faludi, Susan. *Backlash: The Undeclared War against American Women*. New York: Books, 1991.

French, Marilyn. *The War Against Women*. London: Hamish Hamilton, 1992.

Friedland, Roger. "Religious Terror and the Erotics of Exceptional Violence." In *Anthropological Journal on European Cultures*, Roger Departments of Religious Studies and Sociology, University of California, Santa Barbara, July 16, 2004.

Gabriel, Hannelore. *Jewelry of Nepal*. London: Thames and Hudson, 1999.

Gadon, Elinor W. "The Hindu Goddess Shashti: Protector of Women and Children." In *From the Realm of the Ancestors*, edited by Joan Marler, 293-308. Manchester, Connecticut: Knowledge, Ideas, and Trends, Inc. 1997.

—."Probing the Mysteries of the Hirapur Yoginīs." In *ReVision: A Journal of Consciousness and Transformation*, vol. 25, no. 1, (2002): 33-41.

—. "Revisioning the Female Demon: Lilith and Her Indian Sisters." *Revision: A Journal of Consciousness and Transformation*, vol. 20, no.3, (1990): 30-36.

Galland, China. *The Bond Between Women: A Journey to Fierce Compassion*. New York: Riverhead Books, 1998.

Gimbutas, Marija. *The Living Goddesses*. Edited and Supplemented by M. R. Dexter. Berkeley and Los Angeles: University of California Press, 1999.

—. *The Civilization of the Goddess: The World of Old Europe*. San Francisco: HarperSanFrancisco, 1991.

Goettner-Abendroth, Heide. *Das Matriarchat II, 2: Stammesgesellschaften in Amerika, Indien, Afrika*. Stuttgart: Kohlhammer, 2000.

—."Matriarchal Societies and Modern Research on Matriarchies." Paper presented at the Second World Congress on Matriarchal Studies, San Antonio, Texas, 2004, www.second-congress-matriarchal-studies.com

—."Notes on the Rise and Development of Patriarchy." In *The Rule of Mars: Readings on the Origins, History and Impact of Patriarchy*, edited by Cristina Biaggi, 27-42. Manchester, Connecticut: Knowledge, Ideas & Trends, 2005.

Grahn, Judy. *Blood, Bread, and Roses: How Menstruation Created the World.* Boston: Beacon Press, 1993.

Griffin, Susan. *Woman and Nature: The Roaring Inside Her.* San Francisco: Sierra Club Books, 2000.

Gross, Rita. "Is The Goddess a Feminist?" In *Is the Goddess a Feminist? The Politics of South Asian Goddesses*, edited by Alf Hiltebeitel and Kathleen M. Erndl, 104-112. New York: New York University Press, 2000.

Gupta, Sanjukta Gombrich. "The Goddess, Women and Their Rituals in Hinduism." In *Faces of the Feminine in Ancient, Medieval, and Modern India*, edited by Mandakranta Bose, 87-106. Oxford: Oxford University Press, 2000.

—."Women in the Saiva/Sakta Ethos." In *Roles and Rituals for Hindu Women*, edited by Julie Leslie, 193-209. Rutherford/Madison/Teaneck: Fairleigh Dickinson University Press, 1991.

Gupta, Sanjukta, Dirk Jan Hoens, and Teun Goudriaan. *Hindu Tantrism.* Leiden/Koeln: E.J. Brill, 1979.

Gutschow, Niels. "The AṣṭaMātṛkās and Navadurgā of Bhaktapur." In *Wild Goddesses in India and Nepal: Proceedings of an International Symposium Berne and Zurich, November, 1994*, edited by Axel Michaels, Cornelia Vogelsanger, Annette Wilke, 191-216. Bern: Peter Lang, 1996.

Gutschow, Niels, and Bernhard Kōlver. *Ordered Space, Concepts and Functions in a Town of Nepal.* Komissions Verlag Franz Steiner, Wiesbaden, 1975.

Harper, Katherine Anne. *The Iconography of the Saptamatrikas: Seven Hindu Goddesses of Spiritual Transformation.* Lewiston, New York: Edwin Mellin Press, 1989.

Hopkins, Thomas J. *The Hindu Religious Tradition.* Belmont, California: Wadsworth Publishing Company, 1971.

Humes, Cynthia Ann. "Is the Devī Māhātmyā a Feminist Scripture." In *Is the Goddess a Feminist? The Politics of South Asian Goddesses*, edited by Alf Hiltebeitel and Kathleen M. Erndl, 123-150. New York: New York University Press, 2000.

Irigaray, Luce. "And the One Doesn't Stir without the Other." Translated by Helene Vivienne Wenzel. *Signs: Journal of Women in Culture and Society*, vol. 7, no.1, 1981.

—. "Divine Women." In *Sexes and Genealogies*, translated by Gillian C. Gill, 57-72. New York: Columbia University Press, 1993.

—. *An Ethics of Sexual Difference.* Translated by Carolyn Burke and Gillian C. Gill, London: Athlone Press, 1993.

—. "The Forgotten Mystery of Female Ancestry." In *French Feminists on Religion: A Reader,* edited by Morna Joy, Kathleen O'Grady and Judith Poxon, 68-75. London and New York: Routledge, 2002.

—. "How Old Are You?" In *je, tu nous: Toward a Culture of Difference,* translated by Alison Martin, 113-117. New York: Routledge, 1993.

—. "Practical Teachings: Love—Between Passion and Civility." In *French Feminists on Religion, A Reader,* edited by Morna Joy, Kathleen O'Grady and Judith Poxon, 76-81. London and New York: Routledge, 2002.

—. "This Sex Which Is Not One." In *French Feminism Reader,* translated by Jennifer Hansen, edited by Kelly Oliver, 201-211. Boston Way, Lanham, Maryland: Rowman & Littlefield Publishers, 2000.

—. *This Sex Which Is Not One.* Translated by Catherine Porter. New York: Cornell University, 1985.

—. *Why Different: A Culture of Two Subjects. Interviews with Luce Irigaray.* Edited by Luce Irigaray and Sylvère Lotringer. New York: Semiotext, 2000.

—. "Women, the Sacred, Money." In *Sexes and Genealogies,* translated by Gillian C. Gill, 75-88. New York: Columbia University Press, 1993.

Irigaray, Luce and Elizabeth Grosz. "Sexuate Identities as Global Beings Questioning Western Logic." in *Conversations,* 123-137. London: Continuum, 2008.

Ironbiter, Susan. *Devi.* Stamford, CT: Yuganta Press, 1987.

Jayakar, Pupul. *The Earth Mother.* New York: Harper & Row, 1989.

Jenett, Dianne E. "Menstruating Women/Menstruating Goddesses: Sites of Sacred Power in South India." In *Menstruation: A Cultural History,* edited by Andrew Shail and Gillian Howie, 176-187. New York: Palgrave MacMillan, 2005.

Jha, Makhan. *The Sacred Complex of Kathmandu, Nepal: Religion of the Himalayan Kingdom.* New Delhi: Gyan Publishing House, 1995.

Johnsen, Linda. *Daughters of the Goddess: The Women Saints of India.* St. Paul, Minnesota: Yes International Publishers, 1994.

—. *The Living Goddess: Reclaiming the Tradition of the Mother of the Universe.* St. Paul, Minnesota: Yes Publishers, 1999.

Jordan, Donna. "A Post Orientalist History of the Fierce Śakti of the Subaltern Domain." PhD diss., California Institute of Integral Studies, 1999.

Kālī, Devadatta, trans. *In Praise of the Goddess. The Devī Māhātmya and Its Meaning. A New Translation, with Commentary, of the Sacred Hindu Scripture and Its Angas.* Berwick, Maine: Nicolas Hayes, Inc., 2003.

Khanna, Madhu. "The Goddess-Women Equation in Śākta Tantras." In *Faces of the Feminine in Ancient, Medieval, and Modern India,* edited by Mandakranta Bose, 109-123. Oxford: Oxford University Press, 2000.

—."The Ritual Capsule of Durgā Pujā: An Ecological Perspective." In *Hinduism and Ecology: The Intersection of Earth, Sky, and Water*, edited by Christopher Key Chapple and Mary Evelyn Tucker. Harvard University Press, Harvard, 2000.

—. *Yantra: The Tantric Symbol of Cosmic Unity*. London: Thames and Hudson, 1979.

Kinsley, David. *Hindu Goddesses: Visions of the Divine Feminine in the Hindu Religious Tradition*. Berkeley: University of California Press, 1986.

—. *Tantric Visions of the Divine Feminine: The Ten Mahavidyas*. Berkeley: University of California Press, 1997.

Knight, Chris. *Blood Relations: Menstruation and the Origins of Culture*. New Haven and London: Yale University Press, 1991.

Kosambi, Damodar Dharmanand. *Myth and Reality*. Bombay: Popular Prakashan, 1962.

Krishnananda, Sri Swami, "The Esoteric Significance of the Devi Mahatmya," from India: The Divine Life Society. http://www.dlshq.org/ (accessed March 13, 2002).

Kruszewska, Margaret. "Saraswati: Goddess of No Husband/No Child." In *The Constant and Changing Faces of The Goddess: The Goddess Traditions in Asia*. Newcastle upon Tyne: Cambridge Scholars Press, 2008.

Levy, Robert I. *Mesocosm: Hinduism and the Organization of a Traditional Newar City in Nepal*. Delhi: Motilal Bandarsidass Publishers, 1990.

Lorde, Audre. "Uses of the Erotic." In *Sister Outsider: Essays and Speeches by Audre Lorde*, 53-59. Trumansburg, New York: Crossing Press, 1984.

Magee, Michael, trans. *The Yoni Tantra*. Harrow, England: Worldwide Tantra Project, 1995.

Majupara, Indra and Patricia Roberts. *Living Virgin Goddess: Kumari*. Kathmandu: M. Gupta, 2007.

Mani, V.R. *Saptamatrkas in Indian Religion and Art*. New Delhi: Mittal Publications, 1995.

Marler, Joan. "An Archaeomythology of the Gorgon." In *Revision: A Journal of Consciousness and Transformation*. vol. 25, no. 1, (2002): 15-23.

Marshack, Alexander. *The Roots of Civilization*. Mount Kisco, New York: Moyer Bell Limited, 1991.

Marshall, John. 1931. *Mohenjo-Daro and the Indus Civilization*, Vol. I, Indological Book House, Delhi, 1973.

Meador, Betty DeShong. *Uncursing the Dark: Treasures from the Underworld*. Wilmette, Illinois: Chiron Publishers, 1992.

Michaels, Axel, Cornelia Vogelsanger, and Annette Wilke, editors. *Wild Goddesses in India and Nepal: Proceedings of an International Symposium Berne and Zurich, November, 1994*. Bern: Peter Lang, 1996.

Misra, Om Prakash. *Iconography of the Saptamatrikas*. Delhi: Agam Kala Prakashan, 1989.

Monterey Bay Spice Company. http://www.herbco.com/p-622-marigold-calendula-petals.aspx (accessed June 21, 2009).

Mookerjee, Ajit. *Kali: The Feminine Force*. Rochester, Vermont: Destiny Books, 1988.

—. *Kuṇḍalinī: The Arousal of the Inner Energy*. London: Thames and Hudson, 1982.

Mookerjee, Ajit and Madhu Khanna. *The Tantric Way: Art. Science. Ritual.* England: Thames and Hudson Ltd., 1977.

Morton, Nelle. "The Goddess as Metamorphic Image." In *Weaving the Visions. New Patterns in Feminist Spirituality*, edited by Judith Plaskow and Carol Christ, 111-118. San Francisco: HarperSanFrancisco, 1989.

Muscio, Inga. *Cunt: A Declaration of Independence*. Emeryville, California: Seal Press, 2002.

Narayan, Vasudha. "Brimming with *Bhakti*, Embodiments of *Shakti:* Devotees, Deities, Performers, Reformers, and Other Women of Power in the Hindu Tradition." In *Feminism and World Religions*, edited by Arvind Sharma and Katherine K. Young, 25-77. Albany: State University of New York Press, 1999.

Neumann, Erich. *The Great Mother: An Analysis of the Archetype*. London: Routeledge and Kegan Paul, 1954.

Noble, Vicki. "The Auspiciousness of Being a Woman." In *Matrifocus Crossquarterly for the Goddess Woman*. vol. 8-3. Beltane 2009. http://www.matrifocus.com/BEL09/noble.htm.

—."Dakini: The Goddess who Takes Form as a Woman." In *Goddesses in World Culture. Vol. 1: Africa, Asia, Australia and the Pacific*. Edited by Patricia Monaghan. Santa Barbara, California: Praeger, Spring 2010.

—. *Double Goddess. Women Sharing Power.* Rochester, Vermont: Bear & Company, 2003.

—."From Priestess to Bride: Marriage as a Colonizing Process in Patriarchal Conquest." In *The Rule of Mars: Readings on the Origins, History and Impact of Patriarchy*. Edited by Cristina Biaggi. Manchester, Connecticut: Knowledge, Ideas & Trends, 2005.

—."Motherhood and Matriarchy." Paper presented on International Women's Day at Sonoma State University, Sonoma, California, March 8, 2008.

—. *Motherpeace: A Way to the Goddess through Myth, Art, and Tarot*. San Francisco: HarperSanFrancisco, 1983.

—. *Shakti Woman: Feeling our Fire, Healing our World, The New Female Shamanism*. San Francisco: HarperSanFrancisco, 1993.

Padoux, André. "What Do We Mean By Tantrism?" In *The Roots of Tantra*, edited by Katherine Anne Harper and Robert L. Brown, Albany: State University of New York Press, 2002.

Pal, Pratapaditya. *Art of Nepal.* Berkeley: University of California Press, 1985.

—.*The Arts of Nepal. Part I: Sculpture*. Leiden, Netherlands: E.J. Brill, 1974.

—. *The Arts of Nepal. Part II: Painting*. Leiden, Netherlands: E.J. Brill, 1974.

Pande, Mrinal. *Devi: Tales of the Goddess in Our Time*. New Delhi: Penguin, 1996.

Panikkar, Shivaji K. *Saptamatrka: Worship and Sculptures: An Iconological Interpretation of Conflicts and Resolutions in the Storied Brahmanical Icons*. New Delhi: D.K. Printworld(P) Ltd., 1997.

Patel, Kartikeya C. "Women, Earth, and the Goddess: A Shakta-Hindu Interpretation of Embodied Religion." Hypatia 9 (4), (1994): 69-86.

Perera, Sylvia Brinton. *Descent to the Goddess: A Way of Initiation for Women*. Toronto: Inner City Books, 1981.

Peters, Larry G. "The Tibetan Rituals of Dorje Yŭdronma: A Fierce Manifestation of Feminine Cosmic Force." In *Shaman's Drum*, Number 45, 1997, 37-47.

Plaskow, Judith, and Carol Christ, eds. *Weaving the Visions. New Patterns in Feminist Spirituality*. San Francisco: HarperSanFrancisco, 1989.

Prioleau, Betsy. *Seductress: Women Who Ravished the World and Their Lost Art of Love*. New York: Penguin Books, 2003.

Ray, Amita. *Art of Nepal*. New Delhi: Indian Council for Cultural Relations, 1973.

Reid, Vanessa. "Supernova Editorial." *Ascent Magazine: Yoga For an Inspired Life*, Issue 41 Union, 2009.

Rigoglioso, Marguerite. *The Cult of Divine Birth in Ancient Greece*. New York: Palgrave Macmillan, 2009.

Rodrigues, Hillary Peter. *Ritual Worship of the Great Goddess: The Liturgy of the Durgā Pūjā With Interpretations*. Albany: State University of New York Press, 2003.

Sakya, Jnan Bahadur. *Short Description of Gods, Goddesses and Ritual Objects of Buddhism and Hinduism in Nepal*. Lalitpur, Nepal: Subhash Printing Press, 1996.

Sanday, Peggy Reeves. "Antigone in Sumatra: Matriachal Values in a Patriachal Context." In *The Rule of Mars: Readings on the Origins, History and Impact of Patriarchy*, edited by Cristina Biaggi, 95-110. Manchester, Connecticut: Knowledge, Ideas & Trends, 2005.

Saraswati, Dharmanidhi. "Mahasiddhas and Relationship." Paper presented at Yoga Mandala, Berkeley, California April 28, 2008.

Saraswati, Swami Satyananda. *Kundalini Tantra*. Bihar: Bihar School of Yoga Publications Trust, Inc., 2000.

Schaefer, Carol. *Grandmothers Counsel the World: Women Elders Offer Their Vision for Our Planet*. Boston: Trumpeter, 2006, 7.

Shakya, Rahsmila and Scott Berry, *From Goddess to Mortal: The True Life Story of a Former Royal Kumari*. Kathmandu: Vajra, 2005.

Shaw, Miranda. *Passionate Enlightenment: Women in Tantric Buddhism*. Princeton, New Jersey: Princeton University Press, 1994.

Shuttle, Penelope and Peter Redgrove. *The Wise Wound: The Myths, Realities, and Meanings of Menstruation*. New York: Grove Press, 1986.

Silburn, Lilian. *Kundalini: The Energy of the Depths: A Comprehensive Study Based on the Scriptures of Nondualistic Kashmir Saivism*. Albany: State University of New York Press, 1988.

Sivananda, Sri Swami. "Durga Puja or Navaratri." In *Hindu Fasts and Festivals*. India: The Divine Life Society. http://www.dlshq.org/ (accessed March 13, 2002).

Sjöö, Monica and Barbara Mor. *The Ancient Religion of the Great Cosmic Mother of All*. Trondheim, Norway: Rainbow Press, 1981.

Slusser, Mary Shepherd. *Nepal Mandala: A Cultural Study of the Kathmandu Valley*. Vol 1: Text. Princeton: Princeton University Press, 1982. 2 vols.

Spretnak, Charlene. *States of Grace: The Recovery of Meaning in the Postmodern Age*. San Francisco: HarperSanFrancisco, 1991.

Sri Mata Amritanandamayi Devi. "The Infinite Potential of Women: An Address by Her Holiness Sri Mata Amritanandamayi Devi," Jaipur, Rajasthan, India, March 7, 2008, 13.

—. "The Universal Motherhood." Speech given at A Global Peace Initiative of Women Religious and Spiritual Leaders, Palais des Nations, United Nations, Geneva, October 7, 2002.

Srinivas, Mysore Narasimhachar. *Caste in Modern India: And Other Essays*, Bombay: Asia Publishing House, 1962.

Stratton Hawley, John and Donna Marie Wulff. Editors. *Devi: Goddesses of India*. Berkeley: University of California Press, 1996.

Tachikawa, Musahi. "Materials for Iconographic Studies of the Eight Mother Goddesses in the Kathmandu Valley." In *Anthropological and Linguistic Studies of the Gandaki Area in Nepal II*. Monumenta Serindica No.12, Tokyo: Institute for the Study of Languages and Cultures of Asia and Africa (ILCAA), Tokyo University of Foreign Studies, 1985.

Tattwananda, Swami. *Sri Sri Chandi*. Calcutta: Sri Nirmalendu Bikash Sen Gupta, 1962.

Tedlock, Barbara. *The Woman in the Shaman's Body: Reclaiming the Feminine in Religion and Medicine*. New York: Bantam, 2005.

Thapa, Deepak. *Understanding the Maoist Movement of Nepal*. Kathmandu: Chautari Center for Social Research and Development, 2003.

Toffin, Gérard. "A Wild Goddess Cult in Nepal. The Navadurgā of Theco Village (Kathmandu Valley)." In *Wild Goddesses in India and Nepal: Proceedings of an International Symposium Berne and Zurich, November 1994*, edited by Axel Michaels, Cornelia Vogelsanger, Annette Wilke, 217-251. Bern: Peter Lang, 1994.

Tourreil, Savithri de. "Nayars in a South Indian Matrix: A Study based on Female-centered Ritual," PhD diss. Concordia University, 1996.

Urban, Hugh B. *Tantra: Sex, Secrecy, Politics, and Power in the Study of Religion*. Berkeley and Los Angeles: University of California Press, 2003.

Vaughn, Genevieve. *Women and The Gift Economy: A Radically Different Worldview Is Possible,* Toronto: Inanna Publications and Education Inc., 2007.

Walker, Alice. "Coming in from the Cold." In *Living By the Word*. New York: Harcourt Brace & Company, 1981.

Walker, Barbara G. *The Woman's Dictionary of Symbols and Sacred Objects*. San Francisco: Harper Collins, 1988.

White, David Gordon. *The Alchemical Body: Siddha Traditions in Medieval India*. Chicago: University of Chicago Press, 1996.

—. *Kiss of the Yoginī: "Tantric Sex" in Its South Asian Context.* Chicago: University of Chicago Press, 2003.

—. editor. *Tantra in Practice*, Princeton, New Jersey: Princeton University Press, 2000.

Ziolkowski, Mari. "The Return of the Yogini." Unpublished Paper for Hindu Tantra class, San Francisco: California Institute of Integral Studies, 2001.

Index

F

G

H

About the Author

LAURA AMAZZONE is an author, teacher, jewelry artist, and Yoginī. She completed her master's degree in philosophy and religion, with an emphasis in women's spirituality at the California Institute of Integral Studies in 2001. Laura teaches Goddess classes and workshops in southern and northern California and is adjunct faculty in the Yoga Philosophy program at Loyola Marymount University in Los Angeles. She has published numerous articles discussing myth, ritual, adornment and South Asian Goddesses. She lives in Venice, California.

For more info: www.amazzonejewelry.com and www.lauraamazzone.com

61483636R00165

Made in the USA
Middletown, DE
11 January 2018